"There's a reason why Alexander the Great used to sacrifice all night to the god Phobos. Elite performers in all fields—military, corporate, political, academic, creative—know the demon they must face before all others is FEAR.

Neurosurgeon Mark McLaughlin faced his own terror in life-and-death crises under the OR's hot, pitiless lights. His answer is this brilliant, paradigm-blasting book, *Cognitive Dominance*, and the even deeper, more profound philosophy it defines and espouses. *Cognitive Dominance* takes Colonel John Boyd's OODA loop to the next level. This book is wonky. It unapologetically dissects (and even diagrams) fear and the types of paralysis and faulty decision-making it can engender. *Cognitive Dominance* is for fighter pilots and CEOs, for SEAL team members, Olympic athletes, and every other aspirant to the highest levels of performance and achievement.

—Steven Pressfield, bestselling author of
Gates of Fire and *The War of Art*

ALSO BY SHAWN COYNE

Story's Golden Rule:
The Necessity of Phere (2020)

The Story Grid Universe:
Leveling Up Your Craft (2020)

The Story Grid:
What Good Editors Know

The Ones Who Hit the Hardest:
The Steelers, the Cowboys, the '70s,
and the Fight for America's Soul
with Chad Millman

COGNITIVE DOMINANCE

A BRAIN SURGEON'S QUEST TO OUT-THINK FEAR

Mark McLaughlin, MD
with Shawn Coyne

Black Irish Entertainment LLC

Black Irish Entertainment LLC
223 Egremont Plain Road
Pmb 191
Egremont, MA 01230

First Black Irish Entertainment Paperback Edition November 2019

For Information About Special Discounts or
For Bulk Purchases,
Please Visit www.blackirishbooks.com

Isbn: 978-1-936891-62-7
Ebook: 978-1-936891-84-9

"The unexamined life is not worth living."

–Socrates

To Julie, Kaleigh, Alex, Patrick, Trevor, and AJ.

To Bibb, Bleecker, Waverly, and Crosby.

For inspiring us to examine our lives, to create this book, to birth this theory.

CONTENTS

FREQUENTLY USED TERMS

Cognitive Consonance: A state of harmony between values and actions.

Cognitive Dissonance: A state of discordant values and actions.

Cognitive Dominance: Enhanced situational awareness that facilitates rapid and accurate decision-making under stressful conditions with limited decision-making time.

Cognitive Energy: The mental effort required to perform a calculation, recall a procedure, generate an insight, or any of the other conscious efforts to metabolize a Phere event.

Combinatorial Explosiveness: The rapid growth of the complexity of a problem based upon the number of possible operative options available to move from an initial state to a goal state and the total number of operations necessary to achieve the goal.

CSF: Cerebrospinal fluid, the nutrient protective fluid that is produced and absorbed by the brain.

Exaptation: The use of a particular trait of skill for multiple purposes.

Fear Freak-Out: The phenomena of inactive despondence experienced under seemingly catastrophic Phere events...a state of not knowing what to do.

Homeostasis: An equilibrium or balance between two equal and opposite forces.

Life Value: Subjective relevant judgments that determine the degree to which something or someone matters, which direct individual actions through time.

Objective Fact: Information that is measurable and reproducible through time and space.

Orienting Response: An organism's immediate "freeze" response to a change in its environment.

Phere: An unexpected event that gives rise to fear and influences the behavior of the individual who has experienced it.

Scut List: A medical list of errands, tasks and procedures that must be completed in a timely manner on a day-to-day basis to care for an inpatient service.

Semantic Differential Scale: The gradient measurement of language attributed to large categories of feeling on a comparative spectrum.

Subjective Truth: Information whose value is dependent on its interpreter.

Terrible Knowledge: A worldview perspective of reality that intimately understands the often harsh, chaotic and capricious nature of the universe.

COGNITIVE DOMINANCE

Prologue
Jesus and Anthony

Jesus Rodriguez miscalculated. The microsecond after his head hit the bottom of the pool, he went numb. With lungs still full of air, he rose to the surface and then cried out to his ten-year-old son A.J. for help. A.J. pulled his father to the side of the pool and held him afloat, all the while screaming to his mother inside the house to call 911.

Mr. Rodriguez arrived at Baystate Medical Center's emergency room just before 7:00 p.m. on a hot summer Sunday night, August 6, 2000. I was thirty-five years old, with a dozen years of medical training behind me and one month of private practice experience. As Baystate's affiliated neurosurgeon on call that night, Mr. Rodriguez was now my responsibility.

Scans and examinations led me to a diagnosis. One of his spinal vertebrae bones slipped out of alignment when his head snapped forward after hitting the bottom of the pool. That bone was now crushing his spinal cord. Because the misaligned vertebra was in his neck, and all of the body's sensory nerves wire into the brain at the top of the neck, I knew quadriplegia was almost a certainty. I didn't have much time to open him up, realign the vertebrae to relieve the pressure on his spinal cord, and then stabilize the structure with pins and screws to keep it in place.

Even if I did all of that in record time, the odds were dramatically against us.

While we prepped him for surgery, Mr. Rodriguez slowly lost the ability to distinguish the severity of my poking his torso or legs. By the time we wheeled him into the OR, just after 11:00 p.m., he couldn't feel anything. I couldn't help running the numbers in my mind. The chances he would have any feeling or movement below the neck after the operation had dwindled to 1 in 500. Even after six hours of a meticulous all-nighter surgery, whether or not Mr. Rodriguez would be able to hug his wife or son again was no longer in my hands.

But just twenty-four hours later, he'd made a miraculous recovery.

And a few days later he even walked out of the hospital.

After the town newspaper, *The Springfield Union-News*, snapped a photo of Mr. Rodriguez and me for its front page, I received a copy of the article on my desk with a handwritten note from one of my Neurology colleagues.

"What? McLaughlin saves Jesus?"

Deep down, though, despite holding my emotions in check and acting the part of hotshot "brain surgeon" in public, internally I struggled. I faked a good game, acting cocky among colleagues and confident among patients and families. But each day I had to brace myself to overcome an inner fear that threatened my facade. Despite all of my training, was I really good enough? How could I be sure that I could handle the pressure cooker of neurosurgery? More than a few times I had to excuse myself so I could hyperventilate in private. I soon figured out the one common denominator for those instances. Whenever I faced my most dreaded cases—anything having to do with pediatric care—I just about lost it. Facing the possible destruction of a child, somehow scrambling the wonder and potential locked inside their brains with one stupid mistake, terrified me.

Not long after Mr. Rodriguez, a beautiful eight-year-old named Anthony Liquori came to the emergency room for headaches and vomiting. He also had trouble walking. Before the onset of his illness, he was the number one helper at the family's pizza parlor, an impossibly cute kid with a magnetic smile. Anthony was the local delivery service, the clean-up busboy in the parlor, and the heir apparent of the business all wrapped up in one spirited package. He seemed to me to be the spitting image of what my Italian grandfather, Doc Pizzi, must have been like when he was young and ambitious.

When I met Anthony, something was definitely out of sync. He had intense morning headaches and was sleeping more than usual. Shortly before he came into the ER, he'd fallen down the steps of his school bus and cut his face. His parents reported that he'd been clumsy bussing tables, and he'd begun tilting his head to the right when he looked at customers.

He just wasn't himself.

Anthony's MRI images showed a large plum-sized tumor in the back of his head clogging his cerebrospinal fluid highways and pressing on his brainstem. That's why he had balance issues, intense cranial distress and why his body was shutting him down for so many hours a day.

The tumor looked like it was either a medulloblastoma or an ependymoma, both extremely dangerous growths, and one or the other was likely attached to his brainstem. The brainstem is the brain's most vital survival structure as it takes care of all of the unconscious things we rely on to function (breathing, blood flow, etc.). These tumors, if completely removed (resected) and treated with appropriate additional chemotherapy and radiation, are potentially curable.

But just barely.

It was a Tuesday evening, but I didn't rush Anthony to the OR like I did with Jesus Rodriguez.

Since he was stable and I was on call, which meant I'd be at the hospital a lot if not the entire time on call, I decided I would wait out the next post-call day to rest and operate the following day when I was fresh. I would summon every exploitable tool and resource I could think of and get everything together for Thursday morning. I prescribed some steroids to reduce Anthony's swelling, and thus reduce his head pain, and keep that mass as stable as possible. While keeping a close eye on Anthony and his vital signs, I planned, re-planned, rethought, and planned again the surgery in my mind. Again and again and again I did this for the next thirty-six hours.

Anthony needed a perfect operation. There was absolutely no margin for error. Take out too much tissue and he'd be paralyzed. Take out too little and the tumor would come back…and it would probably not be removable the second time. Like a hedgehog, anything I missed would burrow deeper into his brainstem.

I knew I had the skills for the case. I had handled many similar cases with one of my mentors, Dr. Albright, during my residency in Pittsburgh. I knew exactly what was required.

But there was one very big catch. Anthony's case was the first one I would be navigating alone. I fixated on my newbie status and the fear associated with not knowing what to do when something unexpected happened. And the more I fixated, the more I undermined myself. The more the fear of failure grew. It was a negative feedback machine that I knew I had to somehow turn off.

The more I obsessed over it, the bigger a monster the case became. The MRI indicated it was vascular (many blood vessels feeding the tumor) and there would likely be significant bleeding the second I began cutting into the tumor. Although expected heavy bleeding can be handled with a steady transfusion, hyper-vascularity puts additional pressure on the surgeon because the surgical field is harder to see. With multilayered blood vessels, it can take on the look of a snake pit or a family-sized spaghetti dinner. And if you cut the wrong noodle, the patient will never be the same.

An early lesson in neurosurgery is to get a bleeding tumor out fast because of the visual difficulties caused by bleeding and the mental drain on the surgeon over time. A human being has a finite daily volume of cognitive resources before he or she loses efficacy. We just can't operate with super high intensity for very long. We aren't built for that kind of work. I would need to move quickly and assuredly so my cognitive energy never fell below critical situational awareness.

But there was a huge problem with that approach for this case. You don't really want to rush when you are working on the brainstem. One small, wrong nick and you haven't just damaged intellectual capacity. You've killed or disabled the patient.

The military has a color code for awareness. White is unaware, yellow is relaxed alertness, orange is focused alertness, and red is hyperaware and ready to act mode. The problem is that you can't spend too much time in the hyperaware red mode or you'll fall into the last mode—the black. And black is where the person breaks down mentally and physically; it's what I call fear freak-out.

Another nuance to many brain tumor operations is that the most delicate part of the procedure, requiring the most concentration and technical expertise, is the last thirty minutes of the resection, when you're cutting out the last chunk of the tumor tissue. This is when you have gotten around the edges of the tumor and you need to shave the last nubbin off of the brainstem. Within the brainstem are many of the nerve cells that control the muscles of the face, eye movements, respiration, and even consciousness itself. But getting to that critical place requires multiple hours of meticulous tactical maneuvering. You have to stay in the red mode for hours just to reach the place where you'll need...a super-red mode. Big problem.

Saving up a big reservoir of cognitive energy for the last thirty minutes is not easy. That's a big personal limitation. But I reminded myself that the best surgeons always identify and outflank their limitations.

That's why I tapped another neurosurgeon, my partner Kamal, to be in the room with me. Like pro wrestlers, we would tag team the resection. We'd spell each other so that we both brought our best to every second inside the surgical field. He agreed to be available, but he had a busy Thursday too, including a surgery of his own at 7:30 a.m. with office hours to follow.

He'd do his best to be my wingman, but he wasn't guaranteed.

Still, knowing Kamal, he'd do everything he possibly could to be my backup. His support gave me enough energy to proceed with some confidence. Not a ton of it, but enough.

Thursday morning came and I began Anthony's surgery. After anesthesia put him to sleep, I placed a frontal drain. *Always place a drain.* Drains allow for unexpected fluid pressure inside the brain to flow out of the area automatically. In the heat of battle with a tumor, you don't want any distractions, so preparing for the worst and having the drain ready before you need it is just common sense. It's like having a sump pump in your basement in case a pipe bursts while you're away.

When I finished the drain, the fluid was under control but the intracranial pressure was a bit higher than I would have liked due to the tumor. I gently drained off just a bit. I didn't want to remove too much, though, or the tumor would shift, causing damage to adjacent critical structures. I just wanted to drain enough to maintain the cranial homeostasis—the normal levels Anthony hadn't experienced for quite some time. I secured the catheter with multiple sutures and sewed it to his scalp so that it wouldn't move accidently during the operation. This drain would be his lifeline for the next few days, so I made sure it held.

Then I gently applied a Mayfield three-point head fixation device. This apparatus looks similar to old-fashioned ice-block tongs, but when you're explaining surgery to someone, a fixation device sounds better than "ice-block tongs." The Mayfield holds the head in a fixed position during the surgery. Obviously, when you're removing a tumor from the brain's most complex structure, you don't want any movement of the surgical field.

I anchored the device into Anthony's skull and then, with the help of the staff, rolled him into the prone position. *The most important part of an operation occurs before the incision*—another mantra from my training. Anthony's head had to be tucked with his chin down and tilted just so…slightly to the right. By putting his chin down, I could look up the back of his head to the top of the tumor. By tilting his head slightly to the right, I would be playing into the strength of my right-handedness. Since my hands would be in a more relaxed position throughout the operation with this configuration, I'd have an ergonomic advantage in the late hours of the surgery. It's a way to prevent forearm cramping.

With Anthony's body properly positioned, his head turned just the way I wanted, and with the drain in place, I took a deep breath and asked for the scalpel.

After the midline incision, I slowly and carefully exposed the back of Anthony's skull and upper cervical spine. I then drilled off the occipital bone, carefully shaving the bone off the edge of the torcula, the confluence of two large veins that carry about 20 percent of the body's cardiac output from the head back to the heart. Even a small hole in this structure is life threatening. But I needed to expose this area so I could see the top of the cerebellum. I had no choice.

With bony exposure complete, I began draining more cerebrospinal fluid out of the catheter attached to Anthony's scalp. This would relieve more pressure, relaxing the brain further and thus giving me more room to maneuver the instruments.

I then opened the bluish-white, leathery covering (the dura mater) of the brain by cutting a shape in the form of a capital Y. This gave me an optimal opening to see the top surface of the cerebellum. Another deep breath. This was my first glimpse of the tumor peeking out of the fourth ventricle. I had arrived safely and had good exposure. The first half the battle was going in my favor.

I positioned the operating microscope and began the dissection, literally burning and slicing away the tumor's blood supply one vessel at a time. *Never cut what you can't see.* Another rule from my training came to mind as I opened the arachnoid with my micro scissors. I could now comprehend the extent of Anthony's tumor and began to dissect a plane around it.

Dissecting a plane is important for a several reasons. First, the process progressively cuts off the blood supply to the tumor, and thus it will bleed less and less as the operation proceeds. Minimal bleeding is critical when you open the tumor capsule and begin to gut it from the inside, known as debulking, which is a bit like scooping out melon balls from the center of a cantaloupe. Second, less blood in the field makes it easier to recognize the boundaries of the normal tissue and abnormal tissue, which a seasoned surgeon can pinpoint with precision. These landmarks tell you where to stop cutting, especially around the sides of the tumor.

I gently slid some cottonoid dissectors along the sides of the tumor. Doing this is like stuffing a small towel between a large piece of furniture and a valuable wall panel. Next, I guided the retractor blades in place to hold the now-padded normal cerebellar tissue to the side. The superior-most portion of the tumor was now exposed well.

Retractors allow surgeons to gently push aside the normal brain tissue and keep it out of the operative field. Retractors have been around since the beginning of neurosurgery. The earliest surgeons used hand-held instruments including teaspoons, thin spatulas, and elevators, which were essentially tiny metallic strips of malleable metal. With one hand the surgeon would retract or elevate the normal tissue out of the way, and with the other the tumor would be excised.

Because early surgeons noted significant bruising of the normal brain tissue when the lobes of the brain were moved out of the way using less steady hand pressure, the more modern retractors became mounted or fixed to a mooring—either the patient's head itself or the operating table. With a fixed mount the variability of pressure on the retracted tissue is minimized and thus decreases the overall trauma to the normal structures.

Elevating each side of the cerebellum with two narrow spatulas attached to the retractor finally gave me a good view of the top of the tumor. It was like looking at the dome of an iceberg. I knew there was a hell of a lot more I needed to get to underneath, but I had defined the mass externally. Another deep breath. I punctured the capsule of the tumor and took a small bite of it with a pituitary rongeur, an instrument designed for the task that looks a little like a Tyrannosaurus Rex with a long neck ending at a jaw that opens and closes with sharp teeth. I sent the tissue off for preliminary pathological analysis.

I was about three hours into the procedure, but it felt like twenty minutes.

Thankfully, Kamal arrived and scrubbed in.

Pathology called with the results. It was an anaplastic ependymoma. Not good. Ependymomas are tumors made up of rapidly growing cells that line the channels of cerebrospinal passageways in the brain. The enlarging mass slowly strangles the cerebrospinal tubes, which cuts off the flow of lubrication and nutrient fluid to the rest of the brain. The fact that Anthony's tumor was anaplastic was a double whammy. Anaplasticity is a fancy way of saying that the tumor cells are likely to regrow or about to break off and travel elsewhere, thus spreading malignancy hither and yon.

It was likely that Anthony's tumor was incurable.

Kamal and I worked away at this devil nevertheless. We got around it. We shrank it. We kept encircling it and cutting off more and more feeder vessels, all under the microscope with extremely thin margins for error. Having Kamal working alongside me was a godsend. We spelled each other as we took the tumor out rapidly, efficiently and carefully. Without him, the operation would have taken hours longer. We made it to the back of the tumor without a hitch where it was stuck to the floor of the fourth ventricle, and it was crucial to shave the last layer of tumor off without damaging the healthy tissue underneath. Like scraping an expired registration sticker off the windshield of your car, you need to move slowly and carefully so as to get every last bit of stickum off the glass without scratching its surface. I steadied my hand and made the last pass. Kamal and I examined the area and neither of us could see a spec of tumor left.

Eleven hours had passed since Anthony was wheeled away from his mom and dad, and I closed with the confidence that he had gotten the best possible operation he could have had.

Anthony's father spotted me parting the OR doors into the family waiting room. He nearly tackled me. Stopping short, he hugged me while he shamelessly, openly and violently sobbed. His strong arms pulled me into a bear hug. I never really understood the import of this Shakespearean word before this moment, but now I do.

He *beseeched* me, "How is my boy? How is my boy?"

I reported that everything had gone well and then resorted to brain surgeon speak. There was an excellent resection, but we would have to wait for the final pathology. The technicalities did their trick. Mr. Liquori didn't ask more questions and I didn't have to unload the bad news about the nature of the tumor. After all, the report I had in the OR was preliminary, which could change when the final diagnosis arrived in a few days. Wait for proof.

Anthony awoke in the ICU and moved all of his limbs—a good sign. I kept his breathing tube in overnight and ordered an MRI for first thing in the morning while he was still heavily sedated. The MRI would tell the extent of the resection, in other words, how well I did. I prayed for a clean scan. Occasionally, a small shred of tumor on the follow-up scan requires a reoperation to remove the residual bit, so the initial review of the post-op MRI scan is a tense time. It's pass or fail.

The next morning the good news arrived—a clean postoperative scan, no residual tumor. With a clean scan I headed to my office to see patients in my clinic. I left the hospital cautiously optimistic. As the morning flipped into the afternoon, I got a page and was called in.

"Anthony's parents would like to see you. They have some questions. They don't feel he's acting right," said the ICU nurse.

I froze.

A flood of dismay rushed through my body and I scrambled to collect my thoughts. What I expected to happen, a difficult but progressively improving recovery, wasn't happening. And now I had to figure out why that was…

And then after the dismay rush…irritability kicked in.

Don't they know I was there earlier and the scan was clear? Don't they realize I have other patients? They want me to just drop everything to be at their beck and call?

And then I reminded myself that parents have only one true objective—to safeguard their child.

I asked the nurse if something had changed. "Well, kind of, but I can't put my finger on it. He's awake, but he screams bloody murder when I try to move him. He won't talk. And the parents have concerns."

"I'll be over."

The trip would extend my day further into the evening. I'd have to go back to the hospital and see Anthony again after a busy late afternoon office. I kept seeing new patients and focused on their troubles as best as I could, but I couldn't get Anthony out of my mind.

What was going on? Was he just grumpy from the incisional pain or was it something more? The report of him being nonverbal and extremely sensitive to touch concerned me. *It could be a posterior fossa syndrome with cerebellar mutism causing this response.*

This is a rare yet well-documented pediatric post-neurosurgical phenomenon in patients who have surgery for fourth ventricular tumors. It's a poorly understood mechanism that is thought to be related to postoperative swelling, manifested by mutism (the inability to speak), irritability, ataxia and low muscle tone. Blood flow studies have suggested that it is related to a disruption or irritation of the dentate-thalamo-cortical pathway, a relay system that coordinates motion of the speaking muscles and the muscles controlling locomotion. The thing is, very little is known about how it happens. You might as well say the child is "cursed" for the description has no prescription. It's maddening.

Did I warn Anthony's parents about this potential condition preoperatively? I'm sure I did. It's always part of my pre-op talk, but it's a hard concept for parents to understand, especially when they are already in shock about their child having a tumor and about to undergo surgery. Most parents just sign the papers and try not to overwhelm themselves with brain surgeon speak. It's completely understandable.

I finished my office hours and headed back to the hospital. Anthony was awake with eyes wide open. He looked at me. I asked him to say hello.

Nothing.

"Tell me your name!" I said in a booming, coma-stirring tone brain surgeons use when making rounds of semiconscious patients in the ICU.

I asked him to show me two fingers.

Nothing.

Then I reached out to lift his arm. Just as my fingers made contact, he shrieked at the top of his lungs, startling everyone on the floor. I tried to move Anthony's other arm. He screeched again. And his legs were as flaccid as his arms. His dad anguished witnessing it all. No question, no doubt. Anthony was much worse than his immediate postoperative exam.

I went through the neurological change algorithm drilled into my head from junior year residency and got to work. I checked everything—oxygen saturation, CO_2 level, medication list for idiosyncratic reactions, sodium and electrolytes, glucose level, blood pressure, temperature. Meningitis? Too early, but I sent for analysis anyway. I ordered a stat CT of his head. It could be a hematoma but the symptoms didn't match. I helped wheel him down to the scanner and then sat in the control room, viewing the images.

Negative. Nothing.

No blood clot or fluid buildup. The drain was in good position. Labs were normal.

I updated Anthony's parents that the scan looked clear and there was nothing that could be done surgically. I told them I suspected the early onset of cerebellar mutism and the posterior fossa syndrome. I gently reminded them that I had mentioned it before the surgery but they looked at me like it was new information. I sat down and explained this unusual phenomenon in great detail and that it was, to the best of my knowledge, usually improved over time. Time. Wait it out. See what happens next. That was the only thing we could do.

I got home at around 9:30 p.m.

I wasn't crystal clear that night, but as the days and nights would follow, I'd fall into a brand new life, with Anthony penetrating every moment of my conscious and unconscious thoughts. Remembering his shrieks and envisioning his parents' tormented faces fed my darkest fears and insecurities. I couldn't enjoy time with my own family. I was "home" but far away at the same time.

The next morning Anthony was worse. He spontaneously screeched, without physical stimulus, and scared the hell out of everyone in the unit. The ICU team wanted to sedate him with narcotics. I said no. He wasn't in pain. His brain was simply getting some internal message and firing verbal responses. To drug him up so as not to disturb the rest of us wasn't right. So we moved Anthony to an isolation room. At least there, his shrieks were muffled by the enclosure. As he convalesced from surgery his incisions healed.

And yet…his condition did not improve.

Since I removed Anthony's tumor, I reasoned that the obstruction was now gone and it was likely I could wean him off the drain that was still attached to his scalp. Unfortunately, overnight his intracranial pressure went up and I had to open up the drain again. After several days of trying to wean Anthony off the drain, it became apparent that he needed a permanent internal shunt to drain his spinal fluid.

Back to the ICU family room. Back to Mr. and Mrs. Liquori.

It was another disappointment, I told them, but some kids do need a shunt. I made sure to remind them that I'd mentioned that before the surgery, too. Now I had to do another procedure on this boy to insert a more permanent drain into his head. The parents consented, and I shunted Anthony two weeks after his surgery. I was then able to transfer Anthony out of the ICU because he no longer had an external drain; now it was internal and the risk of infection was minimized.

I'd solved his fluid problem. But nothing else.

A few days went by and Anthony developed another fluid buildup. The scan showed his fluid pockets had enlarged again. This was unusual. I pumped the shunt. Maybe something clogged the tubing? Back to the ICU for Anthony. I reprogrammed the shunt, which can be adjusted for pressures depending on a patient's unique needs.

I adjusted his bed to a sixty-degree angle to promote a syphoning effect with the fluid column in his shunt tubing. I needed him more upright rather than just lying flat in bed. This would promote drainage. Of course, this meant touching him and inciting his loud shrieks too.

Due to multiple complications, infections and intermittent shunt malfunctions, Anthony remained in the hospital for three months. He suffered. His parents suffered too. Every day my rounds brought me to him. Every day I saw what I'd done to this beautiful boy who I egotistically believed I'd cured.

I soon developed symptoms of my own. As he continued to do poorly…depression overtook me.

There were so many phone calls coming from the ICU. Then it was dealing with his waxing and waning neurological exams, medications and complications. And innumerable meetings with his parents in which I had nothing to tell them but bad news. I had no idea why Anthony wasn't recovering and I had no idea what I could do about it.

I thought I had done everything right, as well as I possibly could, using the best medical attention and science available.

And still I had maimed this boy.

Eventually Anthony stabilized, but I got worse.

I felt very alone, despite being around very caring partners and a loving family. I can't truly describe the depths of my sadness but it was profound. I just kept thinking about this young beautiful boy who would never be what he would have become if this tumor had never reared its ugly head.

I kept thinking about my son Alex who was near Anthony's age. Why was I so lucky to have such a beautiful healthy boy and Anthony's dad so unlucky? The randomness and nonsensical nature of life tore me apart.

In his landmark article "Terrible Knowledge," Jeffrey Jay describes a perspective that I personally became familiar with during my Anthony depression. As one of his interviewees with Post-Traumatic Stress Disorder stated, "[I have a sense] of really knowing the truth in a way that other people don't know it. And all the truth is harsh and impossible to really accept, and yet you have to go on and function."

Jay described this victim of PTSD as the carrier of "terrible, but important knowledge." That's exactly how I felt after Anthony. It was like everyone around me was living a life of naiveté and I was the only one who knew how tortured life could be. The more I tried to forget about Anthony the less I could.

If someone asked me to chronologically divide my twenty-eight years of neurosurgery into just two time periods, it would be BA and AA—or Before Anthony and After Anthony. To highlight this turning point in my life, I hung up a plaque in my office that held his photo. He's holding my hand with his mom and dad at his bedside. It's a beautiful gift to have known him even with the terrible knowledge that I'd failed him.

PART ONE

The Problem

ONE
The Fear Freak-Out Problem

It's taken me twenty-eight years to boil down all of my life's difficulties into a single all-encompassing meta-problem. Even more striking, the process of slicing and dicing this problem over the past three years writing this book brought me to an even more striking conclusion.

Even though I've never met you and probably never will…we may be of different nationalities, different skin color, different gender, or even different political or social affiliation…I am certain you have the exact same all-encompassing problem I do.

This is the mother of all problems…the source.

It's what I call the "fear freak-out problem."

Let's say you've been working very hard to reach a goal. It could be the goal of going to your college of choice, saving enough money to buy a house, or convincing another person to spend the rest of their life with you. Or in my case…becoming a brain surgeon.

You're making progress. You're almost there. Or, maybe you have reached that goal and just want to maintain what you've already attained.

And then something unexpected happens that drops you into a dark psychological vortex. Like what happened for me after Anthony.

Things haven't gone according to your plan. And all of the work you put into the process, all of the late nights, all of the sacrifice you've made across every level of your life adds up to…a negative outcome. In fact, the result of all of your hard work is not just a negative outcome; it's a result that you would rank as one of the absolute worst things that has ever happened to you.

The fact torments you because you just didn't see it coming. And it just doesn't make any sense. No matter how much you turn it over in your mind, you can't stop freaking out about it.

You keep asking yourself a slew of impossible questions.

For me, after the Anthony experience, the questions looked like these:

How could I spend tens of thousands of hours of my life preparing and learning a valuable skill and end up maiming a little boy?

How is it that I could do everything according to the "book"—that is, correctly and up to the standards of the most advanced health care system in the world—and end up with a result that is a fate worse than death? Because, make no mistake, my performance resulted in that little boy's life turning upside down.

And after what happened with Anthony, how am I supposed to live with myself? How am I supposed to get back in the OR, put the past out of my mind and perform as if I were unaffected by the deeply traumatic experience?

I operated on Anthony nineteen years ago. I performed at my highest level under the highest life or death pressure imaginable. I could not have done anything better. And still, I failed.

Ever since, I've been running from the fear of failing another boy or girl like Anthony.

In fact, I quit pediatric neurosurgery because of it.

So, the "fear freak-out" (FFO) problem and I are very close companions.

That's my big meta-problem. How can I stop the fear freak-out and perform at my highest standard? How can I make sense of things that don't make sense?

The answer, the solution I've discovered with help from everyone close to me, especially my father, is a mental practice, a psycho-technology I call *cognitive dominance*. Admittedly, this phrase is overly serious and rather intimidating, which are two of the reasons I love it so much. The phrase *cognitive dominance* is like wrapping your mind around

The Force in *Star Wars*. It sounds cool, but it's also cryptic and amorphous. So let's start with the technical definition of *cognitive dominance*, which has been percolating in military circles for some time now.

Cognitive Dominance: *Enhanced situational awareness that facilitates rapid and accurate decision-making under stressful conditions with limited decision-making time.*

Let's unpack it:

1. *Enhanced situational awareness:* Focusing your attention on unexpected information that arises while you are pursuing some goal.

2. *Rapid:* Making decisions quickly.

3. *Accurate*: Making decisions about what to do about unexpected information with the greatest probability of achieving your fundamental goal—that is, accurately solving the problem of the unexpected information.

4. *Under stressful conditions with limited decision-making time*: Acting this way under demanding physical and mental stress.

If *cognitive dominance* represents the ideal way to handle unexpected information, the technical, military-like definition of "fear freak-out" would be:

Fear Freak-Out: *Compromised situational awareness that delays decision-making, which increases the severity of stressful conditions as time rapidly expires, leading to indecision or poor decisions.*

Let's unpack it:

1. *Compromised situational awareness:* Focusing your attention on the response (fear) induced by an unexpected event instead of intellectually metabolizing the stimulus.

2. *Delays:* Slows down decision-making.

3. *Increases*: Makes the physical and psychological experience of the stress worse.

4. *As time rapidly expires*: The time to act is slipping away as the stress and negative feeling double down in a negative feedback loop.

In other words, as a performance goal, *cognitive dominance* is the opposite of *fear freak-out*. It's the goal state for keeping your cool. My take is that cognitive dominance is the process by which you achieve what Ernest Hemingway called "grace under pressure." It's an evolving discipline to get better and better at quickly performing at the limits of your mental and physical capacity under maximum pressure with the highest probability of success.

Nailing the winning free throw for the NBA championship. Successfully landing a plane on the Hudson River after your engines have failed and you're flying in one of the most densely populated places on Earth. Not losing your temper as you pile four children under the age of five into their car seats while making sure your cartful of groceries doesn't careen into the sports car parked next to your minivan as the children wail and scream in protest.

A high bar indeed, but knowing the location of the top of the stimulus/response mountain is extremely useful.

Now all we need to do is pack some supplies and begin the climb up.

My armchair general dad is responsible for focusing me on this strategic heuristic psycho-technology, which is a fancy way of labeling a mind-tool thinking process. I'd first heard my mentor and longtime friend at the Center for Enhanced Performance at the United States Military Academy, the brilliant Dr. Nate Zinsser mention the phrase. It intrigued me but I wasn't anywhere near the level of Nate to wrap my mind around it.

When I debriefed my dad after that visit to West Point and mentioned this new term, Dad got very excited. The next morning, he sent me one of his signature predawn emails shining a light on this concept and implored me to pursue it as a major topic for my book. Dad was familiar with the term, which he came across in his research for a nonfiction military history book he was writing. Somehow he knew this concept was enlightening and transferrable to all areas of one's life. Not just neurosurgeons, who obviously need to develop this skill, but it is applicable to anyone facing a threatening unexpected event.

However, we simply didn't have a name for it. And then my dad pointed out to me…EVERYONE is trying to attain cognitive dominance, no matter what life stage they're currently navigating!

Cognitive dominance is a way of tuning out the noise of the world so you can just focus on the signal, the fascinating but challenging problem at hand. For sports, the signal is clear, the problem is acting in such a way as to increase the probability of winning the game—allowing the muscle memory from practice to take over to make the shot, catch the pass, score the goal, beat the clock. That's just the most obvious application of the discipline.

For real life, *cognitive dominance* is a way of thinking, a methodology to quickly make difficult decisions while remaining clearly in sync with your overall worldview—what you value and perceive to be your most important life principle. I define life value as simply how you would describe winning the game of life. If asked on your deathbed if you had a meaningful life, you'd without hesitation say, "Yes." That's winning the game of life. And yes, I think you need to have a single easily accessible life goal in your mind. If you have that goal readily accessible in times of stress, you'll abide by the principles you've embraced in times of leisure.

The reason I fell so deeply into depression after Anthony was that in all of the drama of my everyday life over all of the years it took me to reach my professional life goals, I hadn't clearly defined what my single life goal was. I didn't know what "winning the game of life" would look like or feel like. So it was only reasonable that I succumbed to the disorientation of happenstance, the unexpected. Fear can easily freak you out when you don't have a grip on what winning the game of life means to you. Stephen Covey described this funk in his landmark book *The Seven Habits of Highly Effective People,* calling it "getting caught up in the thick of thin things."

Just after Anthony, I had no idea what my real problem was, which was my lack of defining and committing to a fundamental life value. In fact, how I reacted to the unexpected—making a herculean effort to run away from its meaning—was to thrash about with substances that would distract me (alcohol, tobacco and escapism) from negative emotions. I was in an ever-present state of fear.

And then while I was struggling, seemingly offhandedly, my dad advised me to zero in on this *cognitive dominance* idea.

I fell for it hook, line and sinker. Shortly thereafter, I committed to integrating what I knew about the brain with what other brain-based scientists had pursued and continued to investigate about how to best contend with fear. Psychologists, anatomists, neuroscientists, philosophers and cognitive scientists—their professional titles didn't matter to me as long as their work connected to this notion of how to solve the fear freak-out problem. To say this mission became an obsession for me is an understatement.

I discovered that becoming *cognitively dominant* is fundamentally simple but extremely difficult to put into practice.

Here's the scoop. When something unexpected drops into your life, pay very close attention to it. Laser focus on it until you can break it into two parts.

Part One is the objective fact of it. What is it as material matter? What are its measurable parts…it's length, size, shape? How would a scientist define it? Have you seen this kind of thing before? Is it known to you? Or is it unknown, something you haven't seen before?

Part Two is the subjective truth of it. Why does this thing or event matter to you? How does it challenge or support the story you tell yourself about yourself? Is it something you can use to reach a goal? Or is it something that will keep you from attaining a goal? How can you define it in terms of your fundamental "winning the game of life" goal? Does it threaten that goal or does it get you closer to that goal? Is it known to you? Or is it an unknown, something you haven't experienced before?

This cognitive dominance process, using your mind to break down the unexpected information or thing and what it means into two parts, is essential to keeping yourself from freaking out, succumbing to fear, or running away from things or events that drop you into a depression. In fact, the concentrated mental energy you employ to break the thing into those two pieces actually releases a lot of fear's influence on you. The more you concentrate on the objective and subjective components of the problem or unexpected event, the less fear you'll feel.

When you behave in a cognitively dominant manner, you'll solve the problem that must be solved in order to get you closer to your global life goal, and you'll faithfully abide by the principles you've committed to when you're not under intense pressure.

This *"how to move beyond fear"* methodology is easy to say, of course, and hundreds of books have been written about how to cope with fear.

However, the *doing* is difficult.

Since I began this project, I didn't wish for *Cognitive Dominance* to join the growing list of other inspirational but impractical *"how to move beyond fear"* titles…just another book offering a complex solution to an ill-defined problem. So I decided to break this psycho-technology into smaller parts. I began by thinking about what would convince me to use *cognitive dominance* as an operating system when I found myself fearful.

As an inherently skeptical person, I would insist on a couple of things before I'd even begin to take this idea seriously.

The first thing I'd need to convince me to give it deeper thought is a clear description of what this "fear freak-out" thing is to begin with. I'd want the author to tell me the objective facts about it. On the surface, it seems a bit broad of a problem. What are the details?

Because I have a unique perspective on the brain and how it functions as well as a penchant for philosophy, I'll begin by describing the fear freak-out problem with quite a bit of resolution.

Where did it come from?

Who suffers from it?

What kind of symptoms does it give the sufferer?

What causes fear freak-out?

What are the constituent parts of the phenomenon that causes it?

How do we deal with the problem already?

After having a firm grasp of fear's origin story, I'd want to know:

How do I identify the thing that causes fear in my day-to-day life?

How does my current way of dealing with the problem go wrong?

If this description of the problem and its source are convincing, I'd want to read about the author's proposed solution to the problem and then ultimately how the author proposes that I could actually do what he recommends. With multiple and interesting clear examples.

So first I'd want description of the problem and then I'd want a prescription for solving that problem—not just a generic description or prescription either. I'd want real-life examples of how this problem surfaced for someone else to see if the description is similar to something I've experienced. Then I could follow the same path as a means to deal with the problems I experience in my own life.

These are the must-haves I set up for writing *Cognitive Dominance*.

So, the first chunk of the book will describe the problem, which is the fear freak-out problem. In my case with Anthony, I was not able to deal with a difficult unexpected event to such a degree it made me obsessive about the "terrible knowledge" I'd discovered and I took myself out of pediatric neurosurgery entirely.

The next part of the book will put us on the road to cognitive dominance, building our understanding of the discipline step by step. *We'll build up a deep understanding of how our brain works and then streamline the nuanced responses we receive into four broad categories.*

The last part will begin the "prescription" part of the book. It's about cognitive consonance, or how to build a hierarchy of beliefs that will serve you in times of serious uncertainty. Taking the time to clearly define what you value most and then living a life dedicated to promoting that value is the key to living a cognitively consonant life. Knowing where your fundamental meaningful value line in the sand is will enable you to practice cognitive dominance.

I'll offer some of the tools I've gathered over twenty years as a practicing brain surgeon that have kept me sharp in the OR, operating at the limits of my capacity. While these tools are specific to brain surgery, they are easily transferable to everyday life. In fact, I suspect the everyday life foundation within them came first and then they became more specific to brain surgeons later.

I'll intersperse all of the theoretical and philosophical stuff with stories from my own life, the sum of which relays my quest to understand how to deal with fear productively. I'm no spring chicken and this process was painful and challenging. But looking back, I don't really see how I could have learned about cognitive dominance any other way. Like Bilbo Baggins setting out to seize treasure from the dragon Smaug in *The Hobbit,* I had to come into myself the hard way. Thankfully, I had plenty of mentors who invested their time and care in me along the way. And while there is no shortcut for any of us on our own private quests toward winning our own games of life, my desire is that *Cognitive Dominance* will become a go-to operating tool for you along the way.

TWO
The Gripper

It's January in New Jersey.
1976.

The early morning trip to school is in darkness. And the end-of-day walk from the gym door to the car ride home is darker still. Drenched in sweat after a grueling mid-season wrestling practice, the frost cuts straight through my sweats, winter jacket and woolen hat. I'm cold and hot at the same time.

I open the door, snatch the gripper wedged in the passenger seat crease, and tuck it under the middle armrest console as I climb into Dad's Cadillac. Mozart's Symphony No. 6 fills the warm air. Dad pulls the car into gear just after he hears the click of my seatbelt buckle.

The nine-minute ride to 10 Farmstead Road will be silent. Too exhausted to talk, I close my eyes.

Dad reaches first, pulling my clammy paw up to the middle of the armrest space between us. His firm calloused hand engulfs my soft sixth-grade fingers.

Squeeze...

Squeeze.

Dad knows everything there is to know about exhaustion. And he knows conversation is the last thing a boy or man wants after confronting and surviving the fear inherent in conflict—be it physical, emotional or intellectual. But he also knows that weathering trials alone, without some kind of heartfelt validation along the way from another human being, can crush your soul.

So connecting hand to hand is our secret Morse code…*I'll squeeze your hand twice and you do it back.*

Squeeze one means *I'm here.*

Squeeze two means *I love you.*

If I don't squeeze twice back, he'll keep repeating until I do.

We honor our code without giving voice to it.

Forty-one years after my boyhood ride in Dad's Cadillac, it's still January. Still New Jersey.

I'm sitting in an idling Acura in a hospital parking lot working up my "brain surgeon mask," a crucial confident and unflappable surgical persona I need to show my patient and his family.

It's not easy.

It's a gray Friday afternoon and my inner critical voice reminds me that by the time my head hits a pillow tonight, I will have logged another eighty-hour week with five intense multi-hour surgeries, daily rounds, and dozens of patients seen during my office hours. Now I'm preparing for a difficult craniotomy—an operation that requires the temporary removal of a disk of skull. It's been delayed by the hospital administrator, pushed back to 2:30 p.m.

The now deceased chef and TV personality Anthony Bourdain wrote in his book *Kitchen Confidential* that you shouldn't order fish in a restaurant on Monday because the fresh fish is delivered on Tuesdays. You'll be eating whatever's left from the week before on a Monday.

The surgeon's equivalent of "don't order fish on Monday" is "avoid the 2:30 p.m. surgery slot." The reason is that a half-hour in, 3:00 p.m., is "handoff" time. This is the hour when surgical nurses change shifts.

Ask surgeons and they'll tell you that having immediate access to their tools without uncertainty or delay allows them to invest all of their cognitive energy where it needs to be…on the operation. And no one has a more intimate knowledge of where everything is than the hands that set the instrument table. The surgical nurse is indispensable.

Having a 2:30 op time means the table will be set by one scrub tech, the one who is usually the most experienced in the procedure, but at the 3:00 click of the clock, the shift change "handoff" will begin. Another equally well-trained (but probably less experienced) scrub tech will then take over. Same thing goes for the circulator…the nurse who manages everything beyond the sterile field of operation.

Invariably, no matter how meticulous and efficient the handoff seems, some instrument will be forgotten or misplaced or hidden in plain sight.

The special instrument I asked scrub tech number one to have handy at 2:30 will not be found at 6:30 when I need it because scrub tech number two is faced with a *Where's Waldo* chaos of instruments laid out by someone else.

Me: "Where is my Sachs Dissector?"
Tech: "You didn't ask *me* for it. Let's go get another."

Now I face (and more importantly the patient faces) a fifteen-minute delay, four hours into the operation while some poor circulator forages in the back neuro room for a tiny instrument that was wrapped and labeled by a nurse who went home at 3:00.

That's how surgical rhythm is destroyed.

So, there's that. Two-thirty in the afternoon is the worst time of day for surgery and I'm at the end of a tough week.

Add on the fact that I typically don't operate on these kinds of tumors in the deep occipital lobe, the domain of vision. I've done many of these operations in my past, but I haven't done one recently.

A cook who makes Beef Wellington everyday gets good at it. If he's asked to change his menu to Lobster Newberg after two years of perfecting Beef Wellington? He'll be able to and chances are he'll be able to do it well, but it will require far more cognitive energy to remember the older skills.

When you're doing brain surgery, though, you don't have the margin for error factor a chef has. The procedure is life and death and you want to reserve as much energy as possible to ensure it results in the former not the latter.

I'm doing this operation because my partner Seth, our practice's tumor specialist, is out of town. And if we let the tumor simmer over the weekend, the patient might get into some trouble—intracranial swelling between the skull and the brain or bleeding kind of trouble.

We're pretty sure the patient has what we call "a tumor that can't wait." One of my great fears in my career has always been hearing the news that one of my loved ones has suffered an intracranial hemorrhage. I've made so many "no surgery" recommendations based on the age of the patient and the severity of the swelling that I'll do just about anything I can to avoid having to make another one. So I'm pressing to get this one done today.

In a medical journal, the conditions would be categorized as "suboptimal."

I'm about to step out of the car, ready to go, when a red "You have voicemail" bubble pops up on my phone. It's from my dad's primary physician.

My spine stiffens.

Dad never could sit still.

If we were stopped at a red light, his need to burn extra internal energy presented itself with a three-note "click ta-tink."

While other men of his generation accepted their lot in life—afraid to push themselves into uncomfortable situations when their mental or physical faculties could prove wanting—Dad had no time to sit on barstools or collapse in Barcaloungers watching younger men play sports on television.

His commitment to shouldering life's load began in 1946, when he was just eighteen. That's when he began lifting weights, a practice considered ridiculous and even dangerous at the time. So much for conventional wisdom as our finest athletes today take strength and conditioning as a given. From day one, Dad credited exercise with giving him not just physical strength but cognitive energy.

He was addicted to consciously applied stress, as evidenced by the cheesy gadgets like the ones sold on late night TV littering his garage—abdominizers, pectoralis plungers, shake weights. You name it. But his ever-present companion, the one that never lost its place in his betterment pantheon, was the classic hand gripper. A talisman for fighting idleness, he'd stuff it under his car's front middle console, its seat crease or its door pocket.

A properly executed closure of the gripper made a distinct coupling of two sounds. First you'd hear the two butts of the handles meeting, a deep wooden pitched "click," followed almost instantaneously by "ta-tink," the contacting jiggle sound of the metal figure eight that held the iron spring between the two handles in place.

"This builds great grip strength, son. Squeeze it multiple times for strength, hold it closed as long as you can to develop a vise-like hand grip. It makes for an impressive handshake and it's sure to help in wrestling."

Dad's hand grippers turned my little sausage fingers, bloated hands and pudgy forearms into the front-line weapons of my profession. I've never worried about losing the grip on a surgical instrument. When I command my hands, they respond.

After two years in the Army, Dad came home to an office job and put his GI Bill to work. Remarkably, he'd work a full day and then he'd go to night school until he got his college degree. Then he went back in the Army when called again and was off to Korea.

Home again after that war, he refused to fade away. He did what he knew gave him strength. He went back to work during the day and back to school at night. This time he earned his law degree. A forty-year commercial legal career followed. That work allowed him to send his kids to the best schools, to stretch themselves like he had. All dues and bills paid, he left law when he was seventy-one.

Now, he was finally free to do what he'd always wanted—to stretch himself mentally as hard as he had physically.

An inveterate polymath, the septuagenarian went back to school again. He enrolled at Drew University for a master's degree in Theology...and then got a PhD in history. By seventy-eight years old, he still had energy to burn. So he wrote his first military history book at age eighty-three and polished off his second tome at eighty-eight.

Dad's love of history, literature and the spirited unpacking of big ideas passed on to me. He shared one of his favorite poems with me just as I faced a major challenge in my own life. Dylan Thomas's *Do Not Go Gentle into That Good Night* arrived when I was in high school struggling to maintain my grades while grinding it out after a harsh wrestling defeat in the state championship finals. I understood the poem on the surface...get the most out of every day. And I did.

Now sitting in the Acura in the doctors' parking lot staring at the red message balloon on my cell phone, I'm talking myself through a decision and understanding the poem at a whole new level... Do I call Dad's primary before I go into the OR at the worst time of the day doing a procedure that I'm not entirely comfortable with? Or do I wait until I'm done with the surgery?

It's Friday. If I don't call him back now, he may be one of those doctors who won't return nonemergency calls until Monday morning. Then I'll have to wait all weekend to hear Dad's diagnosis.

I call him.

THREE
On the Origin of Fear

In his advanced years, after he'd written *On the Origin of Species* and *The Descent of Man*, Charles Darwin turned his mind from the mystery of how species evolve over eons to how individual beings within that species change from moment to moment.

This begged the question, is there a single internal "change" driver? An internal, invisible feature that certain individuals within a species had within them that gave them a survival advantage? These individuals would know as Kenny Rogers would write years later "when to hold 'em, when to fold 'em, when to walk away, and know when to run." This automatic, internally driven process—something baked into life—would safeguard the individual's survival from moment to moment.

Given a relatively stable environment—no ice age or meteor explosion or famine—Darwin reasoned that individual behavior determined survival and reproduction. The individuals who had the best internal adaptation systems would win the reproduction game and pass their traits on to the next generation. Today we'd say their genes would be passed on while those without this system wouldn't. So an entire species' survival depended upon individual internal adaptation to the environment as much as external adaptation like hairy morphology in cold environments or smooth morphology in hot ones. Internal traits were as inherently important as external. More so, even.

If a single individual was more adept at avoiding predators while keeping an eye out for edible berry bushes but her brother wasn't, she would have a greater probability of survival than her brother. In this case, a better kind of warning system inside the female being would alert her to the dangerous territory or the opportunity of the berry bushes compared to the male's warning system. And if the female's system had a very wide range of detection—everything from the danger of an odd-looking poisonous mushroom or the threat of a certain member of her herd all the way up to the danger of a lion—the probability of that female being's survival from moment to moment would dramatically increase with each new identification of threat or opportunity.

So it stands to reason, the better a being's internal warning system, which indicates to them they should consider changing their behavior, the better chance of their survival and reproduction. And the more nuanced the identification of unexpected phenomena picked up by their warning system, the better the being will navigate the world. And the better they navigate the world, the more probable they are to mate and have children. If they are the winners of the mating contest in their tribe, their children will make up the next generation for the tribe. And so on.

So a system that tells beings to pay attention when they are under threat or in the presence of opportunity is critical to create and sustain life. With this survive and thrive advantage system already present in humanity, Darwin believed this trait must have started somewhere and at some time.

Darwin suspected that the system began as an automatic response to life-threatening phenomena and then became more and more nuanced over time. It began with the negative. Threats are more important to deal with than opportunity. We can bypass opportunity and survive but we can't do that with a threat.

When time is of the essence, Darwin thought this warning system would simply override the being's usual navigational systems and trigger a response automatically. Just like he would find himself crossing the street before consciously noticing the stranger lurking in the opposite alleyway. In the presence of a predator, the system would fire first and the being would get out of the area without even consciously thinking about it.

Then he hypothesized that certain stimuli are so dangerous they must trigger immediate responses without the being employing any extraordinary decision-making process at all.

With an Anglican Christian upbringing, Darwin's mind naturally latched on to the notion of the snake in the Garden of Eden. If there were one stimulus man should avoid, it would be a snake. So he hypothesized that jumping back from something like a snake just happened. The being didn't think, "Oh there is a snake. I should move away from it." Instead the system got "snake!" messages from all of its senses, not just sight, and then fired the necessary orders for the being to jump back before conscious thought.

So Darwin set off for the Zoological Gardens in London's Regent's Park to test this idea out. He relates the experience in his final book *The Expressions of the Emotions in Man and Animals:*

"I put my face close to the thick glass-plate in front of a puff-adder in the Zoological Gardens, with the firm determination of not starting back if the snake struck at me; but, as soon as the blow was struck, my resolution went for nothing, and I jumped a yard or two backwards with astonishing rapidity. My will and reason were powerless against the imagination of a danger, which had never been experienced."[1]

Darwin's suspicion that our nervous systems make us do things we haven't thought of doing was an idea that launched hundreds of thousands of hours of future scientific research. And it had no small influence on the rise of an entirely new scientific field of inquiry too—Psychology, and more specifically the psychoanalytical school associated with Sigmund Freud. Darwin used his snake response to put forth a theory that structures inside our body bypass our consciousness to get us to do things we hadn't specifically thought of doing beforehand.

The way the system gets us to do things is by pumping us with an emotion called fear. In the snake response instance, we feel the fear after

1   Charles Darwin, *The Expressions of the Emotions in Man and Animals*, (New York: D. Appleton & Company, 1886) 38.

the response. But in most instances, we feel the fear first before we respond to it. Fear is the warning signal that something's up.

While poets and philosophers have explored the subject of fear since man began telling stories, this scientific description is a relatively new concept. In the one hundred and thirty-three years since Darwin's observation, intrepid investigators set out to find exactly where this "automatic fear of snakes jump" response lived inside our nervous systems.

In 2001 and 2003, in their papers "Fears, Phobias, and Preparedness: Toward an Evolved Module of Fear and Fear Learning" and "The Malicious Serpent: Snakes as a Prototypical Stimulus for an Evolved Module of Fear," Arne Öhman at the Karolinska Institute in Stockholm, Sweden, and Susan Mineka at Northwestern University convincingly presented the empirical evidence for Darwin's snake jump.

So the notion that there is a fundamental behavioral change driver in human beings, a system in place that gets us to change our behavior without our conscious consent, is an objective scientific method proven fact.

What's really remarkable is that the "Snake!" response is still so amazingly strong inside each and every one of us that it fires even though we may never have seen a snake in our entire lives. But when we see one in a zoo—just like Charles Darwin did all those years ago—we freak out and jump back. And to top it off, the neural network pathway called "the fear module," the literal channel in our brain responsible for the snake response, was discovered and documented by neuroanatomists in 2001. It lives inside a place in the brain where our emotional experiences are generated called the amygdala.[2]

So we have an automatic system that protects us from unexpected threats like snakes. This system protects us and makes decisions for us before we have to do any work whatsoever. These fear freak-outs are absolutely justifiable and no one would dispute the necessity of having

---

2   Arne Ohman, Susan Mineka, "Fears, Phobias, and Preparedness: Toward an Evolved Module of Fear and Fear Learning," Psychological Review, Vol. 108, No. 3, (2001) 483-522

them. But what about the other kinds of fear we feel? The ones that somehow lead us to fear freak-out without our being in immediate danger? Let's take a look at those in higher resolution.

FOUR
The Gradient of Fear

If I'm on a quest to out-think fear, it would be a good idea to laser focus on exactly what I mean by fear.

From Darwin, we know the snake response is the first level of defense we have to deal with unexpected events like a deadly predator crossing our path. And common sense tells us that after we jump back from the snake, we experience a rush of fear and anxiety to reinforce our body's attunement to sudden life-threatening environmental changes.

But that description of fear is not even close to a global definition of what fear actually means to each and every one of us. Fear is probably the most nuanced emotion we experience. There are many kinds and flavors of fear.

So what exactly is fear? And what varieties of fear do we experience?

I'm going to first break this big problem into two pieces. I think we experience fear in two separate ways. One is an internal experience, in our own minds, and one is an external experience where we show fear through our expressions and actions.

I learned this when my cowriter Shawn Coyne and I were grappling with the structure of this book. The problem was just bigger than the both of us. So we agreed to bring in a third party, someone who specializes in helping people cope with fear in their life's work. He could bring a fresh and probing perspective to our problem. My friend Ken Davidson is a counselor at the consultancy Workability, and he agreed to help us out.

Wisely, instead of giving us a nine-hour lecture about how he defined fear, Ken put the onus on us. To kick off the exploration, he asked us both to write down how we would individually define fear.

Here's what I wrote down:

Fear is the anticipation of not performing to my highest standards, of harming someone because I was not properly prepared.

For a surgeon, hurting your patients is the worst possible event for you. Obviously my experience with Anthony is testimony to that as was my Grandfather Pizzi's experience that I share in chapter 30. So for me, fear was an internally experienced emotional state in which I anticipated a future event in which I hurt someone. I feared an experience in the future of not performing at my highest level, and this failure of performance would result in another's suffering.

As Ken so eloquently put it, "We're afraid of what we are going to feel." In other words, internally we experience fear as present moment interior torment as we imagine what we are going to feel in the future after failure. So just the contemplation of the action, which we project to fail, produces fear.

Now here's what Shawn wrote down:

Fear is a neurological response to an unexpected event that triggers a negative emotional experience.

So for Shawn, fear was an externally induced experience. Something happens that we don't expect, which induces fear. We physically feel "fear," which is biologically evident by the release of cortisol into the blood stream. Cortisol is a hormone that in turn starts a whole slew of bodily responses that put the body into a state of high alert. The longer we remain in this high alert state, the more damaging it is to our bodies. It's like revving your weed-whacker at high throttle for longer than a few seconds. The whacker eventually overheats and stops working. If you live in a constant state of high alert, the drain on your body is extraordinary and it will eventually lead to death. So fear really can kill you.

In Shawn's estimation, fear is a phenomenon that can be monitored, measured, and externally quantified by evaluating the amount of "fear" substances like hormones in a person's blood stream. We can see people in fear, and depending upon their physical state, we can intuitively know just how fearful they are. Likewise, we can monitor heart rates, blood pressure and blood composition to see a corresponding heightened state when a person is exhibiting fear. There is absolutely a measurable gradient of degrees of fear in the body.

Ken helped us discover that we both accurately described a certain type or flavor of fear—one internal and one external. He then took the exploration to the next logical step and asked us to consider what a "gradient of fear" would look like. He wanted us to consider what is technically called a Semantic Differential Scale for a specific life value. Semantic Differential Scales are akin to those tests they ask you at the emergency room in a hospital. On a scale of one to ten, with ten being excruciating pain and one being no pain at all, what number would you give your pain?

The scale is a way of exploring whether there is a hierarchical approach to quantifying the qualified levels of fear. And checking in with yourself emotionally by pinpointing where on this hierarchy you fall is a great way of understanding just how close you may be to a "fear freak-out." Knowing how close or how far away you are from freaking out would be a great piece of information to have, especially when you're trying to figure out a solution to the problem that's giving you a difficult emotional reaction—one that distracts you from solving the problem. Wouldn't it?

We thought it would, so we put together this graph to illustrate the different levels of fear. From absolutely no fear experienced in the present or anticipated in the future, what we call "transcendent" to what we call the "fate worse than death," which would be living in such a hellish state of fear all of the time that death would seemingly be a mercy.

Now, you may review this schematic and personally feel that one of these emotional states should be higher or lower on the gradient. Your subjective point of view is valid. What I'm proposing is that if you were to ask one thousand people to put these words in order of positive or negative emotion, the probability is that the average of those responses would equate to this scale. I've not done that experimental research, but I sure wish I had the time to do it. This gradient is my best guesstimate based upon the phenomenon of Semantic Differential Scale thinking.

THE GRADIENT OF FEAR	
Transcendent **Certain** **Assured** **Confident** **Secure** **Homeostatic**	**INTERNALLY** **DOMINANT** **FEAR** **STATE**
Anticipating the drop in of an unexpected event on your way from WHERE YOU ARE to WHERE YOU WANT TO BE	
Uncertain **Doubtful** **Skeptical** **Timid** **Apprehensive** **Worry** **Dread** **Anxiety**	
The actual drop in of an unexpected event on your way from WHERE YOU ARE to WHERE YOU WANT TO BE	
Fear **Dismay** **Terror** **Panic** **Horror** **Mortification** **Fate Worse Than Death**	**EXTERNALLY** **DOMINANT** **FEAR** **STATE**

Let me explain exactly what I mean by each of these states of fear.

TRANSCENDENT: You have an infallible ability to cope with unexpected events in all of life's domains.

CERTAIN: You are convinced about your abilities to cope with unexpected events in a particular life domain.

ASSURED: You are predominantly positive about your ability to cope with unexpected events in multiple life domains.

CONFIDENT: You are predominantly positive about your ability to cope with a particular life domain.

SECURE: You have the attitude that the probability of positively coping with unexpected events across a wide bandwidth of life domains is greater than the probability of a negative result.

HOMEOSTATIC: Your attitude is neither positive nor negative about the probability of coping with unexpected events across a particular life domain or a wide bandwidth of life domains.

UNCERTAIN: You are specifically predisposed to believe that you have a lack of ability to cope with particular categories of unexpected events within a defined bandwidth of life domains.

DOUBTFUL: You have a general predisposition to believe that you have a lack of ability to cope with a wide bandwidth of unexpected events that drop into a wide bandwidth of life domains.

SKEPTICAL: You have an active and specific predisposition to consciously ignore unexpected events in a defined bandwidth of life domains.

TIMID: You have a general belief that you lack the abilities to cope with a wide bandwidth of unexpected events that drop into a wide bandwidth of life domains.

APPREHENSIVE: You generally anticipate your inability to cope with a wide bandwidth of unexpected events that drop into a wide bandwidth of life domains.

WORRY: You experience negative emotional response as you specifically anticipate your inability to cope with a specific category of unexpected event that drops into a wide bandwidth of life domains.

DREAD: You experience a severe negative emotional response as you specifically anticipate your inability to cope with a specific category of unexpected events that drops into a wide bandwidth of life domains.

ANXIETY: You experience a chronic and severe negative emotional response as you generally anticipate your inability to cope with a large category of unexpected events that drop into a wide bandwidth of life domains.

FEAR: You experience a negative emotional response after the drop-in of an identified an observable direct threat to your present directed path from "what is" to "what should be."

DISMAY: You experience an aftershock wave of increasing negative emotional response just after you've identified an observable direct threat to your present directed path from "what is" to "what should be" such that you lose your ability to cognitively process the event. You freeze.

TERROR: The aftershock wave of negative response reaches its zenith within the freeze.

PANIC: The freeze shifts into a binary sensory response offering two alternative motor actions—fight or flight. Panic is the moment of cognition whereby you toggle between these two "best bad choices" that offer the greatest probability of possible positive outcome.

HORROR: An overload of negative emotional stimulus that includes emotional, psychological, and physical distress at the moment of the individuals final "fight" or "flight" decision.

MORTIFICATION: The overwhelming emotional, psychological, and physical distress results in cardiac arrest and imminent death or a low-level release of chronic stimulus resulting in long-term degradation ultimately leading to death (PTSD).

THE FATE WORSE THAN DEATH: The interim period between the experience of a horrific event and death. The fate worse than death is the belief that death would be a mercy.

THE GRADIENT OF FEAR	
Transcendent Certain Assured Confident Secure Homeostatic	INTERNALLY DOMINANT FEAR STATE
Anticipating the drop in of an unexpected event on your way from WHERE YOU ARE to WHERE YOU WANT TO BE	
Uncertain Doubtful Skeptical Timid Apprehensive Worry Dread Anxiety	
The actual drop in of an unexpected event on your way from WHERE YOU ARE to WHERE YOU WANT TO BE	
Fear Dismay Terror Panic Horror Mortification Fate Worse Than Death	EXTERNALLY DOMINANT FEAR STATE

You'll see a solid line separates "anxiety" and "fear." This is the moment when "fear freak-out" can initiate and send you spiraling downward.

This bold solid horizontal line is also the place where our internal fears become external, the transitional moment when my internal definition of fear—**the anticipation of not performing to my highest standards, of harming someone because I was not properly prepared**—turns into Shawn's external definition of fear—**a neurological response to an unexpected event that triggers a negative emotional experience.** This is the place where a stimulus (either an anticipated or unexpected event) actually happens, which gets you to externalize your fear emotionally. We aren't worried about the impending event anymore because the event is actually happening. We may be afraid of snakes and worry about them before we set out on a hike, but we don't externalize the fear so much until we actually run into one.

All of the emotional fear experience until that external stimulus moment—the rise of something dreaded or unexpected while you are going about your everyday life—is internalized fear. I defined this type of fear as **the anticipation of not performing to my highest standards, of harming someone because I was not properly prepared.** So this fear of anticipated or unexpected events that haven't even happened is a perpetual state of being gun shy to some degree.

Cool, but what's the point of the gradient of fear? How does it relate to cognitive dominance?

Well, if we know there is a whole gradient of fear states, which our bodies enact internally and externally with very precise responses, those different flavors of fear feeling, it would stand to reason that these fear states are specific reactions to internal and external stimuli right?

The snake response, the unconscious jump back from the threat of a predator, happens in the presence of a snake. The snake stimulates the response. Sometimes we're on a hike and we jump back without even seeing a snake, but the response alerts us very quickly that a snake is in the area. The response gives us very rich clues about the stimulus, which is extremely helpful for us to predict what something means when we have no clue about it. On a hike, a quick, seemingly unnecessary unconscious jump back tells us that there are snakes crossing the trail and that we should pay attention. We end up hyper vigilant for the rest of the hike and thus greatly reduce the probability of being bitten.

We can use this very same concept to think about our other fear responses too.

For example, let's say we know that we have a project due on a specific date at a specific time. If we're students, we have a test this coming Friday at 9:00 a.m. Or if we're in the workforce we have our weekly meeting with our boss on Friday at 9:00 a.m. Those are objective facts of our lives. There's no subjective interpretation necessary.

And generally, we know the structure of "tests" and "meetings." So objectively, we know the routine of what's going to take place on Friday at 9:00 a.m. We're not expecting the test or the meeting to be different from any other test or meeting we've experienced before.

So we should be able to handle that information reasonably. Right? We could break down the number of days and hours at our command to get ready for the test or meeting, do the work required and proceed accordingly. But oftentimes we don't do any of that.

I suspect the second you read the words "test" or "meeting with the boss," something inside you was triggered. It's almost as if the cognition of those words, the stimulus of understanding what they mean, caused an automatic internal response. And that response fell somewhere on that gradient of fear.

If you have a long and deep history of preparing for tests and meetings with bosses with depth and detail, you would think you'd get a charge of positive feeling, somewhere above the "homeostatic" bandwidth when you read the words test or meeting. Your experience with tests and meetings has proven positive throughout your life, so the stimulus of test or meeting you would think would trigger a positive emotional state. But if you have had your share of negative experiences with tests and meetings with the boss, you probably felt an emotional response somewhere between "dread" and "uncertain."

Now here's the real kicker.

Very few people respond positively to the stimulus of "test" or "meeting with the boss." In fact, I'd wager with confidence that greater than 90 percent do not. The reason is that we have a natural inclination to frame the world (that is perceive and see it from our own point of view) negatively. We are risk averse, and taking a test or meeting with a boss is inherently risky. We could "blow it" this time, even though we have never blown it before.

So no matter how many times you've taken a test successfully or had a great dialogue with your boss, your initial response to the stimulus of the words "test" or "meeting with the boss" will fall below "homeostatic" on the gradient of fear. You'll fall somewhere between "dread" and "uncertain." Negatively.

What good is this information?

If we can examine the general qualities of the wide range of stimuli in our world and match them with how our minds automatically process those kinds of stimuli, we'll have a way to examine the nature of why we are feeling the way we do at very specific moments in our lives. Instances of not knowing what to do when confronted with something we've never experienced before will decline if we can think through the meaning of the feeling we're experiencing.

So an automatic jump back on a hike means…look for snake. Dread of a test or a meeting means…pay attention to the work necessary to do well and think through why you are dreading it. Maybe you aren't as up to speed on the coursework as you should be? Or maybe that rumor about your company downsizing will affect you? Pick that problematic emotion apart and suss out what it could mean. You'll quell the fear before it can overwhelm you.

Demystifying the problem we're actually facing (the test, the meeting, the difficult operation in my case) instead of putting our focus on the "fear" response it has generated is what I mean by practicing cognitive dominance.

So in our test or meeting with the boss example, the objective fact of the rise of the information itself (the alert that a problem that must be solved has arisen) triggers a negative emotional response from our brain. That's our primal response to an anticipated challenging or unexpected event. It doesn't signal doom. It just alerts us to pay attention to it and use that big brain of ours to figure out what it means.

We can do two things with this objective fact.

1. We can focus on the fear the fact induces and freak out. We can really go nuts spinning out fantastical negative simulations of what will happen if... This mindful focus inevitably sends us further down the gradient of fear. We soon spiral all the way down to dread...long before Friday 9:00 a.m. arrives. And when it does, we arrive for our test or meeting absolutely drained and dreading what's going to happen. Sound familiar?

Or

2. We can focus on what the fear response means. Why it matters. It means we have a problem. And when we have a problem, we need to pick it apart into smaller bite-sized mini-problems we know we can easily solve. So we put our energy into slicing and dicing the big problem (I have four days to prepare for a test or meeting). Instead of putting our energy into spinning out ever more negative emotional states that will result if we don't solve the problem, we simply shift our attention to breaking apart the problem and then solving it bit by bit.

The more we choose the second path, the better we get at it. We just need to constantly remind ourselves that our emotional response to problems (fear) isn't the problem. It's simply alerting us to problems.

When we feel fear, the way to process it is to figure out exactly how much fear we're feeling, which will tell us just how big the problem is. Armed with that information, we can then go about slicing and dicing that problem into smaller digestible pieces.

This is what I mean by cognitive dominance. It is simply a psycho-technology (a mindful process) that one practices when faced with problems that induce ever-increasing amounts of fear.

And the thing about fear is that it can jolt you when you least expect it.

FIVE

Oksanna

Oksanna is five years old.

 I have a toddler just like her at home. They wear the same kind of plastic hair bows. My daughter Kaleigh likes the blue ones. Oksanna's is white. I know because I'll keep it in my left scrub shirt breast pocket for the next twenty-two years.

I'm in the Oakland neighborhood of Pittsburgh, the epicenter of medical services for the Tri-State area (Western Pennsylvania, Eastern Ohio, and North West Virginia). It's the Mid-Atlantic equivalent of New England's Longwood Medical Center in Boston.

Thirty years old and still greener than the corn in Westmoreland County, I'm smugly wearing one of those official white doctor's coats with Mark McLaughlin, MD on it and covering the emergency room as neurosurgery consult. It's 7:05 a.m. in the humid heart of early summer and I'm eager to put all of the hours of cutting up cadavers and watching other surgeons do their work to the test. The typical neurosurgeon puts in close to fifty thousand hours over a seven-year residency stretch. I'm fifteen thousand hours in…the dangerous time when you have some skills but lack experience.

Five minutes after meeting Oksanna, I've convinced her mother to sign the surgery consent form. Oksanna's head looks like three quarters of the way into a slow inflation of a regulation basketball. She's lethargic, sluggish, delayed, etc. A clear case of hydrocephalus—water on the brain. Excessive cerebrospinal fluid is collecting deep inside her head and it must be drained immediately. If it isn't, the drip, drip, drip, buildup of fluid will slowly squeeze her brain until it shuts down completely, an internal mental drowning.

I explain my reasoning and diagnosis to the attending neurosurgeon and he tells me I'll be doing the operation. He'll be right next to me, but the tools will be in my hands.

Thankfully my hands are my strongest feature.

We get into the room at 7:35 a.m.

What I do today before an operation is different than what I did when I was a rookie. Rookies rely upon rapid memory recall, probably because their minds are so young and sharp. And they've spent so much time practicing technique that the connection between thought and action is fresh, clear, and practically autonomic. The stress of the moment compels them to obsess about what they've been told and repeatedly trained to do, not about what they've actually experienced in the past or what they can anticipate for the future.

Veterans, though, understand that present performance requires intimate knowledge of the past while constantly projecting possible outcomes into the future.

Now I rely on an internal Socratic method to prepare myself for the unexpected.

Here's what I do on this day.

First thing...I ask myself a series of questions and answer them clearly in my mind.

Why is the patient here? The patient is in the OR because I believe her brain is filling up with fluid, a very specific kind of fluid that is critical to the health of the brain.

What kind of fluid? Cerebrospinal fluid, which is the stuff our body produces inside the brain in order to a) cushion the neurons that keep us breathing and thinking b) give a buoyant lift for all of the heavy brain matter inside our heads c) neutralize microscopic bad guys (CSF keeps infection at bay with its high chloride content, like a salt-water pool chlorinator) d) travel up and down the spinal cord so the content it brings back can serve as a status report that is processed in the weigh stations/rest stops of the brain.

How much of this fluid is in the body? There's about half a cup of it in circulation at all times. That's about five shots of espresso.

Where does the fluid come from? If you think of the brain as an expressway, like I-95 or the Pacific Coast Highway, the lanes and access ramps are the crucial places where information moves from one place to another. The information gets processed at all of the destination points and then messages are sent back on the highway to other exits to be processed further. Just like a big interstate highway, the brain has weigh stations and rest stops, places where the messengers can go to the bathroom, get sustenance and generally get reinvigorated before heading back out on the road.

The primary rest stops for CSF in the brain are called ventricles, which are filled to the brim with CSF. There are four ventricular rest stops in the brain.

These ventricles, one on the right and one on the left side of the brain (the lateral ventricles), one in the middle of the brain (the third ventricle) and one at the base of the brain (the fourth ventricle) make CSF, replenishing it when on its travels it absorbs into the bloodstream. Every day these ventricles produce about twenty shots of CSF to maintain the required five shots for homeostasis.

How does the CSF flow? The lateral ventricles have tubes, called the *foramina of Monro,* that attach to the next weigh station/rest stop in the center of the brain, called the third ventricle. The third ventricle is the place where CSF from the lateral ventricles travels next. All of the stuff the messengers carry on their way to their final destinations and have dropped off in the left and right sides of the brain is inside the CSF, which then flows down to the third ventricle. The third ventricle processes the CSF and moves it down another tube to the fourth ventricle. The fourth ventricle processes this CSF yet further and then pushes it back up to the surface of the brain where it is reabsorbed.

So what's going on for the patient? The precise equilibrium of CSF flow is out of whack. There is a clog in the channel between the third and fourth ventricle and CSF is building up. More CSF is coming into the third ventricle than can be pushed into the fourth ventricle. The fluid is building up in the third ventricle and squeezing the brain from the inside out.

What can I do about this? I need to reduce the pressure of CSF buildup in the third ventricle. I can do one of two things.

a) Put in a man-made tube called a shunt to drain the fluid from her third ventricle into another place on her body that can process it…like the chest or the abdominal cavity.

b) Make a new hole on the floor of the third ventricle so that the excess fluid can be released into another cavity inside the brain. These are the basal cisterns that will allow the fluid to be carried off back to the brain surface and ultimately be reabsorbed into the blood.

How can I make that hole? By using a neuroendoscope, which is a tiny high-resolution camera, I'll be able to first find a path to the right ventricle and then follow the *foramina of Monro* line from the right ventricle down to the third ventricle. Then I'll find the right place to make a hole in the third ventricular floor. I'll make the opening, check to see that the fluid is pulsing out of the hole and then pull out my instruments, close and move on to the next case.

Before the endoscope was adapted for neurosurgery, patients like Oksanna were forced to have the shunt procedure, the first option in which permanent silastic (a blend of silicone and plastic) drainage tubing is placed in the brain and tunneled down into the chest or abdominal cavity to absorb the fluid. While this procedure is still used in many types of hydrocephalus and is successful, it is fraught with possible complications including clogging, infection, and breakage of the tubing over time. A shunt often requires multiple revision operations.

The bottom line is all of that plastic inside the body isn't a good long-term solution. The body doesn't recognize silastic as part of its ecosystem and the chances of microbial life figuring out a way to latch on to the tubing and multiply rise. If you've ever seen plastic floating in a pond and the green algae that soon clings to it, you get my point. So if I can avoid putting in a shunt, I do.

We chose the endoscope for Oksanna because she was a great candidate based on a formula that included her diagnosis, whether she'd had a shunt before, and her location of obstruction. She had a compelling chance to come through the procedure exceptionally well. By bypassing the obstruction with an alternate drainage pathway that didn't require tubing and its attendant complications or repeat procedures, it would be a "one and done"—the best kind of brain operation.

Three other cases were scheduled for the day so we needed a smooth launch for Oksanna's procedure, which was the most critical to get done quickly. Like anything else, a good solid start fortifies you for challenges that may arise later. I was excited because we were using a new laser technique to make the hole in the third ventricle floor. My attending was developing the technique, which would make the procedure easier and slicker. Faster too. The less time you spend inside someone's brain, the better.

By using the laser I could create the fingernail clipping shaped hole I needed to puncture the membrane and simultaneously cauterize (burning as a means to close a wound) any vessels that might be nicked when passing the scope through the entry point. The laser technique was working well on the first few cases he had used it on and I was stoked to use it too.

I was a rookie then so I didn't actively run through my internal Socratic method before I scrubbed up. I just couldn't wait to get that laser in my hand.

Ready, steady, go.

The anesthesiologist administers his potions and Oksanna is rapidly asleep. After her breathing tube is inserted, I position her head on a jelly doughnut, a soft neoprene cup that eliminates any pressure sores from forming on the back of the head during long procedures. I unclip her plastic hair bow and, not having a place for it, stuff it into my scrub shirt breast pocket.

Her golden hair parts with ease as I comb the line of our planned incision. Is there anything softer than a child's skin? The clipper cuts through her hair like a lawn mower rolling over alfalfa sprouts. In kids, you have to be extra gentle when prepping the scalp because a rough scrub or clipping can lead to a postoperative infection.

After the betadine shampoo and paint to sterilize the area, I re-mark the mini-horseshoe incision just behind her right frontal hairline and drape the field. I then score the incision line with a scalpel and steady my hand with the Bovie needle tip electrocautery device, a pencil-like dissecting tool that coagulates blood vessels as it cuts. I deepen the incision, taking care not to char her paper-thin skin surface.

"Gentle on the pressure, Mark," my attending mentor guides.

In young children, excessive pressure with the cautery can cut right through the skull and into the brain—a disastrous misadventure that would undoubtedly compromise Oksanna for life.

I anchor the skin flap back with a quick suture and call for the high-speed drill. At seventy thousand RPM, the Midas Rex drill is truly a godsend to modern neurosurgery. This powerful, elegant machine was introduced in 1977 and has made opening the skull and the spine infinitely easier and safer for both neurosurgeons and their patients. Using a Midas Rex drill in the lab, a surgeon can shave the shell of an egg off without damaging its inner membrane.

The most favored drill bit at The University of Pittsburgh, internationally known for its exceptional neurosurgery program because of its brilliant head Dr. Peter Jannetta, at the time was the M8 matchstick, which I still use today. It has a blunt tip with a side-cutting flute so the surgeon can make a dime-sized burr hole in the skull without puncturing the dura mater, the protective outer leathery covering of the brain that adheres to the underside of the skull (the human equivalent of the egg membrane).

I drill the burr hole without incident. So far so good.

Next step: I cauterize the dura and then cut a small crisscrossed nick in it, which will create four little flaps that will form a reasonable seal around the endoscope. Not a perfect seal, more like ones on vacuum cleaner bags that hold back most, but not all, of the dust. I repeat the cautery nick on the brain surface so I can pass the endoscope through the brain in a controlled fashion without tearing any surface vessels.

We choose the pathway of the endoscope to traverse Oksanna's less-essential, nondominant frontal lobe gray and white matter. This area is more forgiving of trauma and surgery (which is a trauma) than the other locations of the frontal cortex. It still astounds me today that I'm capable of passing an endoscope the size of a ballpoint pen through this tissue without hurting the patient.

I bring the endoscope into the operating arena. First I point the camera toward a white sponge to white balance the color image on the high-definition television screen I'll use to see where I'm going. Next I orient the field: 12 o'clock, to 3 o'clock, to 6 o'clock, to 9 o'clock and back to 12 o'clock. The camera has beautiful optics, but you must know what's up, down, right and left before you put the pen inside the brain.

Time to advance the trocar and introducer sheath into the third ventricle. The trocar is the firm blunt leading tip that advances first through the tissue and maintains the patency of the guide tube. This plastic snub-nosed probe is the inner cannula (like a long cork) and has an outer sheath/sleeve wrapped around it, which will serve as a tunnel for the endoscope to pass through. As I reach for this device, it reminds me of a blunt-tipped plastic pencil with a milkshake straw wrapper. The wrapper serves as the tunnel to pass the endoscope/camera in and out of the brain without repeatedly damaging the tissue along the tract.

I put my left index finger on the bridge of Oksanna's nose to gain a mind's eye true north of the midline. With my right hand I push the trocar and introducer sheath through the burr hole, through the nick in the dura, and through the surface of the brain into Oksanna's frontal lobe aiming its tip at the intersection of two imaginary lines I am simultaneously mentally projecting onto Oksanna's skull. My target is the intersection of these two imaginary lines—one originating on the midline, the second originating one centimeter in front of her ear. I guide my trocar and introducer sheath to its home base inside the first destination, her brain's right lateral ventricle.

My right index finger feels the comforting pop and loss of resistance once the probe punctures the ventricle's fluid pocket. I know I am in the correct spot—the right lateral ventricle. I remove the inner cannula and a mostly clear, colorless fluid, CSF, comes streaming out of the introducer sheath.

Bull's-eye!

I quickly reinsert the male trocar partially into the introducer sheath so as not to drain too much CSF. If we drain too much, the ventricle will collapse, and our view of the surgical field will be compromised and more dangerous. I carefully staple the plastic introducer sheath to Oksanna's scalp to keep it from moving around.

I'm ready to introduce the endoscope. Okay, big breath. Nice and easy. I'm doing well. I've accessed the lateral ventricle, the gateway to approach our final destination—the floor of the third ventricle.

The floor of the third ventricle sits in the center of the head at the bottom of the brain, about four or so inches deep into the head. A thin, mildly opaque, somewhat transparent cellophane-like membrane separates the inside fluid pockets of the brain from the outer surfaces of the brain. If we can create a hole in it, Oksanna's excess fluid, her hydrocephalus, will spill/divert/trickle back into her blood stream. This will reverse her life-threatening condition and bring her CSF back into balance.

Under my attending's instruction, I gingerly remove the inner cannula and place the endoscope into the introducer sheath. The first thing I see on the screen is the bleached white wall of the plastic tunnel. I slowly plumb the scope until the walls disappear and a more natural yellow pinkish tissue appears.

I recognize where I am.

I have memorized the pattern of the septal vein coming in at 12 o'clock, the caudate vein coming in at 1 o'clock and the thalamostriate vein coming in from 5 o'clock. At 6 o'clock is the fluffy cauliflower-like choroid plexus. They all converge on my next objective—the dark hole in the center, the connector tube between the right ventricle and the third ventricle deeper down. One of the foramen of Monro. This is the pathway I must follow with the endoscope to get a view of the floor of the third ventricle. Fortunately, as expected, the foramen of Monro was dilated, blown up bigger than it usually is, because of the excessive pressure of CSF buildup. Getting the endoscope into this tube will not be an issue.

Looking at the screen like a video game, I see where I need to go next and begin moving that direction.

"Watch out for the fornix, Mark."

This structure sits at the 12 o'clock rim of the passageway and is critical in memory. If I skewer the fornix by passing the scope a little too high, I could damage Oksanna's ability to remember names, faces, what she did yesterday or what she will do on her wedding day years in the future. *Easy does it,* I say to myself as the tip sneaks past the column of the fornix.

My view now after negotiating the foramen of Monro is breathtaking. Human brain anatomy is beautiful to me.

I love this vista even today after many previous visits—especially the floor of the third ventricle. Through the partly transparent, partly opaque membrane, I see the mammillary bodies, two matching breast-like prominences, at the bottom of my screen. Right in the middle sits a tiny funnel, the infundibular recess that leads into the pituitary gland. Up top at 12 o'clock is the clivus, the front of the skull that sits directly behind Oksanna's throat. I've reached the floor of the third ventricle.

My target is midline, halfway between the infundibular recess and just in front of the mammillary bodies. A hole here will allow the extra CSF to drain into the basal cisterns where it can be processed into the blood stream.

Once the puncture is complete, I will advance the endoscope through the hole to make sure the new channel has been successfully bored. When I see a whoosh of fluid move out of the ventricle correspond-ing with Oksanna's heartbeat, I'll know I've accomplished the first part of our mission. Then all I have to do is get out of there and safely close.

I land the scope right where it needs to be, with the camera tip sus-pended just above the floor of the third ventricle. Ready to go. The laser guide/seeker light is aimed on the point of entry.

The laser beam engages.

I'm looking at the monitor.

I'm expecting to see a nice gush of Cerebrospinal Fluid.

Instead I see a small wisp of red.

Like a puff of smoke floating through the CSF, floating up, then more red, then the screen turns cloudy.

"Hmmmm. I guess the tip of the scope needs to be cleaned. Just back the scope out and wipe it off.

This internal voice telling me to do something to deal with an event I haven't seen before…or prepared for…while reasonable…is cata-strophically wrong.

"Hold the scope right where it is, Mark. Don't move a millimeter," my attending says.

"But I can't see anything. The scope tip's dirt…" I begin to protest.

Now, at last taking my eyes off the monitor to look at my attending to explain myself, I see the real operating field. Not the video screen repre-sentation of the operating field. But the real thing.

My stomach churns as I look in horror.

At the back exhaust portal of the endoscope…blood pulses out of her head… a lot of it.

With every chirp of her heartbeat on the monitor…an even, perfect-ly formed geyser of blood spurts, arcing onto the floor. Nausea almost overwhelms me.

I hold it together.

The next thought that hits me is that with the volume coming out with each heartbeat, it will take only a minute or two before she bleeds out and dies.

Get the scope out! Again, the inner voice tells me to pull out the endoscope.

I didn't know it then, but this was the voice of fear—fear of not knowing what to do in a moment I hadn't experienced before. It's telling me to flee the scene. It wants me to save myself, to undo a mistake as quickly as possible so I won't get in trouble. It is not thinking about what's really happening because I've never experienced what's really happening before.

I begin to listen to it. I want to pull out.

"Hold steady, Mark. Don't move a muscle. Keep that scope right there!"

My attending's voice steels my courage. I hold fast.

As I do, my brain recovers.

In fact it quickly reasons that pulling the scope out would be the absolute worst thing to do. Because as long as the scope is inside the head, the blood has a channel to flow out through.. If I pull that scope out of her head, the bleeding will have nowhere to go...and it would rapidly form a large blood mass within the head and cause her death.

In this microsecond...as long as her blood volume lasts (probably about two to three minutes) and I hold steady, nothing bad will happen to her brain. The blood will just stream through the endoscope channel, out the hole, and onto the floor. It's horrific and scary to watch, but it's what's best for right now.

Hold steady.

"Anesthesia, we're having massive bleeding. Begin high volume resuscitation now and get us four units of blood stat." My attending's calm, cool demeanor and lightning fast actions to solve the next problem on the horizon is intensely reassuring. He's seen this happen before. He knows what to do.

I hold the endoscope steady, we transfuse and transfuse and transfuse.

After the longest ten minutes of my life, amazingly the bleeding subsides. The basilar artery that had been nicked by the laser during the floor cut goes into spasm, temporarily closing the hole in the artery.

Miraculously, the ecosystem of Oksanna's brain comes back to equilibrium without further intervention. We gave her brain the time to temporarily repair the nick in the artery without our having to.

I back the scope out and peel my cramped hands from the endoscope.

I close.

My attending smiles and indicates that the next case will be ready for us in ten minutes.

"Well, Mark...still want to be a neurosurgeon?"

SIX
Fifty Thousand Hours

The career path for a neurosurgeon is, to put it mildly, challenging. Malcolm Gladwell famously stated that it requires ten thousand hours to reach a level of expertise in one's chosen field, which breaks down to about two-and-a-quarter years of twelve-hour days with no weekend or holiday breaks. The estimate for neurosurgeons reaching a master's skill level puts the number at fifty thousand hours, almost twelve years of twelve-hour days with no weekend or holiday breaks. It's grueling.

I trained at the University of Pittsburgh Medical Center, the largest and one of the most prestigious neurosurgery programs in the world. That's where I met Oksanna. Over the course of my eight-year residency and fellowship, and twenty additional years in the trenches of a busy neurosurgery practice (approximately another fifty thousand hours) I've seen approximately 140,000 patients. The vast majority of them had life-threatening or debilitating illnesses that required either my surgical intervention or a decision not to operate.

Of those 140,000 people, I had to tell approximately two thousand families that their loved one had died and another thousand that their loved one survived surgery but that he or she would have tremendous physical or cognitive limitations. I have told more than one hundred patients that they are permanently paralyzed, more than five hundred patients that they have a malignant brain tumor, more than five hundred families that their loved one is brain dead and they should consider terminating his or her ventilator. I have told two thousand patients or families that they need a craniotomy. And I have decided more than two thousand times not to operate because the injuries were un-survivable.

I have made a minimum of thirty thousand life-and-death decisions in my career.

In the operating theatre, I've applied a seventy-thousand-RPM drill to someone's skull over a thousand times and to someone's spine over three thousand times. That drill has been in my hand shaving the delicate edges of bone off of a vital structure of the Central Nervous System for approximately two thousand hours.

I've spent another five thousand hours of my life pulling the trigger of a Kerrison rongeur. This pistol-like instrument bites tiny pieces of bone to clear an instrument pathway or to decompress a squeezed nerve. I have pulled the trigger on this device over a million times. With each bite of the rongeur comes a risk of crushing vital nervous tissue. More than seven hundred times I have had to make the decision to sacrifice (close off) a blood vessel knowing there was a possibility it might cause a stroke.

Of my last twenty-eight years, I've spent almost nine of those years on "call," meaning ready, willing, and able to drop everything and laser focus on a specific person facing a life-threatening situation. "Call" is typically for a twenty-four-hour shift, unless in our practice, you are on for the weekend and then it is seventy-two hours straight.

In training, when I was at the lower end of the totem pole, "call" would be far more laborious than it is for me now. It would routinely require me to be awake the majority of the time caring for patients, doing paperwork or operating. In those days, as a resident and fellow, it would be unthinkable to take call for more than a twenty-four-hour stint. You just wouldn't be able to function.

Now that I have reached middle age and am a senior member in my practice, I am significantly higher on the ladder. And while I don't need to be awake twenty-four-hours straight, I still take my equal share.

In the early days, I would carry a pager. Now it's my cell phone. In the course of a twenty-four-hour call segment I will receive on average forty text messages, twenty phone calls, twenty-five emails, all while performing two or three operations a day. On the days I am not performing surgery, I'll see twenty-five patients during office hours.

Most of the time now the "on call" nights are less intensive and I can steal some sleep. Other times I'm not as lucky. My partners and I have put into place certain buffers that make present day "on call" more manageable.

In academic settings, the professors use the residents as buffers. The residents are the first line of defense. They field triage phone calls from the emergency room and take care of minor orders and surveillance of the inpatient service. In private practice we use Physician Assistants as our residents, paraprofessionals who are specifically trained in our field. If a question is too complex or if a surgical decision needs to be made, then the PA contacts the doctor on call.

No matter the procedure, when you are the neurosurgeon on call, regardless of whether you are actually getting called or someone else is in front of you fielding the first calls, it's akin to being a fireman. You can have down time, but in an instant, you can be called to deal with a life-threatening emergency. No matter how seasoned you become, the responsibility weighs on your psyche, and I believe over the long haul this yo-yoing between calm and emergency has detrimentally affected my personality.

I describe the dilemma as "gear shifting"—that is, going from normal daily functioning to shifting into life-saving mode and back again. Often multiple times a day.

I can be sitting with my family at the dinner table asking for more broccoli stir-fry and my phone rings. Suddenly, my fear-based orienting response kicks in and I am pulled out of relaxation mode. I'll answer the phone, usually by the second ring, knowing that any number of people could be on the other end of the line.

It could be a drug-seeking chronic pain patient calling to request more pain medication. Or a nurse asking for a medication clarification on an inpatient. Or my partner calling about an unusual scan that he wants to confer with me on. These are quickies and I can dispense with them deftly.

Or it can be the trauma surgeon telling me they are on the way to the operating room with a patient who has a blown pupil and a big subdural hematoma (a life-threatening emergency caused by a blood clot that is so big the patient's pupil is now dilated, indicating a need for emergency surgery that I'll need to scrub in for). Or it could be a nurse in the ICU telling me that Mrs. Smith's CT scan is a lot worse and she needs to go back to the operating room. Or it could be that my patient I operated on last week now has meningitis and needs to be seen urgently.

Probably 95 percent of calls are something I can give a quick answer or remedy or stall until after we finish dinner. The other 5 percent I have to either deal with immediately or sometimes drop everything, grab my car keys and speed in.

But even if it's something I can dispense with immediately over the phone, when I hang up, the residue of the call lingers with me. I think about it after I hand the broccoli back to my wife. It can rattle around in my head sometimes for the rest of the dinner or into the night. I'll have thoughts like:

Don't you think you should go to your computer right now and look at that scan the nurse called you about rather than wait until after dinner?

Don't you think you should go in and actually see that patient rather than trust the ER doctor's analysis?

Don't you think you should do more?

Calculating these internal conversational decisions that I ruminate over can prove maddening. I think of very little else.

Why?

It has to do with fear.

The phone calls and the ensuing mental wrestling matches continue until the clock turns to 7 a.m. and I am no longer on call. Then I'm off duty for the general onslaught of covering our entire practice and only need to worry about **my** patients and surgeries. Unless it's the weekend. Then I have to do it until Monday morning comes.

Within seconds I have switched from a dinner or party conversation to a life-and-death decision more than five thousand times, that is going from *pass the broccoli* to *what's his pupillary exam and I'll meet you in the operating room.*

My statistics represent a relatively average-volume neurosurgeon in a private practice (nonacademic) setting. In fact, many neurosurgeons have performed these tasks more times than I have.

My only differentiating feature is that I have a strange proclivity to chronicle the sheer volume of micro tasks that my colleagues and I do. I study these actions in order to gain a better understanding of what this profession can contribute to coping with the complexity of the world around us. **More specifically, how we can use a neurosurgeon's knowledge to perform at our highest possible potential, in our chosen profession or personal sphere, while under the influence of an extremely powerful and nuanced emotion—fear.**

I set my compass to become a doctor very early on, but I intuitively knew I needed to learn how to think in far broader ways than the micro resolution necessary to be an effective surgeon. I needed a global system to keep me grounded, so in college I majored in Philosophy while holding down the pre-med track. The philosophical macro approach to dealing with things that happen when we don't anticipate them happening, a way to figure out what to do when we don't know what to do, has been indispensable for me. I've since discovered that the micro and the macro training are both required when contemplating something as ever-present and yet hard to understand as fear.

But let's start with the macro point of view. It will lead us back to where we left off on our journey to figure out how to solve very difficult problems, like my post-Anthony problem. Now that we have sketched out a map of the gradient of fear, which represents our internal and external responses to familiar (known) or unfamiliar (unknown) unexpected events, let's take a hard look at the global nature of these events themselves.

What are they? What is their nature?

SEVEN
What Is and What Should Be

Let's think about how we move through life as if we were an other-worldly figure looking down on humanity from a very high perch. As if we were on Mount Olympus and the Greek gods asked us to explain what we thought about the way the humans below us navigated their world.

With my B.A. in Philosophy on my wall and thousands of hours of autodidactic reading to complement it, here's what I would say:

The present is the process by which we order our plans, which have been informed by our pasts, to achieve desired future states. That ordering is a form of thinking, problem solving to move from an undesired present to a better future.

For example, ever since I was a kid I knew I wanted to be a doctor just like Grandpa Pizzi. My undesired present was me as a young man who wished to get accepted into medical school and my future desired state was to become a physician just like Gramps.

Even if the undesired present is simply lying in bed just before we set out to tackle the day (the future), we all look ahead in the present while informed by our past. Like Thanksgiving travelers who must go over the river and through the woods for the rewards of pudding, pumpkin pie and the safety and love inside grandmother's house, we all long to breathlessly break through the barnyard gates of our external and internal lives to reach our short-term, middle-term and eventually long-term goals.

With a wide and deep inventory of unique past experiences (each person has their own singular, personally framed worldview), our minds think up ordered paths from our unfulfilled present states to foreseeable futures where their desires find satisfaction. Our past experiences tell us what paths to avoid (cautionary narratives) and what paths to follow (prescriptive narratives) in our present moment planning for the future.

We think up a way to behave such that our actions transform the "what is" of our lives presently into the "what should be" lives of a better future. And while the tenor and landscape of our longed-for dream lives update and transform the longer we live, the process by which we aim and shoot for our goals remains the same. We think up a goal state and then behave in the ways we believe will allow us to attain that goal.

Let's look at those goals with more resolution.

Can I be more specific about them?

Can I break that big category that includes everything from becoming CEO of a Fortune 500 company to eating that perfect piece of cheesecake after dinner into two distinct parts? If I had to categorize all of human beings' goals from birth through death and put them into two main buckets—a binary division—what would I come up with?

In his seminal 1976 work *To Have or To Be?* social psychologist and humanist Erich Fromm theorized that we have two kinds of global goals.

First, we wish to attain and possess material **objects**, to **have** things. We want a delicious meal, a nice car, a safe house, etc.

Second, we wish to become someone, to **be** a meaningful **subject** in the world.

While the notion of "being" today is associated with just sort of hanging out and not doing anything, Fromm didn't see "Being" as a hippie-ish or vague ideal of being one with the universe. Rather he defined it as a deep human need to put forth a purposeful and heroic effort in a chosen life arena in such a way that the person's very name and life force becomes associated with his or her highest life value.

The great baseball player Ted Williams famously said that his only goal when he retired was to have people look at him walking down the street and say, "There goes Ted Williams, the greatest hitter who ever lived." That's what Fromm meant by being a meaningful subject in the world—becoming a synonym for a prized value. Williams valued hitting a baseball purely and consistently as his highest value and his life came to be defined by that value. My son Trevor has the exact same aspiration with his skateboarding career.

If we wish to be a master carpenter, we learn the fundamentals of woodworking. We apprentice with a mentor. We work on our craft until we're known far and wide as the epitome of the profession. The ultimate goal then is when someone says carpentry within our community…our face is the first image and representation that come to others' minds. That's "being" at the top of the hierarchy of value. And that desire drives all of the creation in the world. And for that matter all of the destruction too.

The "have" goal and the "be" goal categories are both critical to our surviving and thriving. One isn't better than the other. Both are necessities. We need to acquire food, shelter, water, clothing, etc. to survive. And we need to have a sense of purpose, to understand our place on the planet and the necessity of our contributions as a means to find meaning and contentment. If we don't have a core level of personal meaning, we find ourselves lost, unable to make sense of the world and all of the very complex objects and subjects in it.

Objects (matter) and subjects (what matters) are the two big buckets of phenomena on Earth.

So we have two sets of must-have goals to ground us in the world. And we have the ability to think up plans to reach future states where we attain them. This process requires us to externally take actions in the world (behave) using our past experience to guide us.

Here's a graphic to represent the process:

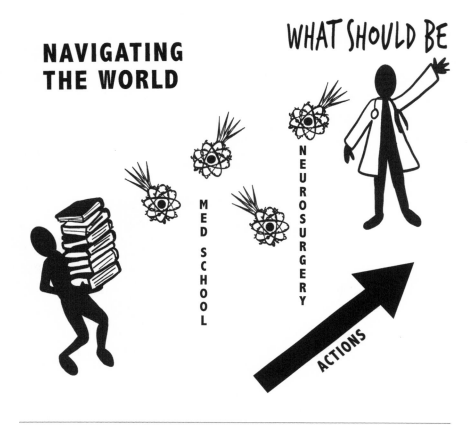

NAVIGATING THE WORLD

WHAT SHOULD BE

MED SCHOOL

NEUROSURGERY

ACTIONS

Inspired by schema in Jordan Peterson's *Maps of Meaning*,
(Routledge: Abingdon-on-Thames) 1999. Figure 1.

Put your quotidian life on top of this concept.

Waking up in the morning begins your daily "what is." And as you progress through your day, you move from that "what is" to progressively more complex states of "what should be." The ways in which you transform those "what is" instances into "what should be" instances is based upon your past life experience. If you know there is no toothpaste in your bathroom when you wake up (you remember the previous evening's experience having to go into another bathroom to find a squeeze) you plan accordingly. You put "go to the store and buy toothpaste" on your to-do list for the day.

We think up ways to negotiate our movement through the world, and we just repeat the plans that work well until we no longer have to consciously "think" about how to do them anymore. Our routines eventually become unconscious. After a while, we don't think about how to put toothpaste on our toothbrush. We just magically do it. These unconscious behaviors are energy efficient because we don't have to spend any cognitive energy rethinking up plans that have worked very well for us before. That's a practical example of the law of conservation of energy, in which energy is neither created nor destroyed. Energy is transformed.

So what's the problem? When do things go wrong? When does the fear freak-out problem emerge?

Something happens, an unexpected event, which knocks us out of our routine. And we must expend energy in order to figure out what the event means.

Circumstances arise while we are moving from A to B that we didn't expect would happen. An obstacle or an opportunity gets in the way of our moving from "what is" to "what should be." It shakes us out of our unconscious, tried and true behavior and signals to us that we need to pay attention. The signal is simply alerting us to the fact that the world isn't conforming to our wishes/plans. What we routinely imagined would result in our action isn't happening. The world is resisting us.

Obviously, having a *stop and pay attention* message is indispensable to our very survival. If we don't stop and jump back when a snake is in our path, guess what happens? The snake bites us and we die.

We do have a message, but this message makes us most uncomfortable. So uncomfortable that we often freak out. The signal message is in the form of fear.

So if fear is simply a message to tell us to pay attention, what is it telling us to pay attention to? It's telling us to pay attention to what just happened—the unexpected event that dropped into our lives on our way from "what is" to "what should be." We need to focus on that thing, figure it out and adjust ourselves accordingly to what it means to our goals.

Now you may be saying to yourself, I do pay attention to the unexpected thing that happens. I certainly paid attention when Anthony didn't respond to my operation in the way I thought he would. And I certainly paid attention when I could no longer see during the operation with Oksanna. But the key here is that in both of the previous examples, I focused on the alarm signal and not the actual phenomenon that triggered the alarm. I used my brain to figure out how to turn off the fire alarm. Instead I should have investigated why the alarm was blaring in the first place. Find the fire and put it out before you turn your attention to the fire alarm. I didn't look for the fire and figure out how to contain it and eventually put it out. I just focused on getting that nasty fire alarm sound to turn off.

The sound from the alarm is what we experience as fear. And the louder that alarm gets, the further down the vortex of the gradient of fear, the closer we get to freaking out. And freaking out, just like in a horror movie when the victim faces the monster, is the process by which we shut down (the freeze response), which then triggers into a rush to get the hell away (flight response) and as a last resort wild flailing at the universe (fight response). Watch any good horror movie and you'll see the fear freak-out over and over again.

That's the problem we're trying to solve. We're trying to figure out a way to stop ourselves from putting all of our attention on the alarm bell and instead put our attention on the phenomenon that triggered the alarm.

EIGHT
The Unexpected

If fear is the fire alarm, the "unexpected" is the fire.

And the unexpected always begins with a negative emotional jolt. As Darwin explained, we have evolution and the phenomenon of snakes to thank for that. Our natural inclination is to not really focus on an object unless it poses some sort of threat to us.

Obviously, all of the human beings in the past who got a positive emotional input when a snake crossed their path ended up dead. And dead people don't have children. They probably went to pick up the snake to explore it, were bitten, and soon thereafter died. So over time, only the humans who had a negative emotional experience when they sensed a snake lived. And that natural alarm system—a negative response to the unexpected first, positive if applicable later—kept us alive. Adapting a system to serve another purpose is one of the incredibly efficient hallmarks of evolution. It's called exaptation.

So how can we deal with the unexpected? Just like the objective and subjective nature of our "have" and "be" goals, the unexpected has two core components. And while unexpected events can certainly threaten us, they can also be filled with promise too. Unexpectedly breaking your leg is certainly a threat to your overall health, but if you were to break your leg the day before a disaster struck at your office, that negative threat would transform into a positive event that kept you from mortal danger.

You can see that these unexpected events in our lives can become quite complex. In fact, they make our lives interesting and are compelling narrative complications that interrupt our goal-directed journeys. They are the stuff of stories that we share with others. Without these jolts in our lives, we'd quickly lose our way in the world. Everything would come to us with little effort and we'd soon find ourselves lost in a meaningless void of satiation. Life would become like an episode from the old TV series *The Twilight Zone*.

Some of these unexpected phenomena aren't such a big deal. Our alarm clock doesn't go off and we sleep five minutes longer than we usually do. Or we wake up five minutes early and realize we may be able to "beat the traffic" to work today. Those are unexpected events that don't seem all that life changing. Some are a bigger deal than a short loss of time but not enough to really upend us, like our toothbrush accidentally tumbling into the toilet bowl. And some grow larger still. We step on a dog toy at the top of our stairs and severely twist our ankle.

We find these external challenges irritating and oftentimes, in the case of a serious personal injury or depravation of fundamental physical resources, life threatening, but psychologically we don't get confused about what is necessary for us to get back on our goal-directed path. We move a little faster, we find another toothbrush, and we take the day off from work to heal from the ankle sprain.

However, the internal challenges posed by unexpected events can really upend us. These can hit us with such force that we find we will never be the same again. We discover the terrible knowledge that what we'd always held to be real and true isn't real and true. We may discover that a loved one has betrayed us. Or that the big new job at work isn't as exciting or rewarding as it seemed from afar. Or that all of the training and work we'd done and were assured would be enough to cure someone isn't enough to bring about that desired event.

Occasionally, these unexpected events confuse us to such a degree that we reach an "all is lost" moment in our lives, when nothing makes sense anymore. We fall out of our narrative path and struggle to find our bearings again. We must reconfigure the very goal-directed path we'd set sail for all those years before we knew the truth of the world. Our "what should be" and all of the actions we took to move toward it turn into a tumble down into depths of darkness.

But we also have life experiences when we are perfectly in sync with our environment. Our "having" goal is perfectly attuned to our "being" goal. We "feel" like we can't miss, like we are exactly where we should be at exactly the right time and that our personal skills (agency) are perfectly aligned with our specific environment (arena). If we're Ted Williams and we come to the plate for the last at bat of our career, we "know" we'll hit a home run. And we do.

But we're also very good at ignoring these beautiful moments or forgetting that they actually happened with far more frequency than we can put our "all is lost" moments out of our minds. Again, that speaks to our evolutionary development—our negative emotional bias that keeps us aware and alert rather than the positive emotions that keep us naive and dull.

Now if we are able to think about our goal-directed behavior in terms of a global concept like the diagram above for micro movements of time (getting ready for work) and macro movements of time (getting a promotion at work), how would we represent those unexpected "problem" events in this meta schema?

Can we create another diagram like the one we made for "what is" to "what should be?"

Yes. But we need to pick apart the nature of unexpected events, like we did with the global concept of "goals" into "having" and "being" goals.

So what is the fundamental nature of unexpected events?

These events either:

1. Accelerate our movement from A to B ("what is" to "what should be").

2. They hinder our movement from A to B.

No matter the degree, the emergence of the unexpected event that does not aid us forces us to change, to transform our behavior.

Let's go back to our diagram and drop one of these unexpected events into the picture. Here's what it would look like.

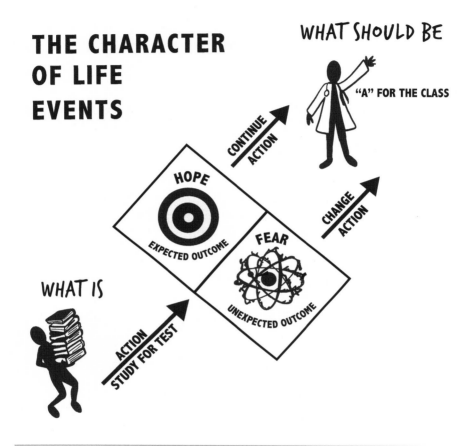

THE CHARACTER OF LIFE EVENTS

WHAT SHOULD BE

"A" FOR THE CLASS

CONTINUE ACTION

HOPE

EXPECTED OUTCOME

CHANGE ACTION

FEAR

UNEXPECTED OUTCOME

WHAT IS

ACTION STUDY FOR TEST

Inspired by schema in Jordan Peterson's *Maps of Meaning*,
(Routledge: Abingdon-on-Thames) 1999. Figure 6.

The thing we are currently calling "the unexpected event" in between "what is" and "what should be" drops into our life, and two possibilities may result when it does.

1. We experience what we think we will experience. This is the predicted outcome of an action. When we wake up at the alarm clock's warning and make it to the bathroom on time, that's a predicted outcome. We experience a level of positive promise (with a micro dose of pleasure, in the form of a neurotransmitter in our brain called dopamine, which incrementally pumps up a hopeful disposition) that we'll be able to make it through the day as we planned. So we continue with our sequence of planned behavior with a bit of positive momentum. We pick up our toothbrush.

Or

2. We don't experience what we think we'll experience. This is an unpredicted outcome of an action. We wake up and discover that our alarm clock didn't engage and we're running late. We experience this unpredicted outcome as a level of negative threat (with a micro dose of fear, in the form of cortisol, which incrementally pumps up an anxious disposition) to our ability to make it through the day as we originally planned.

The first possible event isn't all that interesting. When things go according to plan, we're living in a positive emotional state and feel at one with the universe. There is no "fear freak-out" problem in the moment or on the horizon. We're moving along above the watermark on the fear gradient—from promise to hope to pleasure—and that's a peaceful ride.

However, the second possible event is the subject of our pursuit to out-think fear, the one that triggers the fear alarm with the first external signal on our gradient of fear—dismay.

At this place we have to pay attention, use cognitive energy, and think up a new sequence of behavior in order to metabolize the unpredicted event and quiet fear's alarm bell. We have to find the fire, contain it and put it out. We pay attention to the fact that we're five minutes late, so in order to shave off some time in our normal routine, we take our pre-tooth-pasted toothbrush with us into the shower and eliminate the time we usually spend at the sink by brushing our teeth while we wait to get fully wet in the shower. Or we come up with another way to save some time.

Let's take an even closer look at the unpredicted outcome event. Can we learn even more about it in such a way that we'll be better able to come up with ways to think through what to do about it? Carl Jung had some pretty cool ideas about it.

NINE
The Primary Substance

Our goal is to understand the stimulus, *the unexpected event* that trips our body and mind response, *the fear alarm bell*. Thankfully, Carl Jung, the famous explorer of the unconscious mind as a natural and cross-cultural phenomenon, took a long hard look at unexpected events. He insightfully hypothesized that the core nature of these phenomena represent the critical moments of life change, or transformational moments.

He came up with an easily digestible symbolic representation for these "change agents" from his studies of what was generally Science 1.0, the study of alchemy. Alchemy in its day was a cutting-edge thinking person's discipline. What's fascinating is that it has a much longer history than contemporary science does. For eleven hundred years, from the eighth century through the nineteenth century, alchemy was independently explored in China, Greece, and India.

Technically viewed today as a precursor to what we now call chemistry, alchemy was much more than that in its time. It was a combination plate of "half-science" and "half-philosophy," an attempt to bring together the material world and the meta-material world.

The core hypothesis of alchemy is that a primary substance contains both the external and internal essence of life, the primal substance of change. If we could isolate this primary substance, we'd be able to transform our world in any way we believed most desirable. Sir Isaac Newton, the founder of Newtonian physics, self-identified as an alchemist. It was a serious pursuit of inquiry, despite us laughing it off today as a bunch of silly people trying to convert lead into gold.

Rather than throwing the philosophical baby out with the scientifically flawed bathwater, like his contemporaries in the early twentieth century, Carl Jung reasoned that the alchemists had homed in on the moment when something unforeseen occurs that changes the world. Sometimes these events can catastrophically create change in our worldview for the better—like the Gutenberg printing press, Einstein's Theory of Relativity, or Neil Armstrong stepping on the moon—or in a destructive sense—like the falling of the Twin Towers—can adversely affect that worldview. The alchemists were interested in these types of events. They focused and took great lengths to isolate the problematic drop-in of something unexpected. Where did it come from? What was its source? Answering these questions, the alchemists theorized, would isolate the transformational energy source for external (lead into gold) and internal (madness into sanity) change. Harnessing the stuff that facilitates creation or destruction would convert men into gods.

Let's step back a bit and review how we generally categorize life here on Earth.

There is:

1. The matter of the world. All of the physical **objects** we can measure consistently through time, independent of the measurer—such as water, mountains, pencils, Fruit Loops, our physical bodies—makes up the "matter" of the world. We refer to this world as the **objective world**. It is a world made up of **facts**.

2. What matters in the world. This is the world of **subjects** that our conscious minds sort into gradients of value. If we have constant access to clean water and we can easily find it when we're thirsty, our minds don't place a very high value on water. We don't even really think about it. Unconsciously, drinking water is cheap and flows out of our kitchen sinks whenever we want it to.

If we don't have access to clean water, though, we consciously think about how we are going to get it. And we think about that a lot. It matters. We understand that if we don't get access to clean water, we will die. So while water as an objective fact is made up of matter (two hydrogen atoms attached to an oxygen atom) as a **subject** it can take on all sorts of value to us. We call that value **meaning**. Water for people who get it whenever they want it doesn't mean very much. But for those who don't have easy access, it is very meaningful.

We refer to the world of meaning as the **subjective world**. It is a world made up of **truths**. What is true for me (water is cheap and easy to access, thus its value isn't consciously of concern to me) isn't true for someone stranded on a desert island. So while the objective fact of water is the same for both of us, the subjective truth of water is on opposite ends on a gradient of value subjectively.

Jung thought about how the alchemists identified the novel moment in time when the unexpected arises as the transformational moment. A piece of "matter" changes. It is bombarded by some kind of energy that forces it to change. It either changes creatively into something new (sunlight transforms a seed into a plant) or destructively (sunlight melts ice into water) into what it once was. The alchemists reasoned that if they could isolate that ball of energy (that primary substance the sun shoots into the world), they'd be able to transform a common objective stone (rock without much value) into extraordinary subjective gold (rock with lots of meaningful value).

And they could do it at will.

Jung took the alchemists seriously as philosophers rather than literally as empirical scientists. He thought they were really onto something about the primary nature of the universe. But the energy they sought was not made up of "matter," rather it was "super matter," metaphysical in nature, something that dwelt in a similar realm to what we experience as consciousness.

Jung reasoned that the ball of energy the alchemists were searching for was nothing less than the prima material of everything—the stuff from which all things are created and of how all things degrade. It was the great gob of potential and possibility as well as the force of decay and inevitable dissolution.

Here's what Jung wrote in his work *Aion: Researches into the Phenomenology of the Self*, which I interpret as his tangling with the chaotic stuff that comes into our lives when we don't expect it to—unexpected events.

> This primary substance is round (massa globosa, rotundum) like the world and the world-soul; it is in fact the world-soul and the world-substance in one. It is the "stone that has a spirit," in modern parlance the most elementary building-stone in the architecture of matter, the atom, which is an intellectual model.[3]

The reference within this passage, "stone that has a spirit," is from a very old work of alchemy written by someone named Ostanes in Zosimos pulled from a footnote reference in Jung's masterwork. And the stone that has a spirit became in contemporary culture what J.K. Rowling and a host of other literary figures refer to as *The Philosopher's Stone*. Here's what Rowling has to say about it:

> I did not invent the concept of the Philosopher's Stone, which is a legendary substance that was once believed to be real, and the true goal of alchemy. The properties of "my" Philosopher's Stone conform to most of the attributes the ancients ascribed to it. The Stone was believed to turn base metals into gold, and also to produce the Elixir of Life, which could make you immortal. "Genuine" alchemists—the forerunners of chemists and physicists— such as Sir Isaac Newton and (the real) Nicolas Flamel, sought, sometimes over lifetimes, to discover the secret of its creation.[4]

---

3 C.G. Jung, *Collected Works of C.G. Jung* (Princeton: Princeton University Press, 1981), Volume 9, Part 2, 237, Kindle Edition
4 J.K. Rowling, https://www.pottermore.com/writing-by-jk-rowling/the-philosophers-stone

Carl Jung goes further to align this round primarily spiritual substance (a primary inspiration for Rowling), his massa globosa, rotundum, with the primary building block of matter, the atom. Jung suspects that if the atom is the model for the **matter** of the world, this primary substance is the model for **what matters** in the world.

So if we believe that the primary building block of "matter" is the atom, which we symbolically represent as a sphere with a nucleus that has a progressive series of orbiting electrons revolving around it (akin to our planetary system revolving around the sun), then Jung puts forth the notion that there must also be a primary building block of "what matters," which we today consider as the universe of the mind. Or traditionally, the "spirit."

That's about as far as Jung went in his description of this atom-like unit of transformative "what matters" energy. In summary, stuff out there in the disorganized and chaotic universe is the primary mover of minds. It provides the energy necessary to create mindful change, and it's thought to be spherical.

So, let's flesh this ball of energy out a bit more.

This building block material would also be round, like the atom, and it would probably mirror the structure of the atom. One thing about the nature of evolution is it is extremely efficient. The simplest, most workable model, the minimum viable solution, is what evolution is all about. When a system works for one problem, it adapts itself to solve other problems. That's called exaptation.

So if the atom model works for matter, it stands to reason that an "atom-like" model works for what matters too. If the primary substance is atom-like, there must be varying sizes of the primary substance too. This means there would be progressively more dense units of this matter that energize our minds to change in larger degrees. **If there is a periodic table of "matter," there is probably a periodic table of "what matters" too.**

That is, a small speck of this stuff (perhaps the size of a hydrogen atom, one proton/one electron, which comprises 75 percent of the matter in the universe) drops into an everyday unconscious life event and provides the mental energy necessary to find a spare toothbrush when your everyday toothbrush falls into the toilet. But a big boulder-sized sphere (like the inert gas Radon which has a mass number of 222) of it would be required to make a huge change in your life—one that would upend you enough that you find yourself so lost after years of the pursuit of a major life goal that you quit that journey entirely.

To make this more concrete, let's suppose the prima material would generally resemble something like an eyeball, with a central mass of sorts and a progressive series of energy shells revolving around it.

Like this:

THE ATOMIC MODEL FOR THE PRIMARY SUBSTANCE OF CHANGE

PHERE BALL

So we're theorizing that the model of "what matters" looks like the model of "matter." No need to reinvent the wheel.

What else do we know about unexpected/novel events in our lives? Can we parse out some more features of this "what matters" energy?

They're paradoxical in nature. Aren't they? Meaning that they can first seem like negative events and then they can transform into positive events. And vice versa.

For example, a letter from the IRS may seem negative at first, until you learn you're getting a tax refund. Similarly, the friendly new partner in your practice turns out to be a double crossing enemy who is trying to steal your job.

Our first experience of them is most often negative, meaning we get a jolt of negative threat emotion when they first arise. When our alarm clock doesn't go off and we wake up with the realization that we're running late, we get anxious. However, we often discover they can end up having a positive effect on us.

Perhaps because we are running five minutes late, we leave the house five minutes later than we normally do, thus avoiding an accident that occurs at the exact same intersection we usually reach five minutes earlier in our day. The unexpected misfiring of our alarm clock ends up saving our life. That's how these odd balls of energy transform from negative to positive.

The chaotic, unexpected event that precipitated us being late actually ended up saving our life.

Conversely, positive events can transform into negative energy. You'd think that winning a multimillion-dollar lottery would free you from having to "work" the rest of your life, but those who do win the lottery discover that the positive cash flow can uncover deeper personal problems than they'd ever imagined. Many find the relief of the positive unexpected event ends up driving them into a deep psychological funk.

They discover that "work" isn't something to be avoided. To not have any work is problematic psychologically, and money has little to do with the real work of life.

So these spheres of "what matters" energy transform our preplanned linear paths from "what is" to "what should be"—rollercoaster emotional ups and downs that we can experience as initially negative or positive.

But further down the road on our goal-directed journeys, those same chaotic, unexpected happenings can transform into the opposite experiences. That's the paradox. Negative can become positive and positive can become negative.

What's also interesting about these "what matters" spheres is that they goose us to "wake up" from our everyday unconscious routines. They force us to think, to apply cognitive energy to a problem we didn't anticipate.

So these unexpected events are not just threats to us but also open up great promise. They have a dual nature. Their emergence can be an obstacle in the short term that proves to be an opportunity in the long term. Or vice versa. They can also be an opportunity in the short term that proves to be an obstacle in the long term.

Let's diagram that paradoxical feature schematically.

THE CHARACTER OF UNEXPECTED EVENTS

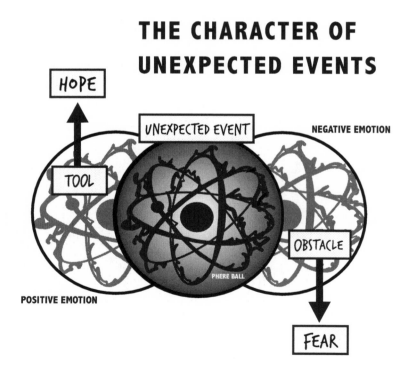

Inspired by schema in Jordan Peterson's *Maps of Meaning*, (Routledge: Abingdon-on-Thames) 1999. Figure 5.

So the sphere represented here—the unexpected novel energy that drops into our path from "what is" to "what should be"— has two possible transformative effects. It can be a positive event, an **opportunity**, which induces promise and its corresponding emotional response, hope. Or it can be a negative event, an **obstacle**, which threatens and stimulates emotional anxiety, fear.

Great, so why are unexpected events a problem for us?

The problem is that, for very good reasons—the origins of which go back to the emergence of Homo sapiens into the world—we experience them as **fear**. No matter what.

So what I propose is, a more specific, metaphorical name for what Carl Jung called *"This primary substance is round (massa globosa, rotundum) like the world and the world-soul."* Let's drop the "S" in spheres.

Or Pheres, pronounced "fears."

So the primary substance change catalyst that induces the external objective and internal subjective reactions can lead to the very big problem we defined at the start of this project, "fear freak-out." We'll call it a Phere.

And we'll define Pheres as:

1. Varying degrees of paradoxically complex chaotic energy that

2. Randomly drop into our lives unexpectedly and

3. Alert us with a fear-based alarm system to

4. Force us to break our routine,

5. Reconsider our current path from "what is" to "what should be," and

6. Change the course of our "what should be" goal or

7. Change the projected destination "what should be" goal itself.

You may be saying to yourself, this is all very interesting and everything, but if these Phere things are actually real phenomena in the world, we probably already know how to deal with them. We certainly don't need this sort of egg-headed analysis of the nature of the general principle "shit happens" in order to get on with our lives.

And you'd be correct.

We do have a very effective system already in place that automatically metabolizes the unexpected happenings in our lives. This amazing system keeps us alive and stable day to day. And it's so effective that we're really great at ignoring signals that don't literally threaten our lives or our plans in the moment.

But there's a problem with it too.

The problem is that we don't live in the scarcity world that the system evolved to navigate anymore. This system was really indispensable when every moment in a person's daily life could cause his or her death, like walking along a snake-invested landscape. But it's not so perfect when it comes to the world we live in now, which is one of abundance and creature comforts. We don't need to worry so much about wild animals or our fire going out or the loss of our best digging tool anymore.

So the system that evolved to deal with scarcity is incredibly powerful for keeping us alive, the micro details of existence. But it's not so great when dealing with the macro concerns of modernity, or modern life, like how I could spend so much time learning how to be a brain surgeon and do everything by the book and still have a terrible result. What was the point of all of that work if I ended up maiming a little boy? That kind of macro problem is what can really freak us out.

Which brings me to a very odd dream I had recently after I'd learned that my son Patrick had received his dream commission upon graduation from the US Naval Academy.

TEN
The Steeplechase Dream

In the dream, I'm in a race. I'm riding an incredibly powerful horse. What's fantastical is that I'm both the jockey and the horse. That is, I'm thinking like a person—thinking, imagining, reasoning, making calculations and decisions like a jockey would—but I'm experiencing the race like the horse would.

Everything I'm seeing, touching, smelling, tasting and hearing is from the point of view of the horse. I can feel the blinders attached to the sides of my skull. So, my sight is very tightly focused on what is in front of me. I can feel my hooves sink into the ground as my legs push off and propel me forward. I can smell the damp and the heathered fields surrounding me. I hear the incessant hum of the crowd as it rises and falls in pitch with the successes and stumbles of my individual steps.

It's as if the crowd is only watching me, this strange jockey/horse combination, even though I know there are lots of other horses to my left and right, in front of me, and behind me too. The crowd is cheering just for me, encouraging me as I move forward and berating me when I slow down. The crowd's response is dependent upon how well I'm doing in the race.

Here's where the dream gets really weird…as if being both a jockey thinking about the race and the horse itself in the race weren't weird enough. I sense another part of "me" too. It's as much a part as the jockey thinker and the horse doer are.

This other part of me is in the form of movie star Jack Nicholson. He's a part of me too and he's communicating with me as I'm running.

But it's not the real Jack Nicolson. It's Jack Nicholson as Marine Colonel Jessup, the character he played in the movie *A Few Good Men*.

Do you remember the climax of *A Few Good Men*? Tom Cruise plays the hero of the movie, a super smart hotshot Navy lawyer given the impossible task of leading the prosecution of a group of Marines who have hazed a recruit to death. At the end of the movie, the Cruise character summons Nicholson's Jessup to the stand in a last-ditch effort to win the case. Cruise gets very frustrated with Nicholson's ability to bat away all of his best questions without revealing anything incriminating, until Cruise gets so upset that he screams at Nicholson-Jessup…

"I want the truth!"

And this is what Nicholson-Jessup tells him.

"You can't handle the truth! Son, we live in a world that has walls, and those walls have to be guarded by men with guns. Who's gonna do it? You? … I have a greater responsibility than you can possibly fathom. You weep for Santiago [the dead recruit] and you curse the Marines. You have that luxury. You have the luxury of not knowing what I know, that Santiago's death, while tragic, probably saved lives. And my existence, while grotesque and incomprehensible to you, saves lives! You don't want the truth because deep down in places you don't talk about at parties, you *want* me on that wall. You *need* me on that wall. We use words like 'honor,' 'code,' 'loyalty.' We use these words as the backbone of a life spent defending something. You use them as a punchline. I have neither the time nor the inclination to explain myself to a man who rises and sleeps under the blanket of the very freedom that I provide and then questions the manner in which I provide it! I would rather you just said "Thank you," and went on your way. Otherwise, I suggest you pick up a weapon and stand a post. Either way, I don't give a *damn* what you think you are entitled to!"

Back to the dream.

Remember that I'm both the jockey and the thoroughbred horse, but I'm experiencing the race from the point of view of the horse, with blinders on etc. And as this sort of jockey/horse avatar, I can sense that

Colonel Jessup/Jack Nicholson is also part of me and has a direct line of communication to me.

The problem is that Nicholson-Jessup has lost his voice. Makes sense because at the end of the movie, Nicholson has screamed so much it's only reasonable to think he's gone hoarse.

Now as I'm running the race, it's as if Nicholson-Jessup has one of those 360-degree camera views you can now get in high-tech cars when you put the car into reverse. It monitors all of the space around the car so you don't hit anything when you're backing out. If you come close to something that you wouldn't be able to see, but the camera can, it makes a beeping sound to force you to stop and reconfigure your approach to the parking space.

Nicholson-Jessup has that high-tech car ability for me in this dream. The dream continues.

I'm in the race and I'm fully committed to getting ahead. I don't see the finish line, but I know my purpose is to run as fast as I can to get over the water-filled ditches and jump the ornate privet fences…to use my hooves to dig into the perfect loamy earth and spring forward as fast as I can.

I realize I'm in a steeplechase race, the kind they've been running in Ireland for centuries from one church steeple in one town to another over the natural ditches and jumps of the land. The dream race is akin the Grand National, the horse race made famous in the novel and movie *National Velvet.*

I'm feeling great as I navigate the course. The crowd is happy, cheering me on like they've bet their life savings on me. The jockey part of me is mentally one step ahead of my horse body, and when he checks in with Nicholson-Jessup, even the actor/colonel seems to be calm and pleased with the way things are going. But this putting my attention on Nicholson-Jessup slows me down a hair, so I go back to feeling my hooves on the turf and focusing on the jump in the distance. The jockey part of me has the direction and reins on me working perfectly. The three parts of me—my horse body, my jockey leader, and my 360-degree safety system controlled by Nicholson-Jessup—are perfectly in sync.

And then Nicholson Jessup sends me a jolt of warning. The warning literally feels like an electrical jolt. Like when you're a little kid and you stick your finger in a light socket. It's an alien shock that gives my horse body pain and then a follow-up fear of more pain in the offing.

My jockey-self tells my body to forget about Nicholson-Jessup and press on...keep running.

And then a larger jolt from Nicholson-Jessup. It's as if he's angry that I didn't stop when he gave me the first jolt, so I slow down and I start to wonder why Nicholson-Jessup has sent his message. What does he want?

And then I see something strange about the next jump in the distance. My jockey self is not clear if it's a ditch or a fence or if it goes to the left or to the right. It seems to be all of those things at the same time, a left jump and a right jump, a ditch and a fence. It's not clear at all what I should do.

Nicholson-Jessup sends another jolt. This one is even more painful than the first two. It's obvious that I have to do something or he'll just keep on firing more and more jolts into me of progressively greater intensity.

My jockey-self takes control and tells me not to worry. Just keep moving forward. He'll figure out what to do.

But now the crowd starts to boo. It starts to let me know that it is not happy I've slowed down. They put all of their faith in me by investing all of their savings on my winning and I'm slowing down. They want me pushing forward with everything I have.

Nicholson-Jessup is relentless with his painful negative jolts too, signaling that there's something I need to figure out and do about the indefinable thing looming in front of me. But Nicholson-Jessup doesn't give me anything more than that, just an ever-increasing amount of pain and the follow-up terror of knowing more is on the way.

I know the unknown thing ahead is something I need to pay attention to, and I desperately plead with my jockey-self to do something because I'm hurting. But my jockey-self isn't sure what it is either and he can't turn his attention to it while my body is bothering him. So the pain and panic keeps escalating.

The other horses pass me by. I'm terrified, panicked, full throttle fear freak-out. The other horses seem to have no problem with the thing in front that's got me so mixed up and not knowing what to do. And the crowd starts cheering for them while booing me...

I don't know what to do. Nicholson-Jessup is now firing a constant stream of jolts into me while my jockey-self fumbles around giving me no information, no instruction, nothing. I don't know whether to start sprinting forward and get back in the race or head back to the stables and hide.

In this hyper state of panic...

I wake up.

ELEVEN

The Trinity of Experience
The Body, Brain 1.0 and Brain 2.0

Before I lay out my minimum viable model of the way the brain handles incoming stimulus, I have a short disclaimer to my fellow neurosurgeons and science professionals. In the interest of simplifying the most complex object on the planet (the human brain), I've decided to make some broad representations about how the brain works in relationship to fear. Taking a page from the brilliant scientists Daniel Kahneman and Amos Tversky and their representation of our thinking processes as System 1 and System 2, I'll be referring to Brain 1.0 (broadly speaking, the limbic system) and Brain 2.0 (broadly speaking, the seat of consciousness as well as the processes associated with the frontal neocortex) as the two brain systems that monitor and control our behavior. I struggled for months with this decision and thankfully, the right hemisphere of my own neocortex fed me the dream (what I now refer to as my steeplechase dream) to use as a metaphor to illustrate the brain's distribution of responsibility.

So let's get back to that weird dream. Where did it come from?

While working on this project, my middle son Patrick graduated from the US Naval Academy and informed me that he'd been awarded his first choice for post-graduation service. He'd received his requested commission in the Marine Corps as a second lieutenant in the infantry. While immensely proud and respectful of Patrick and his choices, being his dad, I'm also extremely concerned about his future. There is no shortage of combat zones in the world today and while Patrick is a very capable man and a highly trained warrior, he will still always be my beautiful boy. I'd be devastated to lose him or to see him hurt in any way. So how do I metabolize the fear-inducing knowledge that he has chosen to live a life of sacrifice and peril?

In the meantime, in between surgeries and office hours, I was grappling with how to best communicate how we process the unpredicted Phere events that drop into our lives. And then the mother of all fears, the very real possibility of losing your child, drops into mine.

My Brain 1.0, the hub where the fear module/snake response lives, threw me onto the gradient of fear. By paying very clear attention to that fear I was experiencing, the fear of losing my son plus the fear of never being able to complete this project, my Brain 2.0 fed me solutions to these two very difficult problems. That's what the steeplechase dream meant.

Here's how I unpacked it. I'll look at the dream abstractly so as to generalize a meaning from its seemingly improbable narrative.

Three components made up my whole thoroughbred being in the dream.

1. The body of the horse, which experiences the five sensory sensations of running the race,

2. The jockey who, after getting the sensory input from the body, directs the horse body where to go and what to do, and

3. The odd Nicholson-Jessup figure, while incapable of communicating with language, maintains a protective monitoring force around the horse and signals the other two components that make up the being (the body and the "jockey") with electrical shocks when it identifies unknowns in its path.

In general neuroscience terms, this steeplechase model is analogous to the three-part system we rely upon to explain the way our embodied brain processes information. The neuroscience trinity is made up of the body, Brain 1.0 and Brain 2.0. The thoroughbred body, with its five senses, represents the first indispensable part of the whole that directly experiences the environmental stimuli. The body directs the five sensory objective facts (sight, sound, touch, smell, and taste) of the environmental stimuli to the brain.

Nicholson-Jessup represents Brain 1.0, which is most often referred to as the limbic system. Brain 1.0 quickly processes the five sensory bits of information and delivers a quiet but positive "keep going" message back to the body if no unknown messages are delivered to it within the five channels of information. If there are unknowns inside those five channels, negative messages (electrical jolts that translate into a gradient of fear) fire warning signals into the body to get it to break routine, to slow down its rush toward a specific goal.

The body experiences the fear message on a discomfort gradient of fear. Simultaneously the negative Brain 1.0 message travels internally to the last part of the three-part system Brain 2.0, which is often referred to as the neocortex. Brain 2.0 is the jockey of the dream. The jockey, now consciously awake after being alerted by the discomfort message on the gradient of fear from Brain 1.0 to pay attention, is then relied upon to think through what the alarm actually means and then plan and respond to the unknown accordingly.

Brain 2.0 must decipher whether the alarm means a whole unit is getting closer to its goal (a promising opportunity) or alternatively if the alarm means the unit is getting further away from the goal (a threatening obstacle). Once Brain 2.0 decides which of these two possibilities best describes the unknown, it either directs the body forward to take advantage of the opportunity or formulates a new plan to go around the obstacle.

Let's walk through the dream sequence again to flesh this out a bit more.

In that fantasy steeplechase race, fear arrived just after Nicholson-Jessup (Brain 1.0) jolted my horse body. Because Nicholson-Jessup does not have the capacity to speak to the jockey (Brain 2.0) with language, he zapped the horse body, which then signals its distress to the jockey. Remember that the jolts were responses to the unknown phenomenon just ahead, that strange jump/ditch/right/left problem in the foreseeable future. Essentially, the electrical jolts were signals from my horse alarm system, the Nicholson-Jessup Brain 1.0, to my horse body and then to my jockey mind (Brain 2.0) to pay attention.

It was signaling that some unknown phenomenon was in our pathway to our goal. Whether an opportunity or an obstacle, it needed to be dealt with.

Fear, as represented by Nicholson-Jessup's jolts, is simply a river of negative feeling that our unconscious nervous system (Brain 1.0) regulates as the means to alert our conscious nervous system (Brain 2.0) to pay attention to something that doesn't quite make sense blocking our progress. Our fear is the motivational force that Brain 1.0 issues when it determines that something is actually happening that another part of our brain (the super-duper, upgraded, add-on system...Brain 2.0) didn't think was going to happen. The unexpected event that drops into our lives while we are pursuing a particular goal triggers negative emotion.

I call these phenomena that happen unexpectedly Pheres, in homage to Carl Jung's definition of the primary substance of creation. A great deal of the rest of this book will be about how to distinguish between the varieties of Phere. If Pheres trigger fear, I'm reasoning, the more we know about them, the better. What we'll come to understand is that if we become skilled at identifying what specific kind of fear emotion we're experiencing at any one time (where on the gradient of fear we'd place ourselves) we'll be able to associate that fear response with a specific kind of Phere stimulus. The sooner we know the qualities of the stimulus, the sooner we'll be able to figure out how to act in its presence.

Having a clear understating of the different kinds of Phere will also give us a better understanding of just how complex a job Brain 1.0 is doing. You've probably heard or read about Brain 1.0 before as it is often referred to as the "lizard brain," or the primitive part of our higher faculties. The truth is that Brain 1.0 is responsible for our survival over the past 150,000 years or so. Without it, we'd be dead. No wonder it took on the personality of Nicholson-Jessup in my dream. It deserves some respect.

Now if we understand exactly what Brain 1.0 is asking us to do when it sends us fear jolts, we can turn our minds to that task instead of freaking out over its messaging system. Being cognitively dominant is simply putting on our proverbial thinking caps to figure out what kind of Phere we're dealing with. Once we do that, we can suss out what it means. When we know what it means, we can plan a course of action to metabolize it. The great news is that when we put on our thinking caps, Brain 1.0 turns down the fear volume (the jolts).

The alternative to dealing with unexpected Phere events by exercising our thinking caps is to focus on the fear noise itself. That's what happens when we have a fear freak-out, a negative feedback loop. Brain 1.0 gets irritated when we focus on its fear noise instead of what it is signaling to us. So it just turns up the volume until we do, or alternatively until we get so freaked out that we run away and find familiar safe surroundings.

When we turn our mind to the signal saying we need to deal with an unexpected Phere event, Brain 1.0 rewards us by tempering the fear signal, quieting it to a background hum instead of a piercing alarm.

So, if we want to understand and coexist with the feeling of fear, we need to:

1. Think about Brain 1.0 differently than the derogatory way we currently do. It is in fact embedded hardware with lots of software applications that saves us from premature death.

2. Put forth a theory about the phenomena Brain 1.0 identifies just before it jolts us with fear. That is our global theory of Pheres we've already talked about.

3. Think about how Brain 1.0 determines whether or not a Phere is present. How does it monitor and sort information?

4. Understand the hierarchical model it uses to determine how to signal to the body and Brain 2.0 once it determines a Phere has landed. That is, how does it determine what level of external and internal "fear" jolt to send?

5. Help our Brain 2.0 be better able to categorize the kind of problem it's facing depending upon the gradient of fear it's receiving. Quickly associating the specific fear signals that result from problematic unexpected Phere events is the key to figuring out how to proceed toward or away from a goal. The first thing one must do to solve a problem is to accurately define it.

Lastly, if fear is simply Brain 1.0's motivational juice to get Brain 2.0 to deal with unexpected Phere events, what about the fear that comes when something we know about and anticipate—like the death of a loved one, the end of a career, or the maturation process itself?

Why do these things we know are coming still frighten us when they finally arrive?

I'll explore this difficult problem in more depth at the end of the book.

TWELVE
Combinatorial Explosiveness

"White count is good as per ER doc's report," I conveyed the status of a bounce-back who'd just come into the ER door to my chief. A bounce-back is a patient who'd been discharged after brain surgery with enough complications at home to force them back to the hospital.

"What is it?"

"It's normal."

"What's the f@#king number? I don't want your interpretation… or the ER doctor's for that matter. I want the number. I'll interpret it."

"I don't know exactly what it is. I'll have to check."

"Check now! And next time remember what it is. It's time you trained your mind to remember the details. If you want to be a neurosurgeon you better learn to remember the details. That's not the way I want you thinking, Mark."

It was 7:30 p.m. after another long day as an intern (the lowest rank on the MD totem pole) covering the neurosurgery service. I was motivated, knowing that if I could present to my superior the thirty-six patients on the ward that I was responsible for by 8 p.m., I'd have a shot at getting home before my wife Julie went to bed. We had limited time these days to be together and I missed her dearly.

As the covering intern, though, I was responsible for all of the floor patients' paperwork and care. This included discharge orders, a daily progress note, and checking up on the entire laboratory, CT and MRI scan and pathology results that had accumulated over the day. While trying to accomplish this daunting task, I would also be peppered with questions from nurses, physical and occupational therapists, and social workers. Plus, I was the liaison between the doctors who were operating in the OR and the families, some of whom demanded a lot of attention. With very good reason, too. The last thing I needed was another patient with a problem coming back onto my service because of a postoperative complication. Hence my relief that what I'd hoped would be the report from the ER about the postsurgical bounce-back—*All is well. No need to admit.*—was actually what I'd heard. Wisely, my chief had zero confidence in my interpretation of the objective data.

The patient in the ER had undergone a craniotomy for a benign tumor. I remembered her because I cared for her after she was transitioned out of the ICU onto the neurosurgery floor. Following our protocol for operating procedures, once patients had completed surgery and were out of the danger zone, they typically were transitioned to the ward for another day or two before they were discharged home. It was our step-by-step launching pad to get patients evaluated for postoperative physical therapy and decide if they were functional enough to go home or if they should be transferred to a specialized rehabilitation facility for further structured recovery.

As an intern, I rarely cared for patients in the ICU, as that was the purview of the more senior residents. But when they hit the stable neuro-floor, they were my patients. I had a long scut work list of miscellaneous tasks that needed completion before I could head home, and I was in the process of clearing them when my chief caught my attention.

Evening chief rounds followed a very strict order. We would walk up to each patient's room and stand just outside the door. I would then review with him that particular patient's status in a very orderly, rote fashion. Something like: "This is Mrs. Smith, post-op day three from lumbar spinal fusion by Dr X. She's been afebrile (no fevers) but she was short of breath today, so I checked her for a pulmonary embolus with a VQ scan (a study that looks at the blood flow to the lungs to make sure there are no blood clots there). VQ scan was negative. Her exam shows good strength in all muscle groups. Her hemoglobin is normal. Her post-op CT scan shows good position of the screws, and I expect a discharge to rehab tomorrow as she lives alone and is not yet ready to go home by herself."

This type of a presentation would continue for each patient with the chief occasionally questioning me on something or double-checking my results and paperwork. This report and checkup on patients would continue until we finished the very last patient. Then if I was lucky and could complete all the new tasks he assigned on those evening rounds (do paperwork for more tests, follow up with X, Y, Z doctor etc.) AND I was not on call…I'd get to leave the building. Best case scenario was getting home around 9 p.m.

During this night's rounds I was interrupted by the ER notifying me of the bounce-back's arrival. The patient returned to the ER with a fever and mild headache. When I heard the ER physician's presentation, I was relieved, but my chief was not. The ER doctor had given me his analysis that the patient looked fine, had another family member at home with the flu, and most likely this patient probably had the beginning stages of the flu as well. As backup, the ER doctor told me that the patient's white blood count was "normal."

The white blood cell count is an indicator of how a patient's body is protecting itself. Normally it ranges with slight institutional lab variations between 4.0 and 10.6. And, again "normally," when the white count is elevated it's a sign of infection. So if a patient comes into the ER and their white count (short for white blood cell count) comes back from the lab somewhere between 4.0 and 10.6 it's technically normal. And a novice like me would interpret it like that. However, a seasoned doctor knows the "normal" number of a white count can be misleading.

For instance, if a person comes into the ER with a high fever and they have an obvious wound infection with pus draining out of their incision and their white count is normal, that's a very bad sign. It means the patient is even sicker than the numbers show because the infection is so overwhelming their body can't mount an attack on the invading organisms. Conversely sometimes a super high white count without evidence of an infection can represent other diseases like leukemia. And if patients have any suppression of their immune system by medications or by chronic disease, like diabetes, their white count is also unreliable.

My rebuke began once I conveyed that info to my chief, verbatim from the ER doc.

"Mark, the ER doc has the luxury of having a rosy *'everything is okay'* attitude because most of his patients don't have life-threatening conditions like ours do. I don't like your thinking. It's your job as a neurosurgeon to think of the worst thing this possibly can be and then prove it's not that thing before you dismiss the symptoms. He lowered his voice almost to a whisper: "*Christ, we were inside this lady's head two weeks ago... Sure, she could be getting the flu...OR she could be developing early meningitis. THAT'S what I want you thinking about.*"

He was right of course.

But the flood of information I was dealing with was overwhelming. So overwhelming that my Brain 1.0 just couldn't maintain vigilance for thirty-six different patient scenarios with a fine-tuned resolution for each and every one.

So how could I train myself to think the way my chief wanted me to?

How was I going to look for evidence of Phere events (unexpected changes in the patient) without any positively clear indication that they'd even occurred?

The first thing I needed to do was come to terms with one ironclad simple objective fact. This is the "too much information" fact of life.

Life's sensory information input (the sights, sounds, touches, smells, and tastes of everyday life) is limitless. There are just too many levels of analysis with too little time to exhaust all possible combinations of scenarios for a complex problem. And the phenomena that causes a postoperative brain surgery patient to bounce back with flu symptoms shortly after discharge definitely qualifies as a complex problem. Add thirty-five more patients, all with varying symptoms and diagnoses, and you get complexity at a level that would overwhelm *Star Trek's* Mr. Spock.

So the fact is, I simply could not then and cannot now write down an exhaustive list of all of the possible causes and combinations of causes that could be at play with my thirty-six patients. And I'd be crazy to even contemplate doing such a thing.

Why?

Because of a fact of life called combinatorial explosiveness.

I recently picked up the game of chess, which is a great example to explain how explosive adding up the number of possible combinations of actions I could take over hours, days and weeks for each of my thirty-six patients (i.e., the number of actions over multiple stages of the process from ailing to recovery) really is.

The game of chess is about cornering the king of your opponent into a place where no matter what movement your opponent makes, you will capture the king in the next move. That's called checkmate. Checkmate is the end (the goal state, where you want to be) that will win the game. Now at the beginning of the game (the present state, where you are just before you begin your pursuit of your goal) you have about thirty legal moves at your command to begin solving the problem of capturing the king of your opponent. After analyzing millions of games played in the past, statistics show that the average game of chess with equally matched players both trying to solve the "win the game of chess" problem takes about sixty moves. Those are the average total number of moves made by both players in a single game.

The mathematical formula for calculating the possible number of pathways for this hypothetical chess game (the combination of possible A to B to Z moves to get from no winner to winner) is to take the possible number of operations for every move (thirty) and multiply it to the power of how many stages in the game occur (sixty). Or in scientific formula terms, F to the D power (F^D) where F is the number of possible operations and D is the number of stages to reach a goal state.[5]

---

5   Holyoak, K. J., "Problem Solving," in D. Osiers and E.E. Smith (Eds.), *Invitation to Cognitive Science, Second Edition* (Cambridge, MA: MIT Press, 1995), 267-296.

So the number of alternative pathways between the beginning of the game—when there is no winner and no loser—to the end of the game—when there is a winner and a loser is thirty to the sixtieth power.

Thirty to the sixtieth power is a very big number. If you translate it into standard scientific notation it comes out to 4.29×10^{88}. That's a lot of possible pathways in the chess game search space to map out winning strategies. And that's why it's such a difficult game for human beings. It was very difficult for computers too for quite a long time until the Deep Blue Computer software came online in 1997.

As a comparison, the Google search engine named itself after the very large number 1×10^{100}, which was its founders' way of letting everyone know just how powerful a machine it is. The Google algorithm-driven machine can comb through millions of web pages to find the address for your favorite pizza joint in Naples in a microsecond and deal with complex searches on the order of ten to the hundredth power. Google solves the combinatorial explosiveness problem very well and that's why the company is one of the most powerful on the planet…if not the most powerful.

If I were to begin writing down a list of how many different possible unexpected Phere events may have caused the return of the postoperative patient to the ER that night over twenty years ago, I'd still be writing to this day. Right off the top of my head, I can think of at least ten possibilities that could cause a headache and flu symptoms in a postoperative brain surgery, and the number of steps required to stabilize and eliminate the symptoms would be at least ten too. So according to the combinatorial explosive formula, to write down all of the possibilities would require 10^{10} scenarios.

Keep in mind that the current estimate of how many neurons we have in each of our brains is 10^{11} and the estimate of how many connections between those neurons is 10^{15}. As a comparison, the human genome project estimates the number of base pairs in the entire human DNA strands at around three billion—3×10^9—and it took very powerful computers to map it over years.

The way computers traditionally solve the combinatorial explosiveness problem is through a set of analytical formulas called algorithms. Those algorithms are devised and programmed by human beings, but the speed and computational power of our digital machines today actually allows for algorithmic search of vast domains of information. It's simply a matter of rapidly searching the ocean for all of the seahorses and then listing where those seahorses are on a big chart. It's a ridiculous task, but we've been able to double our computing power (or computational vigor) every twenty-four months or so since Gordon Moore projected computer processing advances in his 1965 paper "Cramming More Components onto Integrated Circuits."[6]

But human-driven brain surgery is pretty remarkable if not miraculous too.

While we do not have the computational power the Google machine does, we have other ways to solve complex problems. It's a different way of processing information based upon limiting the search field rather than exhaustively combing through it. This skill is not just for brain surgery. Every human being has the powerful ability to eliminate 99.9 percent of information that just doesn't matter in terms of solving a particular complex problem so that he or she can concentrate on what information actually matters to solve a problem.

To find the best pizza in Naples, we wouldn't list every restaurant in the city and then start eliminating them one by one until we found only pizza restaurants. We ignore all of the seafood and steak places without even considering them. The way we solve complex problems is by simply ignoring information that does not matter.

We accomplish this specific training for particular skills, like brain surgery, that solves the combinatorial explosiveness problem through the intense mentor/mentee relationship. The mentor brain surgeon

---

6   Gordon Moore, "Cramming More Components on Integrated Circuits," *Electronics Magazine* 38, no. 8, April 19, 1965

teaches the aspiring surgeon how to limit his or her search field by giving them observational and intellectual tools (called heuristics) to pick out the salient information for each patient quickly.

There's simply too much information for us to sort through. The same combinatorial explosive problem arises for you at your job too. Or at home figuring out whether you should hand your seventeen-year-old the keys to your car. You need a way to cope with all of this information so you don't panic and hide in a dark room for the rest of your life. We use heuristics to outflank too much information.

The mentor/mentee relationship is an advanced system, though, that takes years to become ingrained. So how do we deal with the gusher of information before we get "trained"?

We rely upon a dynamic relationship between Brain 1.0 and Brain 2.0.

THIRTEEN
What Doesn't Matter

The trinity of experience system that played out for me in my steeple-chase dream seems like it would work fine if there weren't so many unexpected events (Pheres) dropping into our daily life. Just looking at my problem with the bounce-back diagnosis and treatment from the previous chapter along with the combinations of solutions to chess demonstrates the impossible number of searches to those solutions.

So many that to search for the answer to each and every unexpected Phere that confronts us is impossible.

How does the trinity of experience manage to decide which unexpected Phere to deal with and which not to deal with in the first place?

Let's go back to our earlier examination of fear in "The Gradient of Fear" chapter to narrow down this problem. Remember, we hypothesized that there is a fundamental dividing line between external fear and internal anxiety. That line is defined by the qualities the Phere event itself presents to us.

Let's deal with the external, easy-to-understand threats that induce fear first.

When Homo sapiens first came online in the world, unexpected Pheres that triggered Brain 1.0 were primal and primarily external. Just surviving took up the majority of our time.

Here are some examples of external Phere events:

1. A predator comes into our environment unexpectedly.

2. Another being eats the food we've stored to keep us alive during the winter.

3. A storm destroys our shelter.

This early human being stage is the time period when Brain 1.0 developed into such a potent force. It ruled our world then, and beneath the surface of everyday life, it still rules our world today. Brain 1.0 is simply indispensable for external Pheres, when an observable and direct threat comes into your environment—like a snake or a tiger, a mugger, or someone intent on assaulting you.

Brain 1.0 immediately recognizes these external Pheres as threats and tells us exactly what to do with lightning speed. It takes no time to consult with our higher thinking zone (Brain 2.0). It gets to work without any conscious thought whatsoever.

The first thing it does is jolt us to freeze our bodies. If we stay still and don't move, the external Phere could fail to detect our presence and leave us alone. And then if freezing doesn't work, and the predator begins to move toward us with malicious intent, Brain 1.0 tells us to run away from the external Phere. And lastly, if we simply can't outrun the external Phere, Brain 1.0 tells us to fight it out to the death. We may fail in our efforts to kill the animal, but we have no doubts about what we need to do in the face of the external Phere. Brain 1.0 takes charge and gives us the best chance possible to survive.

But as time passed, civilizations came to the fore, and new technologies took us further and further away from the primal external environment. A new kind of fear began to dominate. This is the internal anxiety fear we experience when we face an unexpected event that is ill defined—something we've never encountered before or are completely baffled by its inevitability (like growing old or death). Not only do we experience anxiety the microsecond this kind of Phere drops into our lives, but we can often further obsess over it in our minds, turning it over and over until we're convinced we will experience impending doom by its effects.

We fixate on it.

It causes us so much agitation because we just don't know what to do about it. We can't spend the rest of our lives freaking out about it, though, or we'd never get out of bed. So our Brain 2.0 fashions a solution.

The first principle of this is the objective fact that Brain 1.0 has reported to Brain 2.0 that it is flummoxed by these Pheres. It's not sure what the phenomenon is, so Brain 1.0 just keeps firing fear jolts to the body and the Brain 2.0 centers of our mind. It's passing the buck to our second-level system to deal with it. Brain 2.0 needs to respond to the signal.

Brain 2.0 has two quick responses:

1. It can't help but focus its attention and conscious energy on the discomfort Brain 1.0 is sending its way. *My God when is this feeling going to stop? Get me out of this situation! This negative feeling is driving me crazy!* Brain 2.0 obsesses over the response while avoiding dealing with the stimulus that actually triggered the response. If Brain 2.0 stays in this state, it devolves into fear freak-out.

2. It quickly places its attention on another phenomenon. It distracts itself from the response by ignoring the stimulus. *What my mother just said about the way I'm raising my children isn't what I expected to hear, but I don't want to get into a fight with her at Thanksgiving. So I'll go into the basement to get the special tablecloth so I can get away from her.* In this case, Brain 2.0 ignores the Phere stimulus and finds something else to do in order to distract Brain 1.0. Brain 2.0 shifts goals so it can avoid the negative.

So the steeplechase dream—trinity of experience—is great for the external observable threats when they're obvious. But it's not so good dealing with the nebulous internal fears of anxiety...those moments when you don't know what to do because you just don't know what the unexpected event (the fear inducer, Phere) means. Brain 1.0 doesn't have a quick fix for these, so it dumps the problem in Brain 2.0's lap. And not in a nice way either. It does so by jolting Brain 2.0, and the entire body, with negative emotion.

Our huge contemporary problem is the practically infinite unexpected events that occur every single day to every single person who lives in this ill-defined, nebulous arena we call Earth. We don't often run into a tiger, but we do run into the old colleague who tells us something we're not sure is good news or bad news for us. It's very difficult to suss out what every bit of information means to us anymore. This hyper state can send us into places we believe are safe and keep us there, or it can send us into a constant state of "shift," distraction away from the things we don't want to deal with—i.e., the chaos.

Obviously, we are still able to carry on with our daily lives even under the duress of ill-defined Pheres that cause anxiety. But I suggest that in our contemporary world with its multiple channels of information flooding into our beings, we are having more and more difficulty doing so. Quick attention-seeking machines like video games and other quick-fix micro entertainments are as popular as they are today for this very reason. They distract us from focusing on the information we can't easily meaningfully process.

So how did this finely tuned machinery, built to keep us alive (the trinity of experience system), adapt to the ever-increasing amount of unexpected and ill-defined events happening in the modern world year after year? Despite all of the noise we humans endure, we are still extremely capable.

By necessity, our brain adapted by narrowing its focus.

It built a feedback system that ignores any information that is not relevant to the person solving a particular problem in a specific moment in time. Brain 2.0 simply tells Brain 1.0 what to pay attention to and what not to pay attention to, thus eliminating a lot of "false alarms." With this directive, Brain 1.0, while still taking in an ocean of sensory input, withholds its fear responses under certain conditions. Those conditions are met when the inputs don't matter to the particular problem Brain 2.0 is trying to solve.

Brain 1.0 ignores all kinds of sensory input with an efficiency and prowess that is simply awe-inspiring. This laser focus, driven by heuristic psycho-technologies evolutionarily developed by Brain 2.0, limits the search domains of our problems. This "ignore the un-meaningful" strategy defeats the environmentally objective fact of combinatorial explosiveness. Our focus, that keen toolbox that limits our conceptual strategies to get what we want, makes our cognitive functions so dominate in our environment. Heuristics are why Homo sapiens runs the world, influencing and willfully changing the natural environment. Heuristic problem solving is the reason we're able to send people to the moon and back. But there's a dark side to them too.

Once Brain 2.0 has its focal point, it's directive about what's important and meaningful, Brain 1.0 silences its alarms unless a very specific kind of unexpected Phere drops in—the one that will aid or pose an obstacle when solving a specific problem that Brain 2.0 wishes to solve. We are saved by our focus and capable of extraordinary creations, yet we are also blinded by that focus too, asleep at the wheel while our avoidance of difficult Pheres allows them to grow ever larger until they reach critical mass and wreak havoc.

The dynamic relationship between Brain 1.0—which deals with the objective facts that drop in to our lives (Pheres)—and Brain 2.0—which deals with figuring out what those facts mean—is how we eliminate distractions from 99.9 percent of sensory information flooding into our beings.

Let's unpack this feedback system a bit more. The better we know how it works scientifically, the better we'll be able to employ it to best effect, allowing us to practice cognitive dominance in such a way that we never lose sight of our most important values.

PART TWO

The Road to Cognitive Dominance

FOURTEEN
Angie

When I was in medical school, my ambition and hyper-focus on micro tasks in service of my childhood dream to be a surgeon led to my being labeled the class "gunner." This was a dubious honor. "Gunner" was a pejorative term spawned from the Tom Cruise hit movie *Top Gun*. It defined the cutthroat student willing to do anything to earn the top spot in the class—essentially, the brownnoser. Although I did want to be at the top of the class, and did everything I could to get there, I did not appreciate the nickname.

The truth was that I had a very large weakness, one that cracked through my confident persona. This weakness returned time and time again throughout my career. It began just after I earned my MD and finished my internship. My first four-month residency rotation put me right smack dab in the middle of my problem arena.

I had to cover the pediatric ward.

I was the admitting physician for patients with neurosurgical problems (head bumps, brain tumors, hydrocephalus) at Pittsburgh Children's Hospital. I was to "work up" (examine the facts of the case and put forth a theory about what the symptoms meant) each case for my chief resident and attending professor to evaluate and then treat the patient after those consultations.

Angie was a twelve-year-old with congenital hydrocephalus (water on the brain) who had been treated as an infant with a ventriculoperitoneal "VP" shunt several years before the existence of third ventriculostomies—the procedure we performed on Oksanna. A shunt consists of small flexible tubing slightly larger than a cocktail straw that is implanted internally from the brain to the abdomen. This tubing allows any extra cerebrospinal fluid built up in the brain to flow down and into the abdominal cavity where it can be reabsorbed into the blood stream.

Brain surgeons are taught early in residency that shunts are kids' lifelines. While they are lifesavers, the tubing must remain unclogged or the patient will die without urgent intervention to repair the obstruction. So, after a shunt is put in, we educate patients and parents about the signs and symptoms of a shunt malfunction so that if they experience or witness any of these symptoms they will immediately head to the hospital.

Angie had been a normal and thriving adolescent until seventeen hours before I met her when she developed a rapid onset headache and nausea, which soon escalated into vomiting and malaise. Her shunt-educated parents suspected this was an early sign of a malfunction, and after checking and realizing she didn't have the flu, they appropriately brought her directly to the emergency room. My attending and chief resident were already scrubbed in the OR working another case, so when the ER called them they dispatched me to "work her up," or sort the information for them. The "gunner" in me knew the "shunt-malfunction-identification" protocol from top to bottom and was confident he would execute the procedure without fail.

Angie was awake but complained of a severe headache and appeared very uncomfortable. She was anxious and couldn't sit still, shifting from sitting yoga-style in her bed to lying on her pillow. My inner taskmaster knew to compare the past with the present to see what the future might bring. Her CT scan, which had already been completed when I arrived, showed an increase in the amount of cerebrospinal fluid as compared to a routine surveillance scan from the previous year's checkup. The increase of fluid indicated there was probably an obstruction of the flow somewhere in her tubing. There was a shunt malfunction, a clog. I confirmed the clog in the tubing after ordering and looking at X-rays, which showed a disconnection of the shunt tubing made of sialastic (a mixture of silicon and plactic) that was supposed to bypass the fluids down to her abdomen at the level of her rib cage.

It was a straightforward presentation. Shunt degradation commonly happens around Angie's age because the shunt tubing that was placed at birth becomes brittle over the years and can fracture like an old rainwater drainage pipe. I made my diagnosis, ordered the appropriate preoperative labs and notified the operating room we had an "add-on" case to follow the one ongoing in the operating room.

I hiked up the stairwell to the OR pretty confident that I had done my job for the team and gotten the case lined up. I walked into the OR and presented the evolving situation in the ER to my attending, Dr. Albright. The attending surgeon supervises the resident and Dr. Albright proved to be not just a mentor, but also a threshold guardian that kept me from tipping into disaster and damnation over and over again in brain surgery's extraordinary world.

"Mark, is Angie crisply alert?" Dr. Albright asked in his extremely precise tone and demeanor.

"Yes, sir."

"Mark, are you sure she can wait until this case is over? We've got a few hours remaining."

"Yes, sir."

He was working under the microscope and seemed slightly distracted by my intrusion. With no further questions from Dr. Albright, I left the room to get to a conference in another part of the hospital. I was late for it and I didn't want to miss one second more.

According to the facts of the protocol and my observations, I felt assured that Angie was in a safe place awaiting the next available OR. She was getting her blood work done and was being admitted to a room on the pediatric neurosurgery floor, which would take about as much time as the remainder of Dr. Albright's case in the OR. If I was lucky, I could return after the conference, scrub in and help with her case.

About thirty minutes later, as I desperately tried to stay focused in the mandatory weekly departmental Morbidity and Mortality get-together, my pager went off. I excused myself and called in. It was the floor nurse on the pediatric neurosurgery floor who had just received Angie from the ER. Angie was screaming at the top of her lungs and holding her head in serious distress. Her parents were insisting that I come see her again. In the meantime, she wanted to know if there was something I could order for her pain?

I wanted to help out, but my chief had beaten into my head on my first day of the rotation "NEVER give narcotics for shunt malfunctions." It was one of the first rules I was taught.

I denied the request.

Giving narcotics for a shunt malfunction headache is a recipe for disaster. As the fluid builds up in the head from the obstruction, pressure compromises the patient's consciousness center. Beyond pain relief, the opiate also causes a decrease in general nervous system functions, especially respiration. Any additional sedative medication will compound the problem. As the fluid pressure increases with the decrease in central nervous activity, which is the effect of the sedative, the brain squeezes in on itself. So a shot of painkiller causes a neurological deterioration code and herniation syndrome where the brain squeezes the brainstem and the patient dies. One of my colleagues once made the error of prescribing pain meds in this case early in his career and lost a patient. It haunted him every day thereafter. I wasn't about to make that kind of mental error.

I reasoned that I hadn't done anything "wrong," but as patient care always trumped being at our departmental weekly conferences and it was only a ten-minute walk to Angie's floor, I made my way back over to the Children's Hospital through the labyrinth of connector tunnels and two sets of elevators to get to Angie.

As the elevator doors opened to face the nurse's station, I was immediately confronted with the foot of a hospital stretcher. In the stretcher Angie sat bolt upright screaming.

Pushing the stretcher was Dr. Albright still in his surgical mask from the last case.

He calmly declared, "Mark, Angie is herniating. We're opening another OR right now. Help me get her in the elevator."

Once down on the operating room floor, Dr. Albright whisked her straight into the operating room, skipping the preoperative area and anesthesia. He just calmly started getting her in position to place an emergency drain to release pressure. Other anesthesia and OR staff milling around the central hallway saw what was happening and, knowing Dr. Albright's methodology and body language, went immediately into action. Soon, five other staff worked alongside Dr. Albright to get the surgery going.

Dr. Albright saved Angie's life.

That evening, before I left for home, he called me into his office.

I began with a sputtering explanation with lots of excuses... "I'm sorry you had to go up there. I was on my way. I knew she needed surgery. I had all the bases covered."

"Mark," he paused and collected himself, "never forget what you saw today. That is exactly what a patient herniating looks like. They don't always get sleepy first. She was right on the edge. We can't always save them when they're that far along. She absolutely couldn't wait. If you ever have another patient like her, don't wait for anyone or anything. Just wheel them up to the OR and get started. We can always make room for a dying child. Somebody will help you. Sometimes there is no time. We have to trust ourselves and act on what we see. Not what we wish to be."

Because I was so tethered to rules and protocol and checklists, gunning to do everything perfectly and by the book, I was completely blind to Angie's life-threatening situation. My level of concern was low because I hadn't been exposed to this unexpected event when hydrocephalus presented as excruciating pain and not malaise as is generally the case. I thought that since I'd made the right diagnosis, I had an OR scheduled, and she was in the hospital she was safe. I couldn't imagine that she could actually die in the hospital before the surgery. I was blinded and distracted by the safety of the hospital, the familiarity of the protocol, and the proximity of the staff. I thought everything necessary had been done.

I now understand I was behaving with inattentional blindness.

It's a phenomenon of a person being so engaged in a particular task that he or she doesn't consciously register an unexpected Phere event. I was still thinking like a student…trying not to "mess up" and get a bad grade. My internal story was still the "gunner" and I hadn't switched over to "this is not a test" mode yet. I saw Angie and her symptoms through the prism of my applying the craft of being a doctor.

However, I lacked the ability to think about Angie from Angie's point of view. My subjective experience as a brain surgeon was negligible at that stage in my career. I hadn't "seen" that kind of case personally yet. So I relied upon my protocols, rules and book smarts instead of placing my attention on what was going on for the patient. I wasn't attuned to my "gut" instincts yet.

I've since discovered that inattentional blindness isn't just a surgeon's phenomenon.

We all experience it. It's a powerful heuristic that helps us solve the combinatorial explosiveness problem, but we cannot be lulled by it into complacency.

FIFTEEN
Inattentional Blindness

Dan Simons was an assistant professor and Chris Chabris was a graduate student at Harvard University's Psychology Department in the late 1990s. Working together teaching a course on research methods, the two decided to recreate an experiment that one of Simons' professors in graduate school, Ulric Neisser, had published in the 1970s.

The idea was to demonstrate the concept of "inattentional blindness." It's the phenomenon of a person being so engaged in a particular task that he or she doesn't consciously register an unexpected Phere event that arises in another life domain. When we're texting our son about where to meet after school, we don't notice that our dog is chewing our best pair of shoes. Unexpected events, what I call Pheres, are akin to the emergence of that indecipherable left and right directed, pit and fence thing in my steeplechase dream. So Simons and Chabris were trying to document the phenomenon of people literally not seeing Pheres when they are outrageously obvious. If they could document people actually not "seeing" something very clearly "'there," their work would support the hypothesis that when our Brain 2.0 is focused on a specific goal, our Brain 1.0 ignores phenomena that doesn't concern or threaten that single goal.

I thought about Simons and Chabris because their research would be indicative of cases in which it would seem that Brain 1.0 was controlled by Brain 2.0 rather than the other way around. In other words, when does the inner Nicholson-Jessup force that I'd come to associate with Brain 1.0 in my dream refrain from sending negative affective information (lightning-bolted fear) to the Brain 2.0 center? That is, when does Brain 1.0 quiet itself or remain silent even when unexpected stimulus enters its hub? Is there an instance when it should obviously fire gradient of fear specific jolts but doesn't? And If I could harness that ability to quiet Brain 1.0 when I felt anxiety, I'd be able to avoid fear freak-out events. All I would have to do was intently direct my Brain 2.0 on a very specific goal and Brain 1.0 would quiet down.

Was it possible that Brain 1.0 would be so controlled by the goal directions from Brain 2.0 that it didn't send panic messages even when it should in a mortal threat situation? Could the Brain 2.0 focus on a goal be so intense that Brain 1.0 ignored even life-threatening information? Like when a fighter pilot has to zero in on a target despite being shot at by an enemy plane.

That's what Simons and Chabris' experiment was all about—testing the power of Brain 2.0 to quiet Brain 1.0. The experiment worked like this.

Simons and Chabris recruited six students from their class to play roles in a meticulously planned performance. The remaining students in the class were to recruit and direct unwitting subjects randomly selected from around the Harvard campus through the experimental protocol. These subjects would observe the pre-staged events with a specific directed goal asked of them, and afterward, they would answer a series of questions about the experience. They would be asked to do something specific before the performance began so they would concentrate on that goal while watching.

The role players in the pre-staged events consisted of three students wearing white t-shirts and three wearing black t-shirts. These six were then filmed playing a game in front of three elevators. The setting was equivalent to a step-off hallway onto a generally familiar office floor, like the kind where a typical dentist or doctor's office would reside. So it was a generally familiar environment that the average Harvard student would have experienced numerous times in their lives.

The six role players moved around the area passing basketballs within each of their black and white t-shirted groups. The white t-shirted players passed aerial and bounce passes to each other, and the black t-shirted players did the same amongst themselves. Simons and Chabris filmed the staged basketball passing and created multiple copies of the videotape so they could test as many subjects as possible within the limited time frame for the class experiment.

Now it was time for the class's recruiter/experimenter students to walk around Harvard's campus and coax other students to take part as subjects in the experiment. When a subject agreed, the experimenter explained that the goal of the test, what the subject needed to focus on, was to count the number of passes the white t-shirt group executed in total and report how many the subject counted after the video ended. They did an equal number of trials asking the subjects to count the black t-shirt group too. The experimenter then showed the subject the videotape, which was seventy-five seconds long.

After the videotape ended, the subjects were asked to write down their answers to this question: how many passes to the (white t-shirt or black t-shirt) players were completed?

Once the subject had written down his/her answer, the experimenter informed the subject that he or she had some follow-up questions.

1. While you were counting, did you notice anything unusual on the video?

2. Did you notice anything other than the six players?

3. Did you see anyone else (besides the six players) appear on the video?

4. Did you see a gorilla walk across the screen?

While filming the bounce passing, Simons and Chabris had in fact instructed a student wearing a gorilla suit to walk into the center of the frame, stop, pound her chest and then exit. She was on screen for approximately nine seconds at just about the middle of the seventy-five-second video.

Remarkably, about half of the respondents didn't see the gorilla-suited actor.

The conclusions drawn from the study confirmed the phenomenon of "inattentional blindness." When we're locked in on a specific cognitive function (Brain 2.0 work)—i.e. the more we focus on a particular goal-oriented task—we have about a fifty-fifty chance of not seeing a glaringly obvious unexpected object that crosses our path. Note: This is one of the reasons you shouldn't use your cell phone when you are driving.

Further tests also showed that the greater the difficulty of the cognitive function required, the less likely we are to pay attention to the unexpected. Simons and Chabris increased the difficulty of tracking the passes, asking the subjects to differentiate between aerial and bounce passes with variations in opacity of the filmed subjects, and these add-ons proved that the increase in difficulty decreased the ability to see the gorilla.

Simons and Chabris' experiment won the Ig Nobel Prize in 2004— the ignoble Nobel Prize given to experiments that make us laugh and think—and wrote a book inspired by it, *The Invisible Gorilla: And Other Ways Our Intuitions Deceive Us* in 2010.

So, what does this have to do with Brain 1.0 and its fear-as-signal alarm system?

Why don't we look at the invisible gorilla through the lens of the "trinity of experience" and think about how a single subject's body, his Brain 2.0 and his Brain 1.0 may have experienced the experiment. Instead of looking at the macro behavior of all subjects of the experiment, let's just look at a single subject and think about his point of view while performing the task.

What if he had a clear goal that the experimenters didn't know about that factored into his inattentional blindness behavior? That is, like me when I was a newbie resident, perhaps he was so tightly focused on a single goal, like my goal of doing well academically or getting home at a decent hour, that he wasn't listening or even capable of listening to his "gut, or Brain 1.0"? There is no question that all of the subjects' visual sensory machinery (their eyes) took in the visual imagery of the gorilla but in 50 percent of the participants that information never made it to their conscious Brain 2.0 centers.

Why not?

Let's suppose I'm an unattached heterosexual male student at Harvard. I'm twenty years old, and as I'm walking along the commons on my way to lunch, my Brain 1.0 alerts me to an unexpected Phere—an event I didn't expect to happen when I planned my trip to lunch.

This Phere turns out to be in the form of a female student who crosses my path and smiles at me. She gives me the general impression that she's heterosexual too, so my Brain 1.0 sends an intriguing message to my body, that funny butterflies in the stomach effect, which triggers my Brain 2.0 to pay attention.

She then asks me if I'd be willing to be part of a fun and easy experiment that she's running for the psychology department. My Brain 2.0 locks in on her request and has a rapid internal debate about whether I should alter my goal to eat lunch and change it to being a part of this experiment. Because she's innately interesting and part of a large set of possible females that I, as an unattached heterosexual male student, would categorize as potential intimate relationship material, my Brain 2.0 recommends that I spend the fifteen minutes of my time this woman is requesting to see if she becomes more interesting or less so.

This action requires that I abandon my previous Brain 2.0 goal, getting lunch. But Brain 1.0 is pretty excited about this Phere (which can be positive as well as negative, in fact both at the same time as evidenced by the butterfly effect) and it sends me the necessary emotional cocktail to change my plans immediately.

My Brain 2.0 thinks that if I can become more interesting to her than just some guy she could rope in to doing a stupid experiment so she can ace her psychology class, my plan-less Friday night problem could be solved. Brain 1.0 agrees and fires more good feeling to let Brain 2.0 stay the course, but Brain 1.0 also sends a tinge of negative-affecting-fear-juice too. She might think I'm an idiot and is just being nice to me to get a good grade her class.

I take a risk that she doesn't think I'm an idiot and agree to her request.

She walks me to the psychology department and explains what she would like me to do. All the while, this yin-yang emotional yo-yo-ing continues. She gives me the goal of counting the basketball passes.

My Brain 2.0 assigns two meanings to what she's asked me to do.

There is the objective factual meaning…that she wants me to deliver a factual answer consistent with the empirical and testable facts of the number of basketball passes that occurs between the white t-shirted or black t-shirted players. That's part one of the two components of the puzzle.

And there is a story-based subjective truth Brain 2.0 is assigning and believing about her request. This subjective truth is that if I get the right answer to the basketball pass request, she will do well on her experiment, and thus she'll do well in her class. And if I help her do well on her experiment, I will elevate in her mind as a human being. Her view of me will gain positive valence. I'll not be just some guy she convinced to do her experiment but the guy who helped her ace her class. And if I elevate in her mind as a male person, my Brain 2.0 believes, I will in all likelihood increase my chances to take the relationship to a possible coffee date with her later on. And if the coffee date goes well, I'll ask her out for Friday night with the likelihood of her giving me a "yes" to that request.

So with the subjective reasoning, my Brain 2.0 concludes she will be more inclined to say yes to my offer of coffee if I give her the right objective factual answer for her experiment. If I deliver the objective fact she's requested, that will mean a subjective positive outcome, which could mean I have a shot with her in a possible romantic setting.

If this is my state of mind, my point of view, my Brain 2.0 isn't exactly neutral when the videotape starts to play. Is it? It has a very strong goal in mind. It's highly concentrated on getting the facts right.

It's loaded with meaning about what completing the task will do for me. If I accomplish the objective factual goal of getting the right answer to the basketball bounce question, I will be able to move from an undesirable present condition (being without a Friday night date or any date for that matter) to a more favorable future condition (a possible future with a date). My Brain 2.0 has framed this experiment subjectively and very personally in terms of an undesirable present and a desired future. And it has assigned deep meaning to the goal of accurately calculating how many passes one of the teams completes.

To reiterate, the meaning my Brain 2.0 assigns to this task has an objective component. I will be satisfied if I get the right answer. And it has a subjective component. If I do this experiment well and make the woman happy, she will be more inclined to go out on a date. It is laser focused and that focus has a dominant effect on my trinity of experience.

What does Brain 1.0 think about all of this Brain 2.0 goal-directed meaning?

Remember that Nicholson-Jessup speech?

It's standing on the wall between what's really going on and what my goal-directed Brain 2.0 is fantasizing about. Right? Brain 1.0 tells Brain 2.0 to pay attention to things it didn't expect to happen as it is pursuing a goal. So, yes Brain 1.0 is under the influence of Brain 2.0's active goals. And it focuses on those goals by comparing the "reality of what is happening" to the "fantasy of what will happen" in the context of those exciting Brain 2.0 wants. Brain 2.0's plans deeply affect Brain 1.0's focus.

So the goal-changing unexpected Phere event of the woman interrupting my walk to lunch thus takes over the focus of Brain 1.0 as much as it does Brain 2.0.

As long as my Brain 2.0's predictions of what will happen next with regard to the woman are not challenged by another pop-up difference between what Brain 2.0 expects and what actually happens, Brain 1.0 is along for the ride. It's monitoring the situation with keen attention.

Barring an emergency environmental situation, Brain 1.0 judges the expectation and reality of this goal and this goal only. And the goal I'm focused on is to "get a date." So Brain 1.0 is pumping positive emotional feedback along with a sub-current of anxious butterflies in my stomach as I make small talk with the interesting woman. If the woman's behavior changes, I twist my ankle on the way to the psychology building or some other event happens that upends the goal-directed behavior, Brain 1.0 will shoot us some different emotional information. But until the environment changes in a threatening way, Brain 1.0 will put its focus on how the goal-attainment mission is going.

In a familiar territory, Brain 1.0 is Brain 2.0's wingman, making sure the "getting a date" goal is on track while ignoring just about everything else.

It's important to point out that in the experiment, the subject's Brain 1.0 is most likely completely familiar with the environment in which he's operating. He's in an office at his college that looks like every other office in his college that he's been in before. He's with an interesting woman who has been very nice to him and seems to be excited to be in his presence. She's giving him her undivided attention. He's watching a videotape of people who seem to be happy passing a basketball back and forth, and all he has to do to move his goal forward is count how many passes happen in the movie. And only for one team.

This isn't exactly a high alert situation for Brain 1.0. Is it? It's no wonder so many of the subjects didn't see the gorilla. Fifty percent is a substantial percentage for not seeing a gorilla. Their Brain 2.0 goals are so compelling that their Brain 1.0 is ignoring something as outrageous as a person in a gorilla suit pounding her chest.

And yet, even though all of those positive general environmental conditions are present, half of the people who watched that video **did see** a person in a gorilla suit walk into the middle of the field of vision, pound her chest, and walk away. That's how good Brain 1.0 is at its job. No matter how familiar and safe and even how silly the person in the gorilla suit looked, it woke up Brain 2.0 and told it to stop his goal of getting a date and pay attention to the gorilla.

What the invisible gorilla experiment proves to me is not just how powerful Brain 2.0 is in terms of directing the attention of Brain 1.0, but how powerful Brain 1.0 is. In a perfectly harmless environment watching a perfectly harmless video, Brain 1.0 is still on the wall alerting the subject to Pheres that break through Brain 2.0's goal-directed behavior. Even when the reality has nothing to do with the goal, fifty percent of the time Brain 1.0 rings the bell to get Brain 2.0 to pay attention!

Considering the fact that the subjects of the experiment were a) taken from the Harvard University student community, b) that as Harvard students they are inherently interested in "doing well for the authority teacher figure," c) on the high end of Brain 2.0 cognitive ability to attain goals, and d) could be influenced by a normal attraction to the solicitor who asked them to do the experiment in the first place... it is remarkable that Brain 1.0 still alerted subjects to the truth of the gorilla-suited figure 50 percent of the time.

Just to give some contrast, in their book, Simons and Chabris tell the story of when they brought a Boston police officer into their psychology offices to test whether or not he would see the gorilla. He did so very quickly. The fact that the environment was alien to him and the fact that his success in life was not tied to his relationship to the professors were probably very large factors in his Brain 1.0 quickly alerting him to the gorilla. He was not a member of the environment and his performance counting the number of basketballs wouldn't have the power over him as it would Harvard students adept at performing in academic situations, so his Brain 2.0 was not as tightly focused on that task. He probably thought it was stupid to begin with. I'd bet that if they brought in one hundred police officers the number of "gorilla misses" would be close to zero.

All of this is to say, that while the invisible gorilla experiment certainly demonstrates inattentional blindness and how we often do not see something that is obviously "there," it does not differentiate the unexpected events in life all that well or the circumstances by which the subjects experience the unexpected event.

And those elements are key to the influence of unexpected Phere events in our lives. The familiar known situations and the unfamiliar unknown situations dramatically affect the inattentional blindness phenomenon.

For example, when I met young Angie, the patient suffering from a block in her VP shunt back at Pittsburgh's Children's Hospital, my young physician's mind was not attuned to the signs of an impending life-threatening herniation. I was more focused on being a gunner and "doing well in school." Only by experiencing the threat under the supervision of a seasoned mentor, someone who took the time to point out the necessity of keeping my focus on the patients first, could I shift my attention. And after navigating a seven-year residency I did. Similar to the police officer who has a trained eye to identify phenomena that aren't "right" in any environment, so would I learn to focus on patient behavior to sense emergencies quickly. In short, my Brain 1.0 became encoded or trained to be on the alert for extremely specific Pheres that forecast a deadly neurosurgical situation. Those events would immediately press my Brain 1.0 fire alarm when they emerged.

I built up that skill over time, facing numerous puzzling cases until their fast sorting heuristics became second nature.

For fun, let's think about the invisible gorilla experiment if the subjects did not watch a video tape of the basketball passing. Instead, what if they watched a live performance? Would that affect their ability to ignore the gorilla? What if they were emailed by a robot with no discernable gender asking them to do the experiment? How many subjects would actually agree to be a part of the experiment? What if instead of someone in a gorilla suit, the Phere was an unsteady man wearing a balaclava holding a gun and drinking from a bottle of whiskey? What if the balaclava guy was staged live instead of on video tape?

You see where I'm heading?

If you were able to run this experiment over and over again with a wide variety of subjects along with varying Pheres introduced that had different degrees of inherent threat or inherent promise, and set these experiments in varying environments from completely familiar to entirely novel to the subjects, you would be able to test the sensitivity of Brain 1.0 across a wide array of fear gradients.

Theoretically, this very large set of experiments could deliver a hierarchy of Pheres and Brain 1.0's corresponding responses to them—from ones not considered relevant and therefore not worth bothering Brain 2.0's framed and goal-directed mission to move from a negative present to a positive future to ones like the drunk balaclava wearing man with a gun that would demand immediate attention. A "no fear" response to "code blue fear" response could be mapped according to the known and unknown qualities of the environment and of the Pheres themselves.

Instead of doing a million experiments, perhaps we could come up with a meta-concept that would give us a general understanding of the hierarchy of fear. And once we could associate the response with the tenor of the stimulus Phere, we could figure out the best way to handle Pheres according to how our Brain 1.0 responds to them.

If we could understand that an "X" amount of fear means a "Y" kind of problem, we could then prescribe a "Y-Problem" solution in moments of calm and use that prescription while under great stress. That process would become our cognitive dominance methodology. Think through possible stimulus and response experiences across the gradient of fear so that we'll have a go-to system to rely upon when we're under great strain.

I propose that we can abstractly diagnose nebulous problems we will face throughout our life based upon the fear response. And we can then prescribe a way to solve those problems with the greatest probability of how we define "success." The way to do that is to take ill-defined unexpected Phere events, break them apart and define them with greater and greater resolution. That process will not only lead to a better opportunity to solve them, but because we are laser focused on that very specific goal, the process will actually reduce Brain 1.0's fear response. Brain 1.0 will calm down and help us solve these problems instead of just escalating its alarm system. This cognitive dominance methodology can prevent fear freak-out.

This is the kind of guide I'll propose later on to break down ill-defined Pheres (the ones that cause us intense anxiety) into smaller more digestible units, defined with clear processes by which we can peacefully solve them without falling into fear freak-out.

Remember that fear is not the thing we must figure out. It's simply the signal from Brain 1.0 telling us there's something unexpected going on that requires our Brain 2.0's attention. Our job is to figure out what the ill-defined unexpected Phere event means. Being highly attuned to the amount of fear emotion we are experiencing will help us do that.

Pheres cause fears.

Breaking down and defining Pheres is the process by which we can make the uncomfortable fear emotion recede. But to come up with this handy dandy guide to define and then break down Pheres, we first need to think about the objective and the subjective.

SIXTEEN
Objects and Subjects

If the trinity of experience (body, Brain 1.0 and Brain 2.0) is the system to deal with unexpected events we're calling Pheres, then all we have to do is remember not to freak out and to work the problem when a Phere event drops into our lives.

Simple enough, right?

Yes and no.

So what's the problem now?

The problem is that there is so much sensory input available to us, so much information to sort, analyze and process (the combinatorial explosion phenomenon) that our Brain 2.0 couldn't possibly be able to do it as quickly as our Brain 1.0 would like us to.

And as our Brain 1.0 has the personality akin to the Nicholson-Jessup character in *A Few Good Men*, our Brain 2.0 can easily be berated and overwhelmed by the fear jolts Brain 1.0 releases. Remember, at the end of the steeplechase dream, the horse body didn't know what to do when faced with the multileveled confusion of the rapidly advancing thing in front of it. And the jockey had no idea of what to do either.

Neither the body nor the Brain 2.0 had experienced this Phere event before. And to top it off, the Nicholson-Jessup part of the trinity hadn't either, so it continuously screamed at the other two parts of the trinity of experience with his jolts of pain and fear to do something about it.

But the body and Brain 2.0 had no idea what to do. And that's when I awoke from that dream, breathlessly released from the fear freak-out nightmare.

The unexpected Phere that has never been experienced before can overload the trinity of experience, causing an ever-increasing negative feedback loop. If that loop is not broken, a critical mass of fear results and we freak out.

So we need to focus our energies now on unpacking the nature of the unexpected Phere events. If we can understand what the component parts of this Phere are, i.e., what it is made of, we can begin to put together a behavioral model. Essentially, we'll come up with a plan for *what to do when things are not working the way we thought they would.*

So, let's break the huge problem of too much information into halves. If we had to sort the infinite volume of information stimulating our five senses into just two categories, what would they be?

Let's go back to Erich Fromm's ideas about the way we behave to see if we can divide the world's information into two parts. As you remember, Fromm put forth that we had two modes of behavior we pursue to attain global goals.

1. We wish to attain and possess material **objects**, to **have** things.

And,

2. We wish to become someone, to **be** a meaningful **subject** in the world.

If we generally agree that those two modes are accurate representations of the two kinds of desires we pursue, we can reverse engineer how our Brain 2.0 normally sorts all of the information that streams into our own private worlds. And what we do normally will help us figure out what to do under extraordinary circumstances.

We normally divide up information into two buckets: 1) quantifiable objective pieces of information (facts) and 2) subjective meaningful information (truths).

For example:

You go to the post office and see me in line with a bag in one hand and an apple in the other. Let's say you're relatively hungry and the apple looks like a good thing to eat right now. You'll ask me to give you some information so you can make a decision about committing to the goal of getting an apple for yourself.

Here are the kinds of questions you would ask:

1. Where did I get the apple? That is, where is the objective and specific location of the object in time and space? How long will it take you travel to where the apples are?

2. How much did the apple cost me? That is, what monetary value will you have to part with to get an apple similar to mine?

3. And probably, because you're not starving and could easily choose to eat something else or not at all, you'll ask me about the quality of the apple. Is the apple ripe or is it mealy? Is it worth the money? You'll want my subjective value judgment of my apple experience.

So you'll want two kinds of information to make your apple decision:

1. You'll want the **objective facts** about the apple. The quantifiable and consistent measurements, which remain stable through time. What the apple "is."

2. You'll want the **subjective truth** about the apple from a similar human being's point of view (me). These are the qualities about the apple experience from a reliable and familiar source. What the apple means. If you see me, and you're comfortable asking the objective questions that establish the quantifiable facts about the apple, then chances are we share a similar community, and thus that shared bond is enough to categorize me as someone similar to you, worthy of trust in my subjective truth.

That is generally how we sort through life from moment to moment. Once we have gathered a critical mass of this information—once we know what the unexpected Phere event means—our Brain 2.0 decides how to behave based on that meaning.

The problem arises when we start having to deal with events and we don't know whether they are threats or opportunities because we haven't experienced them before. In our little story, let's say you've seen me around town and you know what an apple is, so your Brain 2.0 doesn't have much difficulty metabolizing the apple Phere event. You easily and unconsciously divide the Phere event into the objective facts (where are the apples?) and the subjective truths (are the apples valuable, i.e., tasty, not mealy?) and get the answers to both halves of the problem to solve the "unexpected apple" event. You see it as an opportunity to nourish and enjoy a piece of fresh fruit. Likewise, if you saw me carrying an umbrella, you'd suss out whether or not a storm was coming or if I was overly cautious by asking objective and subjective questions.

If our minds are capable of quickly metabolizing known phenomena unconsciously, that is dividing up the phenomenal Phere into its objective facts (what it is) and its subjective truths (what it means) and then acting on the random drop-in of the phenomenon based upon the solution of it as a threat to us or an opportunity, why not use this same technology when we face unexpected unknown phenomena too?

Break the "what to do when you don't know what to do" problem—which if not confronted can quickly become a fear freak-out situation—into two.

Part One is: The objective facts of it… what it is.

Part Two is: The subjective truths of it… what it means.

Our world is divided into the objective and the subjective, facts and truths, so why not examine both when confronted with a mystery.

Remember the subject in the invisible gorilla experiment? The one the experimenter lassoed to be a part of it? He unconsciously examined the experiment in two entirely different ways. First he understood the objective fact that if he were to help out, the experiment would be better and that if the experiment were better, Harvard's psychology department would be a bit better, which would level all the way up to it being generally a positive advance (even though extremely micro) for everyone on the planet. So, objectively, the subject calculates that "doing this is good for the world" is an objective fact.

But remember that he also assigns a subjective truth to participating in the experiment, what it means to him as a subject. If he agrees to participate in the experiment, the subjective truth is that the woman experimenter he is interested in will hold a higher opinion of him. And if she elevates her opinion of him, the probability of her being open to going on a date with him will increase.

So, these Pheres—the unexpected events that drop into our lives as the primary substance that changes us—are made up of objective facts, subjective truths, knowns, and unknowns.

In my emergency room patient scenario at the beginning of chapter twelve, when I was a newbie intern and my chief resident told me, "That's not the way I want you thinking, Mark," I was exploring the cause of the patient's bounce back to the ER, an unanticipated Phere. We didn't expect her to come back after surgery, but she did.

Objectively, the facts were that she had a fever and a headache, and a member of her family was home with the flu.

Subjectively, for me as the physician consulted on what to do about her objective facts, because my Brain 2.0 was so focused on getting home before my wife Julie went to bed, I jumped on the easily identifiable known diagnosis that would get me home as soon as possible. The patient had no complications other than getting the flu from her family member.

What was required of me, though, was to start out-thinking my emotional subjective desires, to steady my desire to get home and to not fear that my wife would be disappointed in me for not getting home in time to see her, and to begin looking at unexpected events in multiples of different, more broadly defined ways. I was required to think about the other possibilities that could present the same symptoms for the patient instead of quickly going to the easiest answer and think the way my mentors in neurosurgery thought about unexpected complications.

So I ordered the lumbar puncture/spinal tap my chief wanted to eliminate the possibility that the patient's headache was a symptom of meningitis. Fortunately, it came out negative disproving the factual representation of the infection. The patient was discharged home later that night with the flu, and I made it home just before Julie's head hit her pillow—a double positive outcome.

SEVENTEEN
Knowns and Unknowns

The solution that evolved to deal with too much information is incredibly simple to begin with (a binary system) and complex later on (hierarchical processing and cross-processing).

Let's lay out the simple solution first.

After Brain 1.0 determines that the message coming from the environment isn't an external mortal threat emergency (if it is code blue, there is an elegant override, which are those reflexive movements like the snake response that do not require Brain 2.0 engagement), the information funnels into one of two pipelines.

This is the binary system.

Pipeline number one is information that Brain 1.0 can ignore for now.

For example, let's look at the pipeline for my hypothetical male subject in the invisible gorilla experiment. Because the environment, a Harvard office, he is led to is "known" to him, his Brain 1.0 is able to ignore a lot of the sensory inputs coming from his body into his brain. His Brain 1.0 is not sweating the layout of the office, the street where the office is, the way the elevators work or the number of books and papers on the shelves. Because the student has been in a lot of these categories of spaces, Brain 1.0 is not sweating the small stuff. It's ignoring a lot of input just out of habitual exposure to a certain environmental category. This is the "known" and familiar world.

Because Brain 1.0 is in familiar territory, it is focusing on what Brain 2.0 has laid out as the student's goal, where he is now versus where he wants to be on Friday night. This goal-directed behavior, which is to impress the woman experimenter who brought him to the office, is Brain 1.0's concern. It's monitoring the state of the goal at all times. If the student is getting closer to the goal of getting a date, it fires positive emotional energy to him. If the student is getting farther away from the goal of getting the date, it fires a negative emotional warning to him so he can change up his behavior and get back on track. So, Brain 1.0 is able to ignore a massive flood of sensory input and just focus on the "am I making points with this woman" directive issued by Brain 2.0 when it's in a "known," familiar place.

More broadly, the "knowns" Brain 1.0 takes for granted are memories of experiences of objects or other beings. Once we are taught how to use a pencil, the object is "known." Once we meet our summer camp cabin mates and hang with them for a week or so, those subjects are "known." And when we're sitting at a desk and with pencils in our field of vision and we don't want a pencil at that moment, the pencil information is pumped into Brain 1.0's "ignore" pipeline. Like the invisible gorilla, we don't "see" the pencil until we need to see it.

The ignore pipeline makes its way into our short-term memory storage tanks, which live in a separate part of the brain but are easily accessible by Brain 1.0 and Brain 2.0. The pencil information stays where it is until it cycles to the end of the draining hourglass of retained information in that storage area and is deleted. The short-term memory storage tanks for our brains are like Random Operating Memory in a computer.

Pipeline number one is filled with the "known" inputs that can be Ignored by Brain 1.0 until such time that it needs to retrieve them.

Pipeline number two is information that requires further processing.

This pipeline is made up of the "unknown." The unknown are objects and other beings we are not familiar with. Before we learned the thumb, index finger, and middle finger grip and practiced it for a while, the pencil was an unusable tool to us. And before we actually walk into the cabin, our summer camp roommates are mysterious creatures. Once we're with them for a few hours and share a meal or two with them, they begin to move into the known pipeline. But it takes a while to feel comfortable with new faces.

This "further processing unknowns" pipeline is dealt with immediately by Brain 1.0. And in familiar territory, getting to the goal state that Brain 2.0 set forth is the focal unknown. Will I get what I'm seeking or not? That's the big unknown in a familiar environment. So Brain 1.0 laser focuses on whether or he or she is getting closer or farther away from the goal. It evaluates the difference between what Brain 2.0 believes will work and executes in the real world versus how the real world actually reacts to those actions.

For example, the male subject in the invisible gorilla experiment is exploring a very intriguing unknown—the female experimenter. He's trying to figure out what her deal is…if she's spoken for…if she's attracted to him…whether she'll show more interest in him if he does certain things…etc. Brain 1.0 doesn't know what the experimenter or unknown being is up to either. So Brain 1.0 rings alarm bells to Brain 2.0 and the body, like the Nicholson-Jessup being in my steeplechase dream, when reality does not align with the goal of the subject. It's telling the truth to Brain 2.0 by using the language of emotional signals.

That is, Brain 1.0 is focused on seeing how the subject's actions are "landing" with the experimenter. If the subject says something stupid in an effort to get the experimenter to laugh and it works, Brain 1.0 signals to the subject's Brain 2.0 a positive emotion. *Keep going! It's working!* But if the efforts of the subject to be silly and funny aren't working, Brain 1.0 sends a negative emotion to Brain 2.0. *Cut it out! She doesn't think that's funny!* Brain 1.0 is evaluating the micro tactics in real time as they relate to the global goal of getting a date.

Now because Brain 1.0 doesn't have to also deal with an alien environment while monitoring the flirting mission, it can really help out with the Brain 2.0 mission. It's not being too distracted by weird stuff that could threaten the existence of the entire three-part system (body, Brain 1.0 and Brain 2.0) as the subject is wooing the woman, so it can focus on that mission instead of worrying about another environmental unknown popping up.

We like to be in the known familiar world for that very reason. Brain 1.0 can really focus on our goals instead of having to deal with some strange street we've never walked before. The only unknown in these cases (theoretically, of course) is whether we're going to get what we want.

Here's the thing we need to know about fear.

All "unknown" phenomena evoke negative emotion from Brain 1.0. Even the cute experimenter woman evokes negative emotion from the subject's Brain 1.0. An unknown member of the gender you are attracted to brings all sorts of emotional havoc into play. Obviously, romantic relationships can really mess up the whole body/Brain 1.0/Brain 2.0 trinity system. As much as they help the whole system in the long run (committed monogamous people live healthier/happier lives), in the short run, they're hell on Brain 1.0.

And if the male subject had just broken up with someone, his Brain 1.0 may have sent so much negative emotion to him when he met the cute experimenter that he took a pass on helping her with her experiment and just went to lunch by himself instead.

The degree to which the "unknown" reveals itself within the information received by Brain 1.0 is the degree to which the seat of our selves (Brain 2.0) experiences negative emotion. If you're swimming in the ocean and you get a tickle on the toes, the unknown source of that sensory experience will cause your Brain 1.0 to generate a rush of negative emotion in your mind. Just how much negative depends upon the individual experiencing the tickle and the intensity of the tickle. Make no mistake, though, the unknown tickle will bring negative emotion— from mild anxiety to full-blown panic—depending upon Brain 1.0's evaluation of memory and the familiarity of its present environment.

What about the first pipeline, the known information? Doesn't any of that make it into Brain 1.0's processing? Or does all of it just dump into short-term memory?

This is where it gets more complex.

The known does get processed by Brain 1.0, but only the known as it relates to Brain 2.0's mission. Brain 1.0 is familiar with the way women who are interested in the subject as a possible romantic partner behave. So, if the experimenter presents that behavior to the subject, that "known—this is the way women behave when they like me" will be picked up by Brain 1.0 and a positive affect will be shot to the subject's Brain 2.0.

Do you see how centrally important Brain 2.0's goal-directed mission is to Brain 1.0's work?

The goal-direction as determined by Brain 2.0 is based upon the affective messages it receives from Brain 1.0 too. It's a feedback loop that is incredibly powerful. We'll explore more about that loop later on. Suffice it to say that these three systems, our trinity of experience made up of the body as it relates sensory messages, work like a finely tuned symphony.

Here's another bit that's interesting about Brain 1.0. It has a baseline messaging system. That is, when there is a run of the mill experience happening, it's still Nicholson-Jessup, on that wall looking for weird stuff in the real world that could 1) kill the whole being or 2) ruin the attainment of goals set forth by Brain 2.0. It's always anticipating something that could go wrong. The environment is so complex that it has to be on very high alert for all of our waking moments. This is one of the reasons why we need to sleep eight hours a day, to give Brain 1.0 some needed down time.

Brain 1.0's baseline message is a trickle of negative emotion to Brain 2.0. That's its standard operating procedure. Because so many different phenomena are flooding our senses all of the time, we need to have a baseline alert system just to keep us generally aware. We need to have a baseline level of anxiety just to be coherent and awake to our general surroundings. Without it, we'd be way too vulnerable.

Happiness is a wonderful state of being, but we need an underlying attentional anxiety too—a sort of yin and yang. Knowing that reality is useful. We don't freak out so much when we know that baseline doubt is Brain 1.0 just pulling guard duty. Somehow it can distinguish between the danger of a single spider or a drunk man with a gun wearing a balaclava as well as the difference between an attractive fellow human being who is a promising prospect as a mate or someone who would just be cool to hang out with for a while. It can sort threats and promises in the familiar worlds in which we live with incredible accuracy.

Brain 1.0 thinks fast when not flooded with alien background noise in familiar territory. And when it is in an alien environment, whether it's on the surface of the moon or at a new restaurant, it's not sure exactly whether some sensory information is threatening or promising—or perhaps could even be both. So it sends a message to Brain 2.0, the slow thinker, to figure it out.

Sorting a massive pile of information into **ignore this** (known) and **process that** (unknown) is a fundamental way our brains deal with the impossible complexity of the universe. It's how we deal with the combinatorial explosiveness of searching for an answer to a problem, reaching a goal state. This binary nature—ignore or process—allows for Brain 1.0's efficient regulation of our emotions, which then greatly influences our conscious decision-making (Brain 2.0).

A binary approach also allows you to channel a problem into an either/or micro process solution. If X occurs, respond with Y. If Y occurs, respond with X. On or off. Off or On. This simple idea is the single most powerful abstraction of the modern world. We've built remarkable machines using the binary system. For all the incredible complexity of computation and evolving artificially intelligent machines, they originated from the simple process containing the number 0 and the number 1. Little wonder that our machines are built in our likeness. The machines are binary because our brain function is binary! Even right down to its two mirror image hemispheres.

To review, sensory stimuli coming in to Brain 1.0 are immediately divided into just two buckets. Bucket number one is the ignorable familiar territory of the known and bucket number two is the attention-seeking mysterious kingdom of the unknown.

But what of information itself? Once we are consciously aware of an unexpected Phere event after paying attention to Brain 1.0's alarm signal, what do we do then?

EIGHTEEN
Descartes and Langheinrich

Neurosurgery residency is a seven-year hierarchical progression: newbie intern possessing medical school book knowledge; junior resident knowing how to do basic neurosurgical care and surgeries; senior resident learning the craft of surgery; and then finally chief resident polishing skills and defining a niche to launch a career.

Chief residents come in a few flavors. Some are scholarly and always teaching. Some are surgery-mongers who scoop up every case they can, practically living in the operating room their last year of training. Some are great mentors and role models, others less so. And then there was Walter Langheinrich.

Walt was a great surgeon. However his residency experience gave him a battle-worn air. By the time I rotated onto his service in the spring of his seventh year, he was a little jaded. He balanced this with a sarcastic and witty humor that was always refreshing and entertaining. He was particularly fork tongued at our daily 7 a.m. team rendezvous breakfast where we discussed all of the patients and their happenings of the previous night and divided the work assignments for the day.

Walt wanted and liked to do cases, but only if they fit into a gentlemanly work day. His interest in some of the rarer skull-base operations had waned dramatically as he approached the end of his residency. Simply put, he wanted to do bread-and-butter routine cases as much as he could so he could refine his skills and leave the longer cases to his senior residents.

This was fortuitous for me as a senior resident on Walt's service because I was one of those never-say-no kind of residents when it came to big operations. At this point in my career there was no case that didn't interest me and having a chief shed cases to me was like throwing a steak to a pit-bull terrier.

Walt had a unique way of dividing up the operating room assignments. The chief generally knew by the evening before which cases were being done by what professor in each room, but commonly there would be a room shift or a case cancellation over the night shift. So, the chief would arrive in the morning and meet the team in the cafeteria for morning rounds, looking to the resident who was on call the night before to get an update on the operating room manifest.

On one particular sunny May morning after a busy night's call I met the team at our usual spot back in the recesses of the cafeteria with the scoop from the night. Walt needed to know about one big change.

I began my morning briefing to the chief:

"Walt, today Dr. Jho is doing that huge petroclival meningioma."

A petroclival meningioma is a deep-seated benign tumor at the lower part of the skull where it meets the top of the neck. Although slow growing and generally not invasive to the brain, they can be very difficult and dangerous to remove in this particular region. Judging by my knowledge and experience at the time, I estimated this was going to be a six- to eight-hour case. A case like this was typically a perfect chief case.

I continued, "You remember, that real juicy case we looked at yesterday on rounds? The only problem is Dr. Jho called me last night and can't start until 10:30 a.m. because he's got a long overdue dentist appointment. He moved the 7:30 start time to 10:30. Also last night Dr. Segal saw that opening of time and slid in a lumbar decompression in that room *before* the Jho case. And I'll bet Segal's likely to run over." As Walt was chief resident he would traditionally scrub in with Dr. Jho.

It was common knowledge too that Dr. Segal was no speed demon in the OR. And the surgery that was shoehorned into the 7:30

slot was wishful thinking if the charge nurse thought it would be completed and the OR ready for Dr. Jho at 10:30. But the OR would do this kind of thing all the time to increase efficiency, i.e., more billing. That's why a 7:30 start time is like gold for a surgeon in any busy hospital. There is no case before you, so there are fewer variables to throw your day off.

I continued with my "bad news" to my chief: "So with the drain that has to be placed first (in the Dr. Jho tumor patient), and all the anesthesia setup, I doubt your case will start before noon."

I followed with: "You still want that case?"

For me, it was kind of a no-lose situation. He would either say "yes" and I would then know I would likely get home at a reasonable hour and get to see my kids. Or he would say "no" and then I would get the opportunity to do an interesting case not many senior residents get to scrub in on. I had adopted this thinking process long ago, playing the chief resident odds to my best favor, as a way of inoculating myself from changes in assignments. It had stood me well.

Then Walt cupped his chin with his right hand, taking on a thinker-like pose. He was a lefty and he pulled out a three-by-five index card from his white coat breast pocket and laid it on the table.

"Hmmm, what should I do? What should I do?" With a theatrical flair he led us all on.

"Let me think about this. Maybe I should graph this out."

He'd put the index card on the table and leaned in a scholarly way, putting pen to paper.

"Let's plot this out like René Descartes would, Mark."

With his reference to the seventeenth-century genius and father of the X and Y axes coordinate graphing system and anticipating some medical pearl to come from Walt's lips, the younger interns and students who were new to the team leaned in too, listening intently. The more seasoned residents knew better.

"On the X-axis, let's make it time of day from now until 6 p.m. On the Y-axis, let's call it Walt's interest level in Dr. Jho's case. Let's say on a one-to-ten scale, ten of course being highest. Here we are. I see the data points coming to me now."

He dropped a point in the upper left-hand corner of his Cartesian coordinate system.

"Here I am right now at 7:00 a.m. It's a nine or so on the Y-axis. Maybe even a 9.5. But let's move out to 10:30 a.m., the proposed 'pie in the sky' start time for Dr. Jho's case." He'd begun to carefully move his pen downward. "I'm sinking…to a four…how about at noon?" He'd raised the line a bit and then violently crashed back down into the X-axis. "That's a ZERO! And that quotient just doesn't work for me!"

After a long pause he confirmed, "The case is all yours, Mark!"

I smirked. "Yes, sir."

This assignment prompted me to put at the top of my scut list to call Julie and tell her I may not be coming home tonight, again. When she asked me why I would reply; "The Langheinrich quotient was too low." She'd sigh and sign off.

This instinct to divide life into two categories and assign values to them is a powerful tool. And it's definitely worth applying when thinking about how we define reality when the primary substance of change, the unexpected Phere event, drops into our lives. Just as Walt's goal-directed frame of reference/worldview notecard illustration shows us he was focused on getting home at a reasonable time, we can use this same technique to unpack why a goal-directed frame of reference/worldview is powerful enough to blind us to the presence of a chest-pounding human in a gorilla suit.

Let's go back to our hypothetical Harvard man's belief in the positive value of finding a romantic mate and how that drives his actions to agree to be part of the invisible gorilla experiment. He's intent on doing the task perfectly to charm the experimenter based on his placing the pursuit of love at a very high personal value. This intent distracts him from the inputs from non-love-attaining stimuli. So much so that quantitatively there was a fifty percent chance that his Brain 1.0 would not alert him to an extremely obvious unexpected event, the presence of a gorilla in his direct visual frame. For half of the experimental subjects, the gorilla became invisible. It fell into their Brain 1.0's "irrelevant" category. While their eyes take in the gorilla image stimulus, their Brain 1.0s block it from reaching the conscious centers of their Brain 2.0s because the gorilla had nothing to do with the goal of adding up basketball passes.

What is it about particular unexpected Phere events that allow this to happen? What is the fear factor at play with Pheres anyway? Obviously, the fear factor induced by the gorilla as it was presented in the familiar environment and as a taped recording only had a coin flip chance of getting the Harvard man to pay attention to it, that is to "see" it. Can we draw any conclusions about other events our senses take in but we don't consciously consider while we're on a laser-focused goal?

Since fear comes in so many subtle semantic shades, as we outlined in "The Gradient of Fear" chapter, and it's difficult to quickly identify the difference between "dread" and "worry," I began asking myself if there was a simpler way of categorizing our personal fear index. Was there a level of analysis in between those micro semantic representations of fear and the global notion of the unexpected Phere event as the stimulus that leads to the fear response?

This got me to thinking about how my old chief resident Walt Langheinrich would approach this idea. We'd want to break down those twenty shades of the gradient of fear from "fate worse than death" to "transcendence" into just four states of being according to the qualities of the unexpected Phere events that brought on particular emotional fear states. That way we'd only have four general fear categories to analyze when we faced situations that cause us nebulous "I don't know what to do" kinds of stress. So let's expand the Langheinrich graph from a single quarter of a Cartesian graph into all four of its constituent quadrants, like this:

A CARTESIAN GRAPH

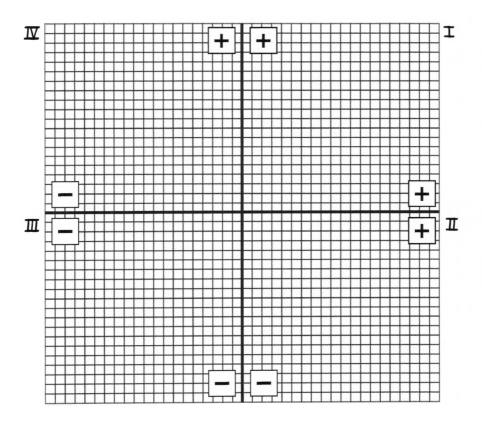

Now, let's categorize each of those twenty-one descriptions from our gradient of fear inside these four quadrants. The one description that would fall right in the center of the graph would be "homeostatic," which is that mystical quality of being neither positive or negative in your experience of the world…simply "being."

Here's what I came up with:

THE GRADIENT OF FEAR MAPPED ONTO A CARTESIAN GRAPH

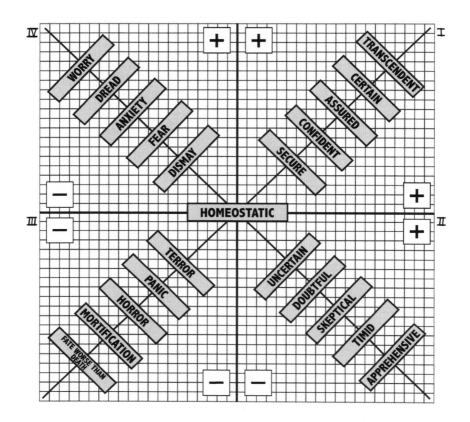

Before I proceed, I'll need to point out that I'm messing with the traditional Cartesian graph quadrant labels. For simplicity's sake, I've labeled them from one to four in a clockwise motion rather than the technically correct counterclockwise way.

I like this diagram because it gives me another layer of analysis, one that is much faster to evaluate than figuring out which of the twenty shades of fear emotion I am experiencing. You'll see that I had to make some value judgments about how I would categorize the critical moment in the gradient of fear when there is an actual drop-in of an unexpected Phere event. That's the dividing line in between anxiety and fear on the hierarchical gradient from "The Gradient of Fear" chapter.

I placed that moment inside of the fourth quadrant of my graph.

The reason I put it inside the vertical positive Y-axis and the horizontal negative X-axis is because we really don't fall into negative/negative territory until we are absolutely certain the event is threatening. Once we find out the noise we heard is that of a tiger in the brush, we fall into the double negative arena. Until we do, there is still a hint of positive hope that the threat isn't so threatening. Hence my belief that we don't tumble into that very disturbing bottom left quadrant three until we have confirmation of a real external threat.

Speaking of the Y and X axes, can we label them better?

Instead of just generic positive and negative valences in terms of our emotional state, can we figure out more details about what those axes represent in terms of the stimulus that causes the fear responses we've placed on the graph?

We know what we're calling an unexpected Phere event (the primary substance that causes us to change our behavior that Jung theorized) is the stimulus that evokes the varying forms of fear emotion. So the X and Y axes in our Cartesian graph represent the qualities of those Pheres. That is, a double positive on the X and Y axes in the upper right-hand corner equals a double positive emotional state that leads all the way up to "Transcendent". Likewise, a double negative on the X and Y axes equals a double negative emotional state that spirals us downward all the way to a "Fate Worse Than Death."

And we've also established that the quality of the Phere stimulus is binary in nature. It's made up of the objective facts of an unexpected event and the subjective truth of the unexpected event. The great thing about Cartesian graphs is they allow us to track the relationship between two phenomena. Walt tracked his interest in a case over time and plotted the data. So reasoning backward, since we know that Pheres cause fears, let's label the X-Axis "Objective Fact" and the Y-Axis "Subjective Truth."

We'll be tracking how much fear we feel as the objective facts associated with an unexpected Phere event move ever more positive or ever more negative in terms of reaching a goal state (the X-Axis) in relationship to how the subjective truths associated with an unexpected Phere event move ever more positive or ever more negative in terms of reaching a goal state (the Y-Axis).

Here's what it looks like with our axes labeled:

OBJECTIVE AND SUBJECTIVE
QUALITIES OF FEAR

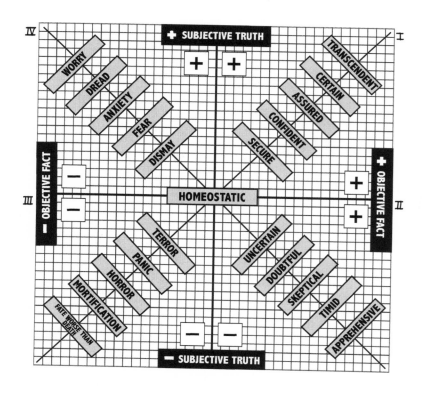

Cool, but what's the point of this graph again?

Let's put it in context by going back to our global mission with this book, which is to:

1. Learn how to manage our "fear freak-out" moments by applying cognitive dominance and

2. Reduce the time it will take to clearly define fear-inducing problems, those nebulous "I have no clue of what to do" dilemmas raised when unexpected Phere events drop into our goal-directed lives. That's our whole cognitive dominance notion to begin with. Remember the definition from the US Military?

Cognitive Dominance: *Enhanced situational awareness that facilitates rapid and accurate decision-making under stressful conditions with limited decision-making time.*

In other words, perform under pressure. Make the foul shot to win the game. Cut out the cancerous tumor growth rapidly and accurately. Say the right thing to our child after he has a tantrum. Make the best bad choices that abide what we value most, quickly and accurately.

And the first thing we needed to do was to clearly break apart what we meant by the loaded notion of "fear." We did that in "The Gradient of Fear" chapter, which picked apart the phenomena and sorted it into twenty-one shades of the emotion that explored the best of all possible fear states (Transcendent) and the worst of all possible fear states (Fate Worse Than Death).

But it's very difficult to keep twenty-one varieties of fear in an easily accessible memory file in your mind. Impossible really. So we need a middle level of analysis—one we can immediately reference when the shit hits the fan and we don't know what to do about some weird event that just dropped into our lives.

This graph represents that middle level of analysis.

The upper right quadrant is that rare psychological place we all would love to be in all of the time. It's what I call the flow quadrant, when we can't miss. When the Pheres drop in, we effortlessly metabolize them and move quickly and efficiently forward to reach our goals. We hit the winning foul shot with ease. We cut forty-one minutes off of our average tumor excision operation, giving the patient a much easier recovery. We buck up our child with love instead of angrily scooting him off to his room. We don't feel "fear" at all.

The lower right-hand quadrant is what I call the calm before the storm quadrant. This is the arena when we have a weird feeling that something is not quite what we think it should be. We're not sure what's going on, but we have a generally disquieted sense of foreboding. We're anxious about the future in general.

The bottom left quadrant is what I call the all is lost quadrant. This is the domain of deep sadness and depression. We feel hopeless and begin to psychologically unwind. We're in trouble. This is the world I lived in for a long time after the Anthony operation I described at the beginning of the book. We can self-destruct here and we often fall prey to anything that will distract us from our sorrow. Alcohol, drugs, tobacco, etc. seem like good coping tools to avoid this arena. Obviously, those are the worst choices we can make as they only delay our rising above the difficulty.

The last quadrant, the one at the upper left is what I call the birth of a new skill quadrant. This is the place where we find ourselves challenged by an unexpected Phere event, but we have the capacity to break it apart, define the problem, and with dedicated concentrated effort solve it. And once we solve the problem, that skill is added to our cognitive arsenal. The next time that sort of category of Phere drops in, we have the power to contend with it much faster. Until eventually, that drop-in Phere doesn't bother us much at all. It is just something we easily handle when we're in that wonderful flow quadrant.

I suspect those four quadrants of fear experience are familiar to you. At times you feel on top of the world (flow). At times you're generally anxious for some reason about the future (calm before the storm). And sometimes you are specifically anxious about current and short-term future events like a test, an interview, or speaking in public (birth of a new skill). And occasionally, you've experienced moments in your life when you've lost your bearings, lost faith in the meaning of your life, and you find it difficult to even get out of bed (all is lost).

That's what I love about this middle level of fear analysis. We can immediately identify where we sit, at any moment in time, inside this four-quadrant system. Let's now explore this graph a bit more and build it out so we can use it to discern the best route when figuring out *What to Do... When We Don't Know What to Do.*

Before we can bring it into an even higher level of resolution, we'll need to walk though how our Brain 2.0 comes up with its goals. Remember how the invisible gorilla experiment proved that Brain 2.0's goals have a tremendous influence on Brain 1.0? The more focused we are on a specific endpoint goal, the less our Brain 1.0 will alert us to unexpected Phere events outside that realm of concentration. That intense focus is great when nothing odd drops into our lives in other arenas outside of that focus. But if we're blind to a predator because we're focused on counting basketball bounce passes, that's not so good for us globally. While we're distracted, the predator could wipe us out.

So how exactly does Brain 2.0 come up with its goals? How does it order them? Does a hierarchy of goals drive Brain 2.0's behavior? And if so, how can we order that hierarchy so we manage to do both things well—concentrate and achieve laser-focused goals while at the same time abiding by our highest values? That is, how do we structure a way to behave to our best advantage?

NINETEEN
Tools and Obstacles

How do we learn to behave in this very intense *too much information* world?

If we're searching for a better way, it's best to understand the present state of the art, one that's kept Homo sapiens alive and thriving for over 150,000 years.

While by no means exhaustive, here's a quick overview of what we generally suspect is going on.

From Erich Fromm's work, we know there are two kinds of goals we'll need to achieve in order to survive and then thrive in this world. First, we'll need to attain material objects, to have things—food, shelter, warmth, etc.—which very early in our lives is taken care of by our mothers and fathers. Without these, we won't survive for very long. So those "haves" are indispensable. And once we have a minimal viable amount of "haves" to properly function, we soon wish to be recognized as a presence on the Earth. We want other beings to acknowledge our existence. To do that we need to become "someone," a recognized member of the ecosystem that other members pay attention to and consider. Becoming someone is as simple as a baby crying out to get another human being's attention. And we do that a lot all throughout lives.

So again we need to have objects and become subjects—to have and to be.

And we learn what objects to have and what subjects to strive to become from the others in our environment. We discover the most valuable object in both categories is information we glean from our family, close friends, frenemies, and those with whom we work. They teach us what to attain to keep us alive and what to achieve to garner acknowledgment. Eventually, we develop a personal value system, what we hold to be the most important to us based upon the messages from others in our world and our own senses. The generation of this personal value system is just one of the jobs of Brain 2.0. It constantly updates as we grow older to form the idiosyncratic source codes that comprise our individual worldview.

Our own private hierarchy of values drives how we choose what we wish to have and what we wish to become. So clearly understanding and thoughtfully curating that hierarchy, rather than not paying all that much attention to it and allowing those around us to tell us what is valuable, is a crucial step toward practicing cognitive dominance. We must clearly define our values and order them from most valuable to least valuable.

I'll not get into stages of development in detail, but the general idea is that babies are born with a whole slew of innate capabilities that allow them to bootstrap a value system (what's "good" to have and how to be "good") within eighteen months. These innate abilities include 1) the startle reflex that signals to his or her mother distress, which is akin to the Brain 1.0 firing the snake response, 2) the signaling to others of the six universal emotions on their faces (happiness, fear, surprise, disgust, anger, and sadness) 3) the proclivity to language, and 4) mimicry.

These abilities come together under the guidance of the mother first, the secondary attachment figures in the nuclear family second, and then the extended family, neighborhood, and greater society and its cultural values last.

Children construct themselves (build a hierarchical value system) by doing what those around them are doing. *My sister kisses me when I smile, and runs away when I scream… If I want a kiss, I'll smile. If I want her to go away, I'll scream.* Eventually, after about eighteen months, a sense of self (another Brain 2.0 function) emerges to begin higher processing of the environment. This sense of self coalesces as the individual's Brain 2.0 of her nervous system begins to take hold. The cognitive functions of her cerebral cortex come online and they begin to build themselves out.

Anyone who has been around young children understands the "terrible twos" that come after the system has booted itself up. It's when the child learns the word "no" as their go-to response. A two-year old's "*No, I won't...*" responses connote that she now understands she is different from everyone else. She now understands her inner "I" drives her body. She embraces her agency and the power of the knowledge that "you," the parent or adult or other child, can't remotely control her body. She becomes her own agent with her own agency in her own arena.

The primary job Brain 2.0 takes on after the person recognizes the phenomenon of her internal self, her control of her agency, is to "frame" the world for her. To limit the information flooding into her nervous system in an optimal way such that she gets what she wants and what she needs. Brain 2.0 builds a worldview, a grand narrative vision from which to set her sights on an ideal future. It reasons and then creates the private heuristics/tool sets she will use to solve the combinatorial explosion problem inherent in everyday consciousness.

It's worth highlighting the combinatorial explosion problem again. If we were to categorize the most abstract problems we face—the ones that could categorize every single problem in our lives from choosing a mate and choosing a profession to choosing what to eat—they would all fall within the parameters of combinatorial explosion. This is the Grand Poobah of all problems. And if we can wrap our minds around it, we can wrestle with anything.

When every problem we face has a practically infinite set of pathways to solve it, like the chess game we discussed in the "Combinatorial Explosiveness" chapter, we need these heuristics or tools just to get out of bed in the morning. Brain 2.0 generates these psycho-technologies, those little processes, methods, and systems that walk us through hard problems. How do I make it through a busy and stressful neurosurgery day? Usually by following my heuristics that I share with you throughout this book.

And the way Brain 2.0 generates them is based upon how we can get what's valuable in our environment, those hierarchy of values our minds have been building since birth. Remember that we observe what other people define as valuable first and use those values to guide us until such time that we can construct our own private hierarchy of values. Obviously, we need to know we're borrowing cultural software until such time as we can code our own. If we don't understand that core concept, we can fall into a difficult place—one that is so reliant upon the consensus of those around us that we lose the thread of our own agency.

Simply put, once it targets a valuable prize, Brain 2.0 fantasizes ways for us to attain those valuable objects or become those valuable subjects. They are either "have" goals or "be" goals. Brain 2.0 breaks down those big "have" and "be" goals into mini-goals it believes will add up to success. And then it sets us on a linear path to attain the mini-goals in order to achieve the big goal at the end of the journey.

For example, in order for me to make it across the room to where a plate full of brownies resides, my big goal being to eat one, I must accomplish the mini-goal of getting out of my chair. So Brain 2.0 directs my body to start doing those little tasks that will, in its estimation, add up to the accomplishment of the larger "have" or "be" goal. I push up out of my chair, navigate across the room avoiding obstacles in my way, until I grasp the brownie in my hand, bring it to my mouth and "have" it. What's remarkable is that I'm so familiar with brownies and what's necessary to get one, I don't have to use any cognitive energy to do any of those mini-tasks. Brownies are a known "have" to me and like the cookie monster of *Sesame Street*, once its stimulus strikes me—I see or smell them—the brownie is practically automatically ingested.

Brain 2.0 formulates means to ends. The rise from the chair and the navigation are the means to the brownie end. It projects into the future to a time and place that is better than it is right now. And then Brain 2.0 fantasizes tactics it thinks are necessary to get us from unfulfilled (the present) to the fulfilled (the future).

But what about Brain 1.0? What's it doing while Brain 2.0 is coming up with the goals? I'm reminded of the great Western film written by William Goldman, *Butch Cassidy and the Sundance Kid.* There's a great scene when Butch Cassidy (played by Paul Newman) is rattling off some crazy plan to rob yet another bank when his partner, The Sundance Kid (played by Robert Redford) laughs at him and says, "You just keep thinking, Butch. That's what you're good at."

That's the relationship between Brain 2.0 and Brain 1.0. Brain 2.0 does the thinking, comes up with the goals, while Brain 1.0 makes sure nothing goes wrong along the way from bank *not yet robbed* to bank *robbed.* Brain 2.0 is Butch Cassidy and Brain 1.0 is The Sundance Kid. And like The Sundance Kid (or my weird Nicholson-Jessup version in my steeplechase dream) Brain 1.0 serves as the sentry on the wall between Butch's fantasies and reality. Brain 1.0 can override Brain 2.0's goal-driven directives whenever it's necessary to protect the entire being.

Here's an example of how Brain 2.0 and Brain 1.0 work together to keep us on target, but properly functioning too.

Years ago, when I was in college, a friend of mine in New England decided to meet me in Florida for spring break. He couldn't afford to fly, so he agreed to drive with four other guys he knew from his school in a beat-up old car straight through from Boston to Fort Lauderdale, Florida. It's about a twenty-three-hour trip nonstop.

By the time he arrived at our meeting spot, he was so bleary-eyed and exhausted he dropped his bag on the beach, curled up in a ball underneath an umbrella and went right to sleep. Every single phenomenon in that "unknown" environment—the ocean, the cooler filled with drinks, the mobs of other people, the fact that he was wearing jeans and a sweatshirt while everyone else was in bathing suits, the sound of the radio—was irrelevant to him. It was as if the shaded sand beneath the umbrella was the only place he could see.

The fact was, he was so tired and so motivated by his lack of a proper night's sleep, that his frame of the world simply focused on finding a dark soft surface to lie down—an abstract "known" place for rest. Brain 1.0 took over after Brain 2.0's goal of getting to Florida had been achieved.

The signals about the drain on his body coming from his Brain 1.0 were so intense that his Brain 2.0 had to put all of its future "Florida fun" plans aside and focus on just getting the guy to find a relatively safe place to sleep. In the moment he arrived, he lived in a "negative present," a place of great discomfort. And everything in his sensory evaluation focused on achieving a "positive future." While there were all sorts of stimuli coming at him—loud music, food available, plenty of visual attraction—his highly motivated Brain 1.0 messages (emotional and physical signals of exhaustion) to his Brain 2.0 were to find a safe place to sleep. And nothing "unknown," except a direct attack by a land shark or an incoming tidal wave, would get him off course. Sort of similar to our Harvard guy participating in the invisible gorilla experiment.

What was going on inside my friend's brain during this fugue state?

His Brain 1.0, the middle primal part of his brain that only deals in emotional signaling, took over complete control. It had been on alert soon after his normal sleep cycle was disturbed (probably just after midnight the previous evening) and throughout the long dark ride that followed. My friend used stimulants—coffee, conversation with the other guys in the car, loud music, cold air from the air conditioner, etc.—to dampen Brain 1.0's demands to his Brain 2.0 to GO TO SLEEP! His Brain 2.0 didn't pay attention to his Brain 1.0's pleas and used coffee to shut it up. Brain 2.0's goal of getting to Florida awake and not letting down the other guys in the car by doing his share of driving compelled him to push forward. The framing of the world pushed down Brain 1.0's control.

But now that he'd reached the finish line of his long drive to Florida, he found the place where his friends were, the familiar tribe that he believed would protect him when he was vulnerable, and his Brain 1.0 went into overdrive. The GO TO SLEEP! signal was so intense that he transformed into a man possessed. For him, the shade beneath the umbrella was everything good in the world. And once he got to that place where he really wanted and needed to go, he curled up and went right to sleep. And any anxiety he might normally feel being at a beach he'd never been to before surrounded by strangers was not being fired into his Brain 2.0 from his Brain 1.0. The surrounding unexpected Phere events were just not enough for Brain 1.0 to turn on any emergency alarms.

Similarly in familiar, nonlife-threatening circumstances, Brain 2.0 uses its future goal as the filter for Brain 1.0 to throw out incredible amounts of sensory input. Brain 1.0 divides the world into two neat categories:

1. Irrelevant Phenomena: Information that will not have any discernable effect on the means (our micro tactics) to move from the negative present (right now our state of being isn't what we want it to be) to the goal state end (the future positive outcome).

2. Relevant Phenomena: which is then further broken into:

   a. Knowns, which it assigns emotional valence to based upon its determination of whether or not the phenomena has served Brain 2.0 previously as a tool or obstacle.

      i. Positive Tool: Information that will aid the means (our micro tactics) to move from the negative present (right now our state of being isn't what we want it to be) to the goal state end (the future positive outcome). In other words, positive news that should be coded to Brain 2.0 with positive emotion.

      ii. Negative Obstacles: Information that will deter the means (our micro tactics) to move from the negative present (right now our state of being isn't what we want it to be) to the goal state end (the future positive outcome). In other words, negative news.

   b. Unknowns, which it assigns potent negative emotional valence to based upon its determination that the being has never encountered this phenomena (which Brain 1.0 has determined is in the arena in which Brain 2.0 is applying its agency to attain a goal).

Let's look at my friend's trip to Florida again from the point of view of this Brain 2.0 filter system.

In the car on the way to Florida, my friend and his mates probably passed twenty really cool places to pull over and check out an amazing view. But if you asked them if they did or even if they knew of any "park to see the view" places on their way, chances are not a single one of them registered the signs or opportunities. That is, while their senses may have taken in the information, the signal did not make it to their Brain 2.0 thinking center. And because it didn't make it to the thinking center, it didn't lodge in their memory banks. It was irrelevant to their Brain 2.0s, so none of them took the time to further process the information.

Because the scenic views were not identified as relevant tools (positive news) to help them on their way to Florida, they didn't consciously register them. They fell into the irrelevant bin.

However, if you asked them where they stopped for gas, they'd probably be able to give you a pretty good idea of not only the state they stopped in, but the status of the mini-mart inside the gas station and how clean the bathrooms were. The sensory information required to identify and use the gas station was a helpful, relevant positive tool in their mission to move from their "negative present" (not at the beach in Florida) to their "positive future" (hanging out on the beach).

Likewise, if their car got a flat tire, they'd be able to give you very clear stories about how they dealt with that relevant problem. The negative obstacle to move from their "negative present" to their "positive future" would be well documented and stored in their memory banks.

If we were to generalize from this little adventure story, we could say the guys in the car all shared a goal to move from a negative present (in the northern climes of winter) to a positive future (sunny Florida). And along the way they had two different kinds of sensory input with regard to that goal.

They recognized:

Relevant Input made up of Known Positive tools (gas stations with food and bathrooms) and Known Negative obstacles (flat tires, bad directions). Chances are they did not encounter derailing Unknown Relevant inputs that threatened their goal (like a roadblock filled with shotgun bearing revolutionaries intent on kidnapping them for ransom), or they would not have arrived in Florida without a very interesting story.

They didn't even register irrelevant phenomena to their goal (everything else).

Just like our vacation travelers, all of our goal-directed experiences can be divided into irrelevant and relevant information, which in turn are made up of Known positive tools and negative obstacles and Unknown phenomena that require deep, immediate, and conscious problem solving skills.

We're after these deep, immediate, and conscious problem-solving skills in our pursuit of cognitive dominance.

No matter the Phere, we solve the problem of moving from our unfulfilled present to our fulfilled goal state with this unconscious means-ends analysis. Scientists Allen Newell, J.C. Shaw and Herbert Simon introduced this extremely useful concept back in 1959 at the RAND Corporation when they were working on concepts that would be used to build artificially intelligent machines. They called it the General Problem Solver and it is one of Brain 2.0's ways of satisfying our desires to have and to be.

Brain 1.0 filters and then sends our Brain 2.0 a whole slew of "known" and "unknown" information that relates to Brain 2.0's goals. But it only sends what it determines is relevant to Brain 2.0 and its goals.

That means the fast-thinking Brain 1.0 quickly determines what unexpected Phere event information it suspects is completely irrelevant to Brain 2.0's goals and dumps it into the "ignore" bin. It dumps 99.99 percent of information into the irrelevant pile of hay.

The .01 percent of information it deems relevant to Brain 2.0's goal makes it way into the slow-thinking processing. What's truly remarkable is that Brain 1.0 tells Brain 2.0 to pay attention to these knowns and unknowns very quickly with perfectly modulated jolts of fear emotion.

So the more fear we experience, the more Brain 1.0 is urges us to apply our Brain 2.0 processes.

So how does Brain 2.0 ideally respond? That is, how does it do what Brain 1.0 is telling it to do?

While we are not consciously aware of it, Brain 2.0 responds to Brain 1.0's "pay attention" commands by cracking "known" and "unknown" phenomena apart into these smaller tools and obstacle units. The label derives from the goal. If it helps us achieve our goal, it's a tool. If it distracts us, it's an obstacle.

TWENTY
Facts and Truths

Our Brain 1.0 sorts the world into two phenomenal buckets, "irrelevant," and "relevant." The "irrelevant" is stored in short-term memory and the "relevant" is pushed on to Brain 2.0 to be further broken down into "known" and "unknown." This two-bucket system is Brain 1.0's (the fear giver) primary way of coping with combinatorial explosiveness on our way from our negative present to our positive future. The huge irrelevant bucket is made up of "knowns" that do not have anything to do with the particular operating mission set forth by Brain 2.0 and "unknowns" that do not immediately threaten that mission.

Knowns and unknowns that do affect the mission, however, are what I've been calling unexpected Phere events. I define Pheres as those change agents Carl Jung thought of as the primary substance of spiritual matter. And I'm submitting that the quality and valence (however positive or however negative it is) of the Phere determines the amount of fear Brain 1.0 sends to Brain 2.0 and the body.

So what happens next?

After Brain 2.0 gets fear jolts from Brain 1.0 alerting it to pay attention, what does Brain 2.0 do about the known and unknown Phere problem? How does it behave in Phere's presence?

Eighteenth-century Scottish philosopher David Hume shined a spotlight into this mystery when he considered Philosophy's first principle problem. That question can simply be summed up as *How should one behave in order to survive and then thrive in one's environment?*

Even back in the eighteenth century there was too much information. Our five senses are so sensitive that simply sitting in a dark room can overwhelm us. After considerable contemplation of the "How to best behave?" question, Hume put forth that you cannot derive an *"ought"* from an *"is."* What *is* and the problem of what *ought* to be done about what *is* cannot be deduced by what *is* is.

Obviously this idea is a mind bender, so let's pick it apart.

Hume's *"is"*…is objective fact, the realm of scientific exploration. It's the length, width, mass, temperature, molecular structure of a thing or being. It's what something or someone is physically made up of…its matter. What *is* are the quantifiable things—i.e., data and measurements that are repeatedly true and consistent no matter who is measuring or where on Earth the matter is measured. Science requires that what *is* be defined as empirically reproducible, regardless of the individual examination. So, if I measure something and then a woman from halfway around the world measures the same thing, we'll both get the same results. That's what Hume meant by an "is."

"Is" are facts and they are objective. They are observable across time and verifiable by every person on Earth. And the scientific method is the means by which facts become facts. They are the facts of matter, which is made up of objects and living beings.

Simons and Chabris' invisible gorilla experiment, while elegant and innovative, was just another iteration of an experiment published in the 1970s by another psychologist, Ulric Neisser. Neisser measured an objective fact about the way we think, and Simons and Chabris reproduced his results a few decades later. They all confirmed that we ignore a lot of phenomena when pursuing a goal. The fact that we don't see things that would seem to be impossible "not to see" is a fact because the experiment can be repeated through time with the same results. An experiment to support this objective fact can be done in the 1970s and it can be done in the 1990s with the same results. So we call that "fact."

What about truth?

Let's remember that the scientific method, on the grand scale of human history, is a very recent psycho-technology with its origin going back just three thousand years or so. Our species is about 150,000 to 200,000 years old, though. So the scientific method has been around for only two percent of our conscious time on Earth. So how did people before the scientific method figure out how to behave if they didn't have a clear methodology to confirm objective facts?

If "facts"—that is, scientifically reproducible measures—have only been in the world since the beginnings of the scientific method, how did people define "truth" before the notion of objective fact came to be?

This is where Hume's "ought" notion comes from. It's the world of human action, what one should do about what is. So what one "ought" to do about what "is" requires another kind of knowledge, which is not dependent upon scientific fact because there was literally no objective fact for 98 percent of the time we've been on Earth. This primal knowledge is called subjective truth.

Let's move slowly here because we often confuse fact and truth.

Human beings know truths about certain objects and beings even if they don't know their particular mass, length, width etc. People were oblivious to scientific facts for more than 145,000 years and still they were able to survive and thrive. And to this day we don't know "unknown" facts about certain objects and beings yet we function perfectly well with that ignorance.

Why can we remain so ignorant with little fallout?

Truth was defined for our predecessors, and still is, as the answer to Philosophy's first principle question "how does one behave to the greatest possible positive effect and affect...to survive and then thrive in the world?" This is what Hume meant by "ought." The objective matter of how many hairs on your body doesn't matter...unless it becomes subjectively valuable.

So objective fact defines matter, but subjective truth is about what matters. You can measure a rock and get to the core facts of the thing, but it will never reveal what you ought to do about it. It doesn't tell you why it matters…only the facts of it being matter. *"Ought"* defines the meaning of an object or being for a single, value-based system as held by a particular human being. Its subjective truth is the ought.

What one *ought* to do about what *is* is the fundamental problem of existence. It's that combinatorial explosiveness problem again. We can measure a thing on so many different scientific levels practically ad infinitum, but it will never tell us what to do about it. What Hume put forth brilliantly in just a single sentence is that the computationally explosive "what to do" problem requires a narrative story to answer. It requires subjective truth.

When you come right down to it, this is the core idea about why I wrote this book. What ought I do about the knowledge I have acquired through my twenty-eight years of brain surgery training and practice?

For me, I set out to concentrate the lessons I've learned and the experiences I've assimilated into my own hierarchy of value framework so I could pass that personal meaning I've generated for myself on to my family. I wanted to leave behind a record for my children and grandchildren of what I learned about what one ought to do in this world in order to best survive and thrive. In this process I've discovered it has been too rich of an odyssey to not share outside of my family circle. And thankfully my writing partner Shawn agreed.

So the way we answer the fundamental question *What should I do?* is by judging matter (what is) and assigning particular values to it (why it matters). If we need to crush a coconut in order to eat something and survive, a rock becomes a tool to do that. We judge the rock as matter that matters to our ability to survive. And thus, the rock's value is extraordinary, especially if we find it in a desert with just one coconut left to eat.

Subjective truth is the meaning derived from a particular object that is specific to the person examining it. What's true for me isn't necessarily true for you, unless of course we share a similar hierarchy of values.

In the "Descartes and Langheinrich" chapter, the petroclival meningioma case was an extremely valuable case that I wanted to handle as a senior resident no matter what time of day the operation began. But for my chief resident Walt Langheinrich, the operation's value diminished as the day progressed. And perhaps in three years when I became chief resident, the petroclival meningioma would be less desirable for me too because I would be focused on mastering other cases. My future self had already experienced the petroclival meningioma case…it had become known to me. So exploring it again would not be as valuable to me, just as it wasn't so valuable to Walt that morning in the hospital cafeteria.

Walt wasn't being lazy. He was focusing on performing surgeries he hadn't mastered yet and was willing to pass up surgeries he was familiar with so another surgeon (me) could learn something new. That was Walt's job and that story-driven job of the chief resident passes on from year to year to other surgeons. And that story makes our medical profession work very well. We value it because mentors pass on their subjective truths to their mentees from procedure to procedure, and Walt's great sense of humor and love of graphs stuck with me too.

Our life experiences define what matters to us, our subjective truths, what we believe and value—in other words, our worldviews. So why one particular student subject in the invisible gorilla experiment saw or didn't see the gorilla is dependent upon that particular person's worldview. The fact that human beings as a category can be so focused on a particular micro goal that they don't "see" something as extraordinary as a gorilla is an objective fact. But the subjective truth for each of the subjects as to why they aren't seeing the gorilla can be extraordinarily divergent.

Thankfully, the great majority of people on Earth share a few core fundamental beliefs or our behaviors would be so unpredictable that none of us would want to leave our particular caves. So each piece of information we examine has two components inherent within. It has objective facts attached to it: What it *is*. And it has subjective truths attached to it: What personally defined value that information has to the observer. What one *ought* to do about the information.

What matters is objective fact and why it matters is subjective truth.

Here's an example of how one thing has characteristic objective facts associated with it and also has subjective truth attached to it.

Life is about assigning value to objects and other beings we share our environment with. The way we do that is through our value systems. If we value higher education, that is we "believe in it" as a meaningful process, the truth embedded in a letter from MIT is a ticket to our dream future or, alternatively a future of lesser value. If we don't think higher education is all that important to the essence of a person and we don't assign a high value belief to it, the letter will be just another piece of paper stuck inside another folded piece of paper. Essentially, it would be considerably less meaningful in our grand conception of the world.

Subjective truth begins with the individual, but it doesn't end with the individual. The key element that makes something true for the individual is the value system held by the individual. And what's true for an individual who shares a value system with a larger group of people will be true for that group too. Like teenagers waiting on their college admissions letters, what's true for one of them (this is the most important letter of my life!) is true for all of them.

So, while subjective truth begins at the individual level, it can grow in truth depending upon how many other people share that subject's value system. Once enough people share a value system, the predictability of everyone's behavior in the community can be increased. And eventually mutual trust between two completely different individuals emerges. For example in my profession, it's true that a Neurosurgery resident feels comfortable talking to another general surgery resident but perhaps would be less interested in interacting with an internal medicine resident.

Those who share value systems share subjective truths. The more people who share a value system, the more potent the subjective truth. And the stronger the belief in the value, the stronger the truth. Martin Luther King's *I Have a Dream* speech is so potent because it clearly states truths that virtually all Americans believe in, no matter the objective facts of our individuality. He spoke in terms of higher ideals, goals that he set forth so clearly for American society to aim for—not for one part of United States, but for all of the United States. He defined our shared values and paved the way for different Americans to communicate in ways they never did before. The speech was so effective because it put forth the global values that all listening shared, the "we hold these truths to be self-evident" values.

TWENTY-ONE
Taxonomy of Phere

We now know that Brain 1.0's job is to alert Brain 2.0 about an unexpected Phere event by jolting it with specific quantities of fear emotion. The amount of fear Brain 1.0 shoots at Brain 2.0 depends upon the global character of the unexpected event. That is, Brain 1.0 is very good at determining just how monstrous the unexpected event is to the entire being. It just doesn't have the resources available or the time (remember the too much information problem inherent in existence itself) to process and break it down into digestible bits. So, Brain 1.0 tells Brain 2.0 to break down the Phere, process it and act according to the global goals of the entire being.

In a brilliant natural feedback system, Brain 2.0 formulates those global goals (the narrative story of the being), which in turn inform Brain 1.0. So the unexpected Phere event is defined by the global Brain 2.0 story that has already been relayed to Brain 1.0, which alerts Brain 2.0 to think about how that Phere event fits into its narrative—a circular system that moves us from our less desirable present to our more desirable future informed by our past.

This elegant circular system works extraordinarily well for us from birth to death, an ever increasing duration of time due to the ever increasing capacity of Brain 2.0. So as a global evolutionary "survive and thrive" machine for Homo sapiens, it's just about perfect. It allows for a tremendous variety of individual adaptations as it protects the survival of the species. It's what Nassim Nicholas Taleb calls Antifragile.

But for the individual member of Homo sapiens (you and me) it can prove buggy.

The bugs arise in the way we're able to ignore Brain 1.0's signals. At times when faced with a Phere, we distract ourselves from the fear emotions it sends us with various mind-altering substances making us very efficient at not dealing with unexpected Pheres in real time. Essentially, we lie to ourselves to avoid the pain associated with engaging our fear. We pretend that an unexpected Phere event didn't happen or ignore it by rapidly switching our micro goal to shut down Brain 1.0.

Cognitive dominance is the process by which we upend that tendency of avoidance that allows fear to overwhelm our critical faculties. It's a psycho-technology capable of walking us through a step-by-step process to face our fears head on. To break them down into smaller and smaller pieces so we can use that big Brain 2.0 of ours to make the choice that best fits our global worldview and live up to our hierarchy of values.

Let's walk through this cognitive dominance process step by step— from the moment an unexpected Phere event drops into our lives, through the digestive stages, and ultimately to the critical decision points when we decide what to do when we don't know what to do.

As we've established, the everyday world is a binary environment that consists of two domains of phenomena.

We know that when an unexpected Phere event drops into our life, it can be quickly cleaved in two.

It is comprised of two qualities, the objective and the subjective.

THE FIRST BREAKDOWN OF PHERE

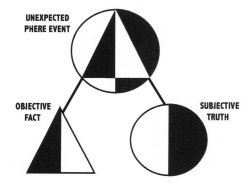

UNEXPECTED
PHERE EVENT

OBJECTIVE
FACT

SUBJECTIVE
TRUTH

A. The Objective Facts:

The objective component is what Hume defined as the "is" of life, the matter. It is the realm of scientific exploration and the scientific method. Empirical facts that are reproducible across time, regardless of the observer, are factual. Newtonian physics, molecular structure, and even complex abstractions like math comprise objective fact. The facts are the same for everyone. They are rational and data-driven. The measurements of matter, be it inorganic or organic, comprise the great body of objective fact.

Brain 2.0 has a specialized zone for operating in the objective world, contemplating and analyzing facts—the left hemisphere of the neocortex. This is popularly called the "left-brain." It's the place where we apply our stored knowledge and activate motor actions. Our Brain 1.0 encourages us to use this hemisphere of our brain by feeding us positive emotion when we use it. We're engaged and focused when we're rationally sussing out a problem with our left hemisphere. Word processing, linear thinking, the details, the micro processing happens here.

We're calm in this realm…fear may be lurking but it is not in control. So this is the first realm we will unpack further.

B. The Subjective Truths:

Hume defined the subjective component as the "ought" of life, what matters and what one ought to do about it. The big story truth informs Brain 2.0 in its determination of actions that enable it to survive and thrive.

Subjective truth is mythic. It is the realm of stories, religions, and the humanities. This system has ordered the world far longer than the science realm. Myths concerning individuals navigating between ordered environments and chaotic environments reveal universal truths. Myth is a boiling down of "what has come to be believed as the way to behave properly to serve oneself best while also serving all those around you" into a richly detailed individual story like Homer's *Odyssey*.

Stories about the ideal "heroic way" to behave serve as prescriptive paths for our own individual journeys while tales about the "wrong way" serve as cautionary paths. Story as universal truth is a powerful paradox.

Brain 2.0 has a specialized zone for operating in the subjective mythic world, contemplating and analyzing myths and story-based truths. It's the right hemisphere of the neocortex—popularly called the "right-brain." Here we fantasize possibilities about what to do about what is. It's where myths and stories, creativity, and lateral thinking reside.

Since the right side of the brain is the place where we tend to fall into fantastical realms, our Brain 1.0 discourages us to use this part of our brain...too much. It can jolt us with negative emotion (fear) in times of stress in order to push us back into left brain mode with its micro practicalities. Remember that Brain 1.0 is a sentry, impatient to neutralize the unexpected Phere events it identifies so the entire being can press on toward its chosen goal. The longer Pheres sit inside our consciousness, the more Brain 1.0 gets frustrated with our inaction. And when Brain 1.0 gets frustrated, it behaves the only way it knows how to behave. It shoots us with more fear.

When we're predominantly focused inside the right hemisphere, we can often find ourselves frozen. We don't act because we're being flooded with images, picking up patterns, generating macro plans. This is the place where dreams come from. Nightmares too. We're not calm in this realm. Fear is palpable and constantly threatening to "possess" us.

The way to out-think fear is to leverage the two different perspectives of Brain 2.0's left brain and right brain power, the objective and subjective. We are absolutely capable of figuring out *what to do about what is* when we use both hemispheres. This is the cognitive dominance protocol. We're able to move unknowns into the realm of the known. It's not easy because Brain 1.0 is quick to hit us with more fear the longer a Phere remains mysterious, but this gift—our ability to toggle between macro fantasy and micro action—separates us from the rest of life on Earth.

Understanding how the left-right brain toggling works and knowing how to unleash its power while under the influence of an impatient but indispensable Brain 1.0 is what we're after. So when an unexpected Phere event drops into our life while we're pursuing a larger goal, the first thing we need to do is crack that Phere in two—its objective and subjective characteristics.

Let's move to the next step, which is breaking down the objective factual components embedded in our unexpected Phere event.

Break this component down first!

BREAKING DOWN THE OBJECTIVE COMPONENT: PART ONE

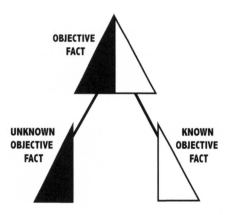

Why? Because it will get Brain 1.0 to quiet down a bit. The objective realm is left-brain processing and Brain 1.0 slows down its fear machinery when we engage the left side of our brains.

Now. Think about what the unexpected Phere event actually *is*. You do this by asking yourself a very simple question... Have I ever encountered this object or being before? Is it known or unknown to me?

1. **The known:** This very large container includes the interconnectedness of the human race and grows as we get wiser—the particular culture we live inside of, the language we speak, the facts of life as we know them, our shared stories, our shared beliefs, and our habits collectively and individually.

The known world is order. It drives our understanding of who we are, how we are to behave, and where we align on the competence hierarchies within the groups we are a part of. Our known relationships include ourselves, our attachment figures, our local community, our state, our country, our ethnicity, our college, our profession, our softball team, etc.

Order provides us with readily available meaning. It's the familiar feel of our favorite chair, and it's generally pleasant and positive. Comforting.

2. **The unknown:** This even bigger container includes everything that isn't known or familiar to us. In our current configuration of reality, the natural environment is for all intents and purposes unknown to the average person. Not being able to understand another's language or communication systems is an unknown. The realm of other people's subjective truth—how their worldviews frame their worlds and their "truth"—is an unknown. We can't possibly "know" everything about another person so from our worldview, each and every other person has strong elements of "unknown" to them. That's what makes strangers strange. Similarly, we are strangers to others. And without hard work and consideration, we can even be strangers to ourselves.

   An alien environment is unknown to us. If a college student were taken out of the lecture hall and put into an auto body shop, she'd find herself in an unknown world. And vice versa.

The most frequent exposure to the unknown is the rise of Phere. We don't know why the world didn't represent itself in the way we predicted it would.

The unknown world is chaos. And chaos drives disorientation of who we are, how we are to behave, and where we align in the impossibly complex universe. It undermines meaning. It's generally unpleasant and filled with negative emotion. And it can quickly suck us deeper and deeper down the gradient of fear.

So first we ask ourselves to list the objective facts of the unexpected Phere event. Are they known or unknown to us?

Can we break the known objective facts and unknown objective facts of the event down further? Yes. We simply ask ourselves whether these facts appear as tools to help us on our way from our negative present state to our positive future state. Or are they obstacles to our attaining our goal? You'll notice that I've assigned valences and values to these smaller broken down pieces.

BREAKING DOWN THE OBJECTIVE
COMPONENT: PART TWO

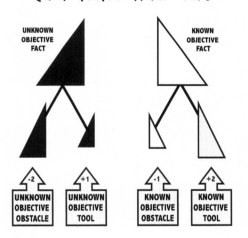

To determine the quality in the first half of Phere, Brain 2.0 can reason four possible objective definitions. Here they are from left to right:

1. An Unknown Objective Obstacle: The Phere is unfamiliar to us, and it appears to be a hinderer to our attaining a micro "having" goal. So I've assigned a negative two (-2) value.

2. An Unknown Objective Tool: While the Phere is unfamiliar to us, we can use it as an aid to get us closer to a micro "having" goal. As an unfamiliar tool I've assigned it a positive one (+1) value.

3. A Known Objective Tool: The Phere is familiar to us, and it helps us achieve a micro "having" goal. So I've assigned it a positive two (+2) value.

4. A Known Objective Obstacle: The Phere is familiar to us as something we've had to deal with before as a hinderer to our achieving a micro "having" goal. So I've assigned it a negative one (-1) value.

Now that we've broken down the objective factual qualities of the unexpected Phere event, it's time to turn our attention to the subjective qualities. We'll break down those qualities in the same way we did for the objective.

BREAKING DOWN THE SUBJECTIVE COMPONENT: PART ONE

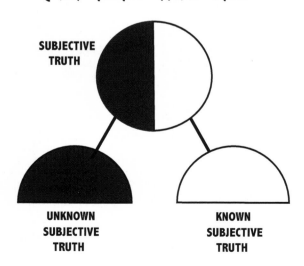

SUBJECTIVE
TRUTH

UNKNOWN
SUBJECTIVE
TRUTH

KNOWN
SUBJECTIVE
TRUTH

1. The first break we'll make is to determine if the unexpected Phere event has a story attached to it inside our minds. Can we dive into our memory banks and recall dealing with this object or being before? If we can, the Phere is known to us. If we can't it is unknown to us.

2. The next break-down stage is determining the value of the Phere as an obstacle or a tool.

BREAKING DOWN THE SUBJECTIVE COMPONENT: PART TWO

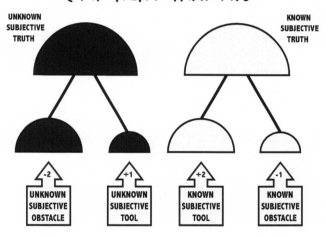

To determine the quality of the second half of the Phere, Brain 2.0 can reason four possible subjective meanings. Here they are from left to right.

1. An Unknown Subjective Obstacle: The Phere has no story associated with it, and it is a hinderer to our attaining a macro "being" goal. So I've assigned a negative two (-2)value.

2. An Unknown Subjective Tool: The Phere has no story associated with it, but it can be used as a tool to attain a macro "being" goal. So I've assigned a positive one (+1) value.

3. A Known Subjective Tool: The Phere has a story associated with it and can be used as a tool to attain a macro "being" goal. So I've assigned a positive two (+2) value.

4. A Known Subjective Obstacle: the Phere has a story associated with it and it is an obstacle to attaining a macro "being" goal. So I've assigned a negative one (-1) value.

To reiterate, we need to remember that objectives are made up of "matter" and we set micro goals to attain them in the "have" mode. Subjectives are made up of "what matters" and we set global macro goals in the "be" mode in order to live up to an ideal way of being.

Let me summarize all of this abstract stuff and then I'll give you a clear example of how this system can be applied to everyday life.

METABOLIZING AN UNEXPECTED FEAR EVENT

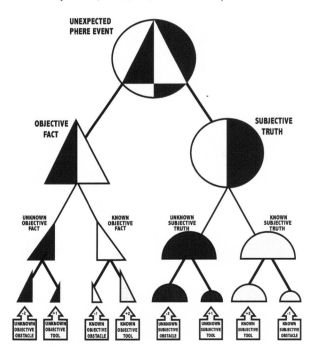

Navigating the known, ordered world and the unknown, chaotic world is how I define consciousness. We are active agents with the power of personal agency, that is the power to change ourselves and thereby our environments, inside a specific earthly arena.

This is humanity's superpower.

So how does the individual make his or her way through this world of known order and unknown chaos? The way in which he does is through the two-brain system each person has embodied within them. Brain 1.0 is the sentry on the wall between the ordered internal world as constructed by Brain 2.0 and the chaotic flood of external information coming into the system from the body's senses—that combinatorial explosion problem.

But just as Brain 2.0 orders its internal world by constructing a story narrative to follow (a goal to get from here to there), chaos emerges in the form of the unexpected Phere event from the external environment. It threatens the internal construction, the personal worldview "story." Brain 1.0 pinpoints the chaos (the Phere, Jung's primary substance) and alerts Brain 2.0 to the fact that the way it is constructing the world (its worldview) is inconsistent with the environmental reality surrounding it. The alarm system Brain 1.0 uses is fear and it has a whole gradient of fear to alert Brain 2.0.

Being cognitively dominant requires that Brain 2.0 immediately pay attention to the fear-inducing Phere, the rise of the unexpected. To do so requires systematic processing with Mr. Spock-like precision. Brain 2.0 must break down the Phere into smaller, more readily and more rationally solvable pieces of information.

Once the Phere is transformed from an unexpected event into a "known," Brain 2.0 uses this fresh knowledge to update its worldview, or frame of reference, by storing this new bit of "known" in its memory.

This process is also called learning.

Cool, but how can we help Brain 2.0 focus its cognitive energy? Is there a psycho-technology (a mind process) we can use to help speed up Brain 2.0's work?

Let's go back to the diagram.

After Brain 1.0 identifies the unexpected Phere event, that is after its lottery ping pong sorting machine drops it into one of the "known" or "unknown" Phere categories, it jolts Brain 2.0 to get working.

Brain 2.0 then takes over.

Whether the unexpected Phere event is known or unknown will be relayed to Brain 2.0 from Brain 1.0 in terms of the amount of fear Brain 2.0 experiences. Remember that four-quadrant graph we created earlier that breaks down Brain 1.0's gradient of fear response into just four global "feelings"? We'll get back to that soon. Suffice it to say that Brain 2.0 understands that gradient and its relationship to known and unknown intuitively. Now we're making that intuitive understanding as explicit to us as possible. So let's get back to how Brain 2.0 would ideally respond to Brain 1.0's messaging.

What Brain 2.0 does next is crack the known or unknown unexpected Phere event into two again. It breaks it into "What it is," which is the objective/scientific facts of the thing, and "What it means," which is the subjective/narrative truth of the thing in terms of Brain 2.0's global worldview.

How does this thing or being affect Brain 2.0's global Story?

How does it do that?

After cleaving the unexpected Phere event into its objective component and its subjective component, it laser focuses one component at a time. With my cognitive dominance protocol, I suggest beginning with the objective facts—that is, break the known or unknown Phere down objectively first.

What are the scientifically measurable facts of the unexpected Phere event? Do the facts indicate the event will be a positive tool to achieve Brain 2.0's micro goal-directed path to a larger goal? Or do the empirically reproducible facts indicate that the unexpected Phere event will be a negative obstacle to achieve Brain 2.0's micro goal-directed path? Is this thing an objective tool or an objective obstacle to my pursuit of my goal?

Once the objective piece has been settled, take a good hard look at the subjective component associated with the Phere. How does the unexpected event align with attaining the micro goal I'm pursuing as a means to the end of a larger macro goal? Does the subjective truth of the event, according to my worldview, reveal it to be a tool or opportunity to push me closer to those goals? Or does the subjective truth of the event reveal it to be an obstacle that I will need to overcome in order to get back on track toward my goals? Is this thing a subjective tool or a subjective obstacle?

Again, Brain 2.0's processing stage is another two-bucket division, figuring out the objective and the subjective nature of the unknown. Our Brain 2.0 explores the Phere by first asking objectively "What is it?" and then subjectively "What does it mean?"

Let's explore the differences between objective fact and subjective truth a bit more with a real-life example.

TWENTY-TWO
A Real-Life Phere

L et's say I can't find my car keys, an unexpected Phere event.

It's getting late and I promised to take care of the grocery shopping while my wife takes a needed nap. The present moment (*what is*) is negative because I need to go to the store to do the shopping before it closes (*what should be*).

So, facing the negative obstacle of not being able to find my own key to my car, I change my micro motivated plan from setting out on the road to first finding a car key so I can then set out on the road.

I remember my wife has an extra key to my car in her purse. So, I head to the entryway and dig my hand into her purse to find it. As I blindly paw through it without really looking inside, I discover something that has the vague shape of my car key.

As I'm pulling it out of the bag, my Brain 1.0 initiates a low-flow negative orienting response signal to my Brain 2.0. The sensory messages Brain 1.0 is getting from my hand are that this object doesn't have the mass of my known car key, and it's making a slight rattling sound too.

This unknown Phere event (I don't know yet what the object in my hand is) intrigues my Brain 2.0.

I finally pull the object out into the light. It's a box of match sticks with a logo from a fancy hotel. It has seven numbers written on it with a dash between the third and fourth numbers.

Looking at it objectively, my Brain 2.0 has already surmised that it's a matchbox from the Four Seasons Hotel with a phone number on it.

What I need to figure out is "what does it mean that there is a Four Seasons Hotel matchbox in my wife's purse with a phone number written on it?"

As a **known** thing, its objective meaning skews on the negative side **(-)** because it is culturally well-known that matchboxes are associated with smoking cigarettes, which have been proven to cause lung cancer and death. But one hundred years ago, the valence of the matchbox would skew on the positive side **(+)** because smoking cigarettes was a culturally significant indication that you were sophisticated and wealthy enough to afford the smoking habit. Plus, in a pinch, a box of matches can be used as a tool to start a fire to keep you warm.

So, **known objective** things can have either positive **(+)** or negative **(-)** meanings built into them based upon the state of their factual knownness at the time they are encountered. That is, the context surrounding the observation of the known object determines whether it surfacing at the time it appears is a positive tool to move my goal forward or negative obstacle for me to attain my goal.

For me, in this moment, the box of matches is objectively negative. It's an obstacle to my goal to find my car key so I can go to the store. Neither my wife nor I smoke and it makes no sense that a box of matches should be in her purse, let alone a box of matches from a fancy hotel with a phone number on it.

My Brain 1.0 has fired an orienting response to the Phere. I'm frozen by it, neither moving forward nor retreating backward, and facing two choices.

The first choice is to proceed as planned. That is, for the time being, ignore the Phere as it will not literally stop me from going to the store (my Brain 2.0 goal that got me into my wife's purse in the first place).

The second choice is to retreat and reassess. That is, abandon the whole going to the store plan and reassess what my near future goal should be, based upon the rise of this unexpected Phere event.

But before I pull the trigger on this decision, I still have about forty-five minutes before I absolutely must get to the store to do what I need to get done. So, my Brain 2.0 explores what this box of matches means to me subjectively.

Subjectively this particular box of matches is an **unknown**. I've never seen it before and I've never seen the phone number written on it either. I allow the right hemisphere of my Brain 2.0 to conjure up some possibilities as to its meaning. If I believe that my relationship with my wife is in great shape, I will remember that our wedding anniversary is approaching. Perhaps the matchbox is a positive subjective thing **(+)**. It could be evidence that my spouse has made a special trip into the city to find a beautiful place for us to celebrate our commitment to one another and jotted down the number of the hotel concierge to follow up with reservations later.

If I believe my relationship with my wife is not especially vibrant at the moment, though, that same matchbox could be a negative subjective thing **(-)**. It could be evidence that my spouse is betraying our marriage vows and is having an affair.

The remarkable thing about our nervous systems is that we have an early warning detection and evaluation mechanism built inside of us… good old Brain 1.0. It's our "gut" reporter. Our gut reporter is feeding us information about the Phere even while our Brain 2.0 is contemplating its meaning.

Now if I have a lot of experience with relationships that ended in betrayal, my Brain 1.0 is going to wallop me with a lot of fear. But if my wife and I and my previous relationships have been generally positive and respectful, my Brain 1.0 won't be jolting me with overwhelming fear. Instead it will give me some anxiety, but not panic—a signal that this Phere isn't the end of the world and that there's probably a reasonable explanation for it.

The fast-thinking gut response from our Brain 1.0 is completely dependent on the past, for good reason, so when we acknowledge it, we do have to take its message with a grain of salt. That is, we have to use our Brain 2.0 to keep exploring the Phere and not jump to the rash conclusions of our gut/Brain 1.0.

Let's step back and think about this Phere in broader more abstract terms. If we were to categorize a matchbox with a logo from a fancy hotel with a phone number written on it that we found in our spouse's bag, how would we do it?

Using the schema outlined in the "Taxonomy of Phere", it would generally be:

A known objective obstacle (-1)—I know what a matchbox is but it has inhibited my goal to go get groceries. And it would be an unknown subjective obstacle (-2) because I don't have a story from my past concerning a matchbox with numbers written on it inside my wife's purse. I don't know what it means in terms of my global relationship with her. With its predominantly negative character (objective -1 and subjective -2), this matchbox has pushed Brain 1.0 to flood my Brain 2.0 with serious panic-inducing fear. It's subjectively upsetting enough to keep me from finding a car key, let alone going to the grocery store. It's turning a critical part of my global story, and thus my entire worldview, negative.

I'm very close to a fear freak-out.

That's interesting, but what can we actually do with this information? A lot.

Let's walk through how analyzing the objective and subjective qualities of a Phere can help us cope and metabolize fear without collaterally damaging ourselves or anyone else in the process.

To review, there are two kinds of phenomena:

The known: the familiar, part of our experience filed in memory, generally a positive (+) place that we know what to do inside of.

The unknown: the unfamiliar, not part of our experience and not filed in memory, generally a negative (-) place because we don't quite know what to do inside of it.

And we have two ways to process phenomena.

The Objective: Matter

The Subjective: What Matters

We experience the world through a goal-driven worldview or frame of reference that determines the positive (+) or negative valence (-) of objects and beings we encounter in the present on the way from our undesirable past to a more desirable future. Objects or beings that aid our attainment of goals are tools. Objects or beings that deter our attainment of goals are obstacles.

Everything else is irrelevant. Unless...

Our Brain 1.0 signals to our Brain 2.0 that its goal-driven plans are not meshing with the real world. The evidence for that disconnection reveals itself via an unexpected Phere event. The Phere itself has both an objective definition and a subjective meaning. Brain 1.0 tells Brain 2.0 that the Phere has dropped in by signaling its presence with fear emotion. Brain 2.0's job after it receives that message is to break apart the Phere into its objective and subjective components.

Let's unpack these eight components again.

1. **A Known Objective Tool (+2)**: We know what this unexpected Phere "is" and our Brain 1.0 quickly tells us that it's a tool to get us to our micro goal-directed future. In search of a spare car key we notice our wife's purse, an unexpected Phere event. Soon thereafter, the stored memory that she has a spare car key in her purse comes into our Brain 2.0. The purse (a thing that was irrelevant to our *buy food at the store* goal before the *I can't find my car key* event) is familiar to us and it is a tool to move us closer toward our micro goal of buying food at the store. So the wife's purse is a positive known and a tool to attain a micro goal to buy food from the store. So a known objective tool equals a +2 objective value.

2. **An Unknown Objective Tool (+1)**: We don't know what the unexpected Phere "is" but we figure out we can use it as a positive objective tool to get us to our micro goal-directed future.

   For example, perhaps my son has some weird-looking thing that he uses to do something or other to adjust his skateboard. It's lying on the driveway when my micro goal is to cut an overgrown limb from our rose bush, so I can "have" nice roses. I don't know what the skateboard thing "is." That is, I haven't used it before nor do I know how to use it for the purpose it was created, but my Brain 1.0 picks up on it lying there and signals to me that if I check it out, I may be able to find a sharp edge on it to cut the branch. So the weird skateboard adjuster is unknown to me but the objective qualities about it prove its usefulness as a tool. So an unknown objective tool equals a +1 objective value.

3. **A Known Objective Obstacle (-1):** We know what it is and our Brain 1.0 tells us it's an obstacle to us getting to our goal-directed future. When we're moving toward our wife's purse on the way to dig in to find our spare key, a "have" micro goal, our Brain 1.0 signals us to step over our son's skateboard on the way. The skateboard is a known object to me and an obstacle to attain a micro goal to find/have the spare car key. So a known objective obstacle equals a -1 objective value.

4. **An Unknown Objective Obstacle (-2):** We don't know what the Phere is and Brain 1.0's fear messaging tells us it is an obstacle to keep us from getting to our micro goal-directed future. For example, the unknown skateboard tool could block our way to pick up the pruning shears. We don't know what the skateboard tool is used for, but we can navigate around it to accomplish our micro goal nevertheless. The skateboard tool is an unknown and an obstacle to attain a micro goal to pick up the pruning shears. So an unknown objective obstacle equals a -2 objective value.

5. **A Known Subjective Tool (+2):** We know what the Phere means within the context of our past, and our Brain 1.0 tells us it's a tool that will get us to our macro goal-directed future. If on my way to my wife's purse, I spot my neighbor Bill pull-

ing out of his driveway, and my previous experience with Bill supports the notion that he'd be happy to help me out (my narrative story). With Bill as tool, I'll be able to accomplish my macro goal of being a good husband and taking care of the groceries by asking Bill to give me a lift to the store. Bill is a known tool to attain my macro goals of being a considerate husband... good man... transcendent being. So a known subjective tool equals a +2 subjective value.

6. **An Unknown Subjective Tool (+1)**: We don't know what the Phere means within the context of our past but our Brain 1.0 tells us it's a tool to get us to our macro goal-directed future. If the person driving my friend Bill's car is not Bill, but looks like him only twenty years younger, my Brain 1.0 signals that the unknown person is a tool I could use to get a ride to the store. It's probably Bill's son home from college. So the man in Bill's car is an unknown but a possible tool to attain my macro goal of being a considerate husband... good man... transcendent being. So an unknown subjective tool equals a +1 subjective value.

7. **A Known Subjective Obstacle (-1)**: We know what the Phere means within the context of our past, but our Brain 1.0 tells us it's an obstacle that will keep us from our macro goal-directed future. If I see Bill approaching my front porch with a clipboard and a box of girl scout cookies, my Brain 1.0 signals to me that he will keep me from my macro goal of being a considerate husband... good man... transcendent being by getting to the store and buying groceries. So a known subjective obstacle equals a -1 subjective value.

8. **An Unknown Subjective Obstacle (-2)**: We don't know what the Phere means within the context of our past and our Brain 1.0 tells us it is an obstacle to our goal-directed future. This

is the matchbox from the four seasons hotel with a phone number written on it from my earlier example. I don't know what the Phere means, I don't know how it came to be in my wife's purse, and it is definitely keeping me from heading to the grocery store. So an unknown subjective obstacle equals a -2 subjective value.

Whew. I'm sure your head is spinning. These abstractions can really tax your mind. But trust me, these four possible valences for the objective and four possible valences for subjective will prove extremely useful to us in our journey to become cognitively dominant. **And cognitive dominance is all about coping with the fear emotion in such a way that you can decode its signals and act in the service of your most cherished values. That's the point of all this.**

If we want to deal with our fears with accuracy and reason (the brain's left hemisphere realm) without losing the global goal of living up to our macro ideals (the brain's right hemisphere realm), we need to be able to break down big problems into more digestible pieces. We need to figure out what to do when we don't immediately know what to do. The way to do that is to get very good at breaking our problems into these objective and subjective components.

So when we encounter something that our Brain 1.0 tells us we need to orient to, we'll be able to put it in the appropriate category of threat or promise to our goal-directed lives.

Knowing all of these objective and subjective values will come in handy if I found a mysterious box of matches in my wife's purse. After toggling through some right hemisphere catastrophic and idyllic fantasies of what those matches might mean, I'd be able to calm myself using the left hemisphere of my brain. That is, I'd be able to think about the possible objective facts and subjective truths associated with those Phere-ful and fearful matches.

I'd be able to reason that my wife hasn't yet left me for another man. She's actually taking a nap in our bedroom. If there's a problem in our marriage, it hasn't reached a point where she's picked up and left me without explanation. The truth is that I'll be able to have a discussion with her about the matches in a much better state of emotion after I've had time to consider it some more. So I don't freak out and start screaming, even though the fear coursing through me wants me to.

With that understanding, I'm able to proceed as planned with my original macro goal. I go to the store, pick up the groceries and decide to simply ask her about the matches after we've had something to eat. When she wakes up and comes down for dinner, I'll ask her about the matches—not in a freak-out panic but in a calm tone.

She'll then be able to explain whether they are an obstacle or a tool for our marriage. And once that truth is exposed, the two of us can operate again in the real world, not a resentful dark world inside my own mind. This cognitively dominant thought process may not be easy to contend with when contemplating the permutations of the meaning of the matches, but it beats ignoring what they mean until it's too late.

TWENTY-THREE
The Four Quadrants of Phere

The taxonomy of Phere is heavy sledding. Being able to pinpoint and break down the constituent parts of a drop-in unexpected Phere event with speed is a tall task.

What happens if you need to quickly diagnose the Phere event? What if you don't have time to calm down and go grocery shopping as you break your Phere apart? In brain surgery you really don't have that much time to deal with a problem. Just like my trying experience with Oksanna in the OR when I was a resident, surgeons need to react quickly and decisively before the problem blows up into a huge mess that can cause irreparable harm or even death to the patient.

With a number of Oksanna experiences in my past, I wondered if it would be possible to map with higher resolution the knowns, unknowns, objective facts, subjective truths, tools and obstacles onto that gradient of fear Cartesian graph inspired by my old Chief Walt Langheinrich. If I could do that, I would be able to divide Pheres into four broad categories that I would be able to pinpoint and "feel" quickly. I could simply check in with myself, evaluate my psychological state broadly, and have an immediate idea of what sort of Phere I was dealing with. Then, when I don't have the time to use my slow-thinking Brain 2.0 to walk through the reasonable series of steps to break down an unexpected Phere event into those nuanced elemental components, I would have a much easier system to inform me about the global nature of the Phere simply based on the level of fear I was feeling. That is, I could translate fast-thinking Brain 1.0's signals rapidly and have a set of diagnostic principles handy to triage my emotions. I could keep my cool and then do whatever necessary to buy time for Brain 2.0 to do its thing.

So let's go back to that "X" marks the spot graph with its shades of Brain 1.0 fear emotional signaling from the "Descartes and Langheinrich" chapter.

Remember that we boiled down those twenty-one nuanced emotional fear states into just four global categories?

THE QUALITIES OF THE FOUR QUADRANTS OF PHERE

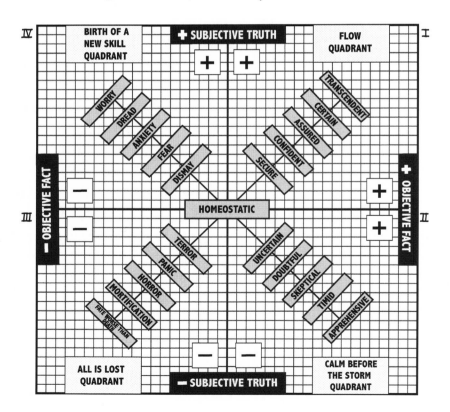

Quadrant I was
THE FLOW QUADRANT

Quadrant II was
THE CALM BEFORE THE STORM QUADRANT

Quadrant III was
THE ALL IS LOST QUADRANT

Quadrant IV was
THE BIRTH OF A NEW SKILL QUADRANT

For simplicity's sake, let's remove the qualitative representations of the gradient of fear from this graph for a moment. Keep in mind that those representations and qualitative descriptions are still valid. We're just going to fade them into the background for a while so we can add additional information without the graph getting too overwhelming.

Let's add what we know about the set of qualities "tool and obstacles" onto their appropriate axes.

Tools aid us in our quest to achieve micro (have mode) and macro (be mode) goals. We use tools to attain a "have" or to achieve a state of "being." So let's put tools on the same positive X-axis as "objective positives" and on the Y-axis as "subjective positives." I like the notion of objectives being sort of "on the ground" pursuits and subjectives being "in the air or beneath the surface" pursuits.

Obstacles, however, impede our progress to achieve micro or macro goals. So let's put obstacles on the same negative X-axis as "objective negatives" and the same Y-axis as "subjective negatives."

Here's where we come out with the addition of tools and obstacles to our graph.

Now, let's add in the qualities of knowns and unknowns. Where would those concepts sit on this graph?

QUALIFYING THE OBJECTIVE AND SUBJECTIVE AXES

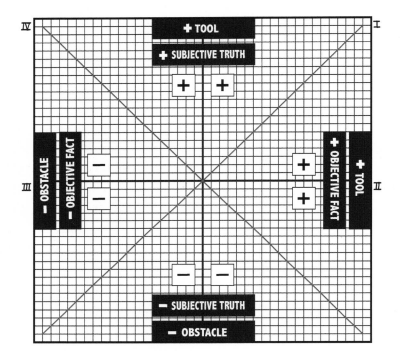

Let's go step by step.

A known subjective tool would be on the positive side of the Y-axis. And so would an unknown subjective tool. Both tools help us get to our target destination. But is one more positive than the other?

Is it more positive to have familiarity with a tool than to never have used it before? Yes. The way I use a scalpel today is far better than when I used it the first time. So if we're tracking the degree of positive subjective tools, a known tool would be worth something like a positive two (+2) on our graph while an unknown tool—though still positive—would be worth less than a known. So it would be worth a positive one (+1).

Now let's look at the negative side of things. Is it worse to be unfamiliar with an obstacle or to be familiar with it? If we know that in order to achieve a good grade in a class, it will require overcoming the obstacle of studying an hour a day for that class, we're in a better position to overcome that obstacle than if we don't know that. Aren't we? So a known obstacle is less negative (while still negative as no one really wants to study an hour a day) than an unknown obstacle. If we don't know that we need to study, we won't. The choice to study hasn't even been presented to us. So if we were to assign negative values to known and unknown obstacles, known obstacles would be negative one (-1) while unknown obstacles would be negative two (-2).

This same reasoning applies to objective tools and obstacles too.

Let's now drop in those degrees of positive and negative on both of our Y and X axes of our Cartesian Langheinrich graph.

QUALIFYING THE VALENCES WITH KNOWNS AND UNKNOWNS

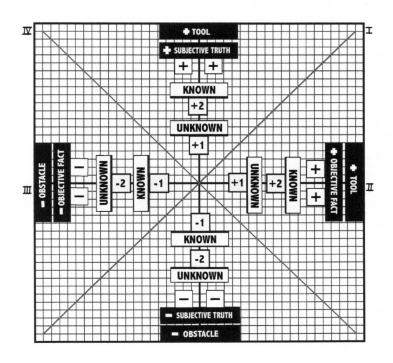

Now we can head back to our Taxonomy of Phere in the previous chapter and lay out where the eight possible Phere qualities sit on this four-quadrant graph. Just by plotting them.

And here's how it comes out:

HIGH-RESOLUTION ABSTRACT QUALITIES OF THE FOUR QUADRANTS OF FEAR

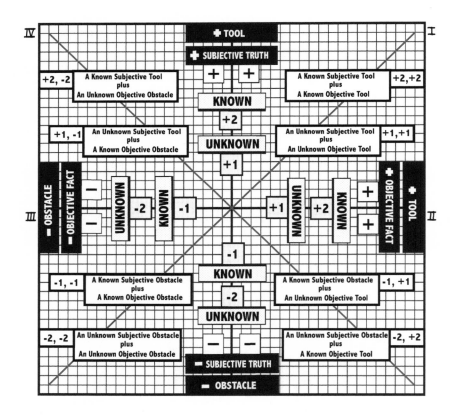

I'm sure you're scratching your head at this point, wondering what the point of all of this graphing is.

The point is that *these* four quadrants of Phere directly map onto the four quadrants of Phere we created when we mapped the qualitative gradient of fear. Now we have a very rich graphic representation that we can use as our practical reference in our cognitive dominance practice.

To contend with our emotional fear responses and avoid "fear freak-out" requires us to pay attention to our general fear state. That fear state, the one our fast-thinking Brain 1.0 signals to us when something unexpected occurs on our journey from a negative present to a positive future, will indicate where we sit on this four-category graph system.

Once we know we're in one of those quadrants of fear, we can use our incredibly powerful slow-thinking Brain 2.0 to laser focus in that one particular quadrant and figure out just what the Phere event is and means.

Let's run this logic through one more time before we get into specific examples.

We know that:

a) Unexpected Phere events rise in our lives that induce our Brain 1.0 to fire fear into our consciousness and into our body (just like the Nicholson-Jessup character in my steeplechase dream).

b) These Pheres can be categorized into two different modes of experience. The first is determining the "matter" of the Phere, the objective facts of it. The second is determining "what matters" about the Phere, the subjective truth of it.

c) Now we need to laser focus on the kind of objective fact and subjective truth the fear represents. The first way to do that is to ask ourselves if we've confronted this fear before or not. Is it "known" to us or "unknown" to us?

d) Begin with the objective facts. Is the objective fact of the Phere known to us? Or unknown to us?

e) Once we determine which channel that objective fact of the Phere is (known or unknown) we can break it down more.

f) We can then evaluate whether or not the objective fact (either known or unknown to us) can serve us as a tool to get us closer to our goal state (an object or state of being of desire). Or is it an obstacle we'll need to overcome in order to get back on that goal-directed path?

g) Once we've determined which of the four possible objective fact states is imbedded in the Phere, we'll turn our attention to the subjective truth component of the Phere.

h) Is the subjective truth of the Phere known to us? Or unknown to us?

i) Once we determine which channel that subjective truth of the Phere is (known or unknown) we can break it down more.

j) We can evaluate whether or not the subjective truth (either known or unknown to us) can serve us as a tool to get us closer to our goal state (an object or state of being of desire). Or is it an obstacle we'll need to overcome in order to get back on our goal-directed path?

k) Once we've determined which of the four possible subjective truth states is imbedded in the Phere, we can better understand our problem.

l) With a well-defined problem, our Brain 2.0 is extremely efficient at running a whole slew of simulations (internal story driven fantasies) from start to finish. Then it will settle upon the choice with the most probability of success that maintains our global hierarchy of value worldview.

Let's now take a closer look at the four quadrants in this graph and think about what kind of emotional response Brain 1.0 would communicate to Brain 2.0 when it identified an unexpected Phere event during Brain 2.0's goal-directed path. If we can have a broad understanding of the emotional fear responses to each of these categories of Phere, when we feel that emotional fear messaging from our Brain 1.0, we can quickly know generally what kind of objective fact and subjective truth the Phere represents.

What quick emoticon could we use to represent the four outermost cells in our four quadrants? 1) the most positive objective and the most positive subjective, 2) the most positive objective but also the most negative subjective, 3) the most negative objective and most negative subjective and 4) the most negative objective, but also most positive subjective .

THE FOUR QUADRANTS OF PHERE

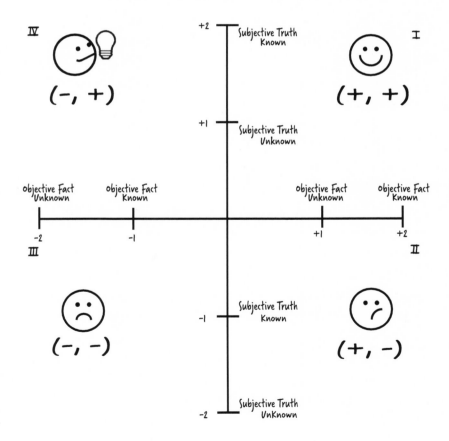

Knowing the broad category of what we are up against by listening closely to our fear response from Brain 1.0 will allow us to turn on our Brain 2.0's formidable left and right-brained processes. Generally, the left brain brilliantly orders the objective world and the right brain fantasizes about the subjective world.

Remarkably, when we place our energies into the unpacking of the category of Phere step by step, using the four quadrants of Phere graph will help us do that very quickly. Our Brain 1.0 takes that effort as a sign that we listened to it. We (that is our conscious processing systems within Brain 2.0) didn't ignore Brain 1.0's signal. And so, Brain 1.0 turns down the fear response messages it sends to us after we calm down and direct our efforts to figure out what the Phere means. And thus, with less fear emotion hitting us, we can think more clearly.

If we don't listen to Brain 1.0's warnings about the Phere it has identified (the signal) and instead concentrate on the message and its negative effect on us (the noise), Brain 1.0 gets frustrated and just sends more negative messaging. That biofeedback loop is relentless and leads us into fear freak-out like in the steeplechase dream.

The biofeedback may not represent itself as an externally visible panic state, but we can all relate to internal panic states that keeps us from heroically pursuing our life's work. Too much fear signal from Brain 1.0 clouds our thoughts. It robs us of being present in the moment when figuring out the problematic mysteries of our day-to-day lives. And for me it can interfere with optimal surgical performance.

Under fear's power, we can't make the nuanced and critical "proceed as planned" or "retreat and reassess" decisions necessary to attain our goals. Instead, we shut down and hide in the places we find the most unthreatening. And the more we do that, the smaller the list of unthreatening places becomes. Over the long term, we'll begin to inhabit smaller and smaller boxes of life, like for me abandoning a subspecialty that I was well trained to do. We don't want to find ourselves so overwhelmed by fear that we find it extremely difficult to leave our home, apartment, or tent in the woods. Practicing cognitive dominance is a psycho-technology that will prevent that retreat from happening.

If we use our formidable Brain 2.0 and systematically explore unexpected Phere events when we learn of them, our fear recedes and we find ourselves creating knowledge out of the unexplored territories of the unknown. The process by which we do this is, not coincidentally, also reflected in the four quadrants of Phere paradigm.

The way in which we move into the unknown and come back again with new knowledge begins in the first quadrant (the upper right) and then shifts down to the second quadrant (the lower right) across to the third quadrant (the lower left) up to the fourth quadrant (the upper left) and then back to the first.

Starting with known levels of personal competence and circling back again with a newly developed skill mimics a clockwise psychological iterative progression.

But I'm getting ahead of myself. Let's look at each of the four quadrants individually so we can understand the feeling Brain 1.0 fires under each condition of Phere with more granularity.

We'll start with the only entirely positive quadrant, the upper right-hand I define as the "flow quadrant."

TWENTY-FOUR
The Flow Quadrant

I'll never forget the first time I completed a Jannetta procedure. It seemed like the world's axis had shifted in my favor. It was late in my senior year of residency. I was on call the night before, but amazingly I had gotten six hours of uninterrupted blissful sleep with no pages! My rounds that morning before the case went smoothly. None of the patients I was responsible for had any issues the night before. They were all getting better.

In the preoperative unit I introduced myself to the patient I would be assisting Dr. Jannetta with that morning. The patient came from Texas for her microvascular decompression, something not uncommon for Dr. Jannetta's practice. She had a three-year history of severe electrical shock-like pain in her right cheek and jaw and was exhibiting all the signs and symptoms of classic Trigeminal Neuralgia. Her MRI scan showed a large blood vessel was crushing a sensory nerve at the base of her brain that was surely causing her pain. She was a thin lady and in relatively good spirits. Many of the patients that came to see Dr. Jannetta had lost their mind to the pain and were quite unraveled by the time we met them. For very good reason. So the composure this woman presented inspired me in great measure.

The patient rested in Operating Room 8, which was Dr. Jannetta's main arena for big cases, a proverbial Yankee Stadium for neurosurgery. Our anesthesia start went off without a hitch. Sometimes there's an abnormal lab that needs to be checked again, a difficult intubation, a delayed arterial blood pressure line or something that slows the momentum down. But this lady was otherwise healthy and was ready to be positioned on the operating table by 7:45 a.m.

I applied the head holder and negotiated her into a Park Bench position for the craniotomy. It's called the Park Bench position for the exact image the words conjure—a person lying on their side in the park getting some quick shuteye at lunch time. The Park Bench position is advantageous for this type of surgery because the brain, which is primarily composed of lipids (fat) will normally float in the watery cerebrospinal fluid that bathes it. When we drain the cerebrospinal fluid away, the brain can no longer float in the fluid. So, the brain sags away from the skull, thus creating a passage for the surgeon to approach the deepest parts of the brain in the most direct way. It's like using gravity as a retractor to move the brain out of the way to get where you need to go.

The patient had the perfect cranial anatomy to palpate, which helped me define the external landmarks to place the incision. One of the most important parts of a microvascular decompression is incision placement. If you misplace it, the craniotomy window will be off the mark, not near the arena that needs to be dealt with, and you will have to push and maneuver the brain more. This miscalculation also makes seeing the offending vessel more difficult and risks traumatizing the brain because too much pressure needs to be applied to see what you need to see.

I marked the incision with the standard issue indelible marker. I felt her skull again, getting purple marker all over my fingers—marks I often carry on my fingertips to this day. We started the case.

The bony exposure looked perfect. I drilled over the landing point and shaved the rest of the bone off with the high speed Midas Rex Drill. She had thin bone, which made the exposure easier. I opened the dura with a scalpel and got at familiar and comforting splash of clear colorless cerebrospinal fluid. As the fluid drained out of her head, her cerebellum began to sag away from the skull and my corridor down to the trigeminal nerve and offending blood vessel began to part. I brought the microscope into view and zoomed in to the deep angle of the cerebellum.

The trigeminal nerve is usually shrouded by a sizable and potentially dangerous vein called the petrosal vein. If it's in the way, you need to dissect the spider web like arachnoid coverings to clear it of any tethering and then coagulate it and cut it in half. I had struggled with this skill early on. But today the arachnoid hung over the petrosal vein like a towel over a clothesline. It was a perfect veil to cut and my micro scissors made quick work of it. The petrosal vein came into perfect view. I coagulated it and divided it.

This gave me an unobstructed view of the glistening sprout of the trigeminal nerve. Coming off of the floor of the rounded brainstem, the nerve looked like a bleached handle of a pumpkin. Just under the nerve lay the culprit—a thick, deep red arterial blood vessel pulsating across and into the base of the trigeminal nerve. With every heartbeat I could imagine the pain it inflicted on this poor woman. I could actually see her pain.

I reached down with my Sachs dissector, a long-handled instrument that looks like an elongated miniature barbeque spatula. Oftentimes the blood vessel that needs to be moved away from the nerve is tethered by another smaller blood vessel below or by deeper arachnoid membranes. That was not the case here. This vessel just flipped away from the nerve like it was waiting for me to introduce myself. Immediately after I lifted the blood vessel away, the nerve's tension relaxed. I was essentially done. All I needed to do was put felt padding in to buttress the vessel away from the nerve forever and I could back out of my micro world and begin closing.

I asked the circulating nurse to call Dr. Jannetta in to take a look. I couldn't believe I had gotten this far so smoothly before he came in, but this was his system of training the residents. First, he would make sure we safely added micro skill on top of micro skill from operation to operation. After he felt secure that we were performing properly, he would give us more and more time to add on and expand our skills. He'd always be available, though, to come in when we were stuck and couldn't go any farther.

Dr. Jannetta came into the room and asked where I was in the procedure. I jokingly said, "You better scrub in before I begin closing." He laughed and went to the scrub sink. I was so excited to show him what I had done. It was a thing of beauty. There was no bloody oozing, no pressure on the cerebellum, and you could see a perfectly placed bony opening and atraumatic approach to the trigeminal nerve. And you could see the vessel now away from the nerve.

PJ hunkered down to the operating microscope and looked in.

"Mark, nice job here." My heart fluttered. Nothing was sweeter to my ears in residency than PJ's praise.

He flipped the vessel back to where it originally was and took a picture. Then he moved it away with the exact instrument and manipulation I had done previously. Then he picked up the felt padding on the nurse's stand and said to me. "You did all the hard work here. And you know how to place this felt. Let me do something in this case. You practically stole it from me."

After the vessel was safely tucked away, he pushed his rolling chair back from the field and looked me in the eyes with seriously tight eyebrows that softened when he began to speak. "Mark, I think I'm going to be on time for my squash lesson. Thanks!"

Precious few cases go this smoothly, but when they do you feel like you've just bottled lightning. This was a feeling I wanted more of... that I craved... that I still crave.

What I'd experienced in those previous minutes in the OR was flow, the upper right-hand first quadrant of our Cartesian four quadrants of Phere graph. Flow represents what our ultimate in sync emotional experience feels like during a goal-directed journey from a negative present to a positive future. The Pheres that arise (the things we didn't expect to happen) are all positive tools to get us closer to achieving our goal.

The four squares that make up this quadrant are:

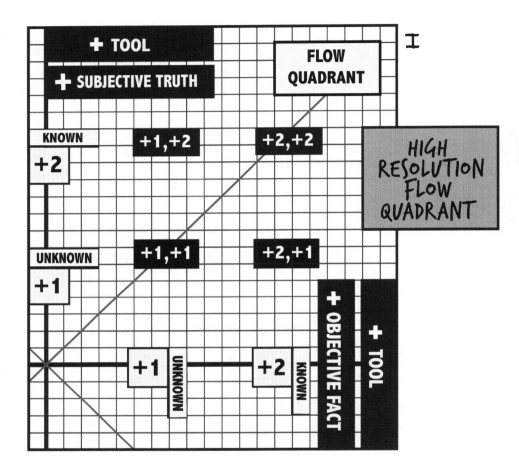

Let's focus on the top right box, which represents the emergence of a +2 positive objective known linked with a +2 of a subjective known. What emotional message is Brain 1.0 sending Brain 2.0 when the Pheres it encounters on Brain 2.0's directed journey from the negative present to a positive future align themselves as double positives objectively and subjectively?

What does that feel like? Here is the corresponding four quadrants of Phere for the flow quadrant.

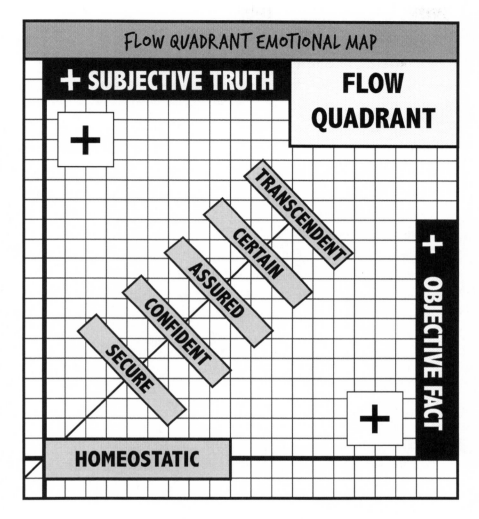

Double positive Pheres get us closer to our objective micro goals (having a successful result from the operation) and our subjective macro goals (being the best brain surgeon I can be). And when Brain 1.0 encounters them, it sends a torrent of positive energy into our Brain 2.0.

This domain defines the realm of what psychologist Mihaly Csikszentmihalyi coined "Flow," in his book *Flow: The Psychology of Optimal Experience*. The objective skillset of the person living in this quadrant is so well-developed that unexpected happenings in this zone prove immediately useful as tools to their micro goals.

The subjective experience of dealing with these rising opportunities proves so natural that the player feels as if "she can't miss." Brain 1.0 has the positive emotional systems firing on full, and as such, the delay experienced as the orienting response to unexpected events (the freeze moment in the freeze, flight or fight response) to the double positive Pheres is practically nonexistence.

Brain 1.0, because of the familiarity of the territory, quickly recognizes double positive Pheres. And the hyper-speed by which it does generates a mystically compelling feeling, a religious experience of sorts that makes the experiencer feel as if he or she were operating at an otherworldly level of competence. This is transcendence.

Transcendence is the feeling we get when we're playing a game and just "know" before we enact a movement that it will work. It's the basketball player who can't miss. The classical pianist who has practiced the individual notes so many times that she can forget about them and let it rip, thus allowing for unique miracles of interpretation to arise while she plays.

Many people may be able to learn the notes of a particular piece of music. But Art (individual specific and unique interpretation) emerges when Brain 1.0 releases Brain 2.0 from self-doubt during these flow experiences. Then the gap between choice and performance narrows to instantaneous. The player becomes reflexive to the flow of the moment. Only in this state can works of art emerge. The dividing line between the thought and action dissolves.

The other three cells in this quadrant represent the varying levels of the "close to Flow" experience, the $(+1, +2)$, $(+2, +1)$ and $(+1, +1)$. All Pheres are positive tools for us, but there is a fractional delay in getting the "proceed as planned" positive affective messaging from Brain 1.0 after the orienting response to the Phere. It's not as transcendently instantaneous.

This entire quadrant is the realm of the "super familiar," a connected territory with a feeling of calm, contented active play. Time seems to stop as our skills display themselves effortlessly. We're part of a greater whole but performing with an extraordinary individual expression that only we can bring to the world. We're "releasing our gift" into the world and expressing new creations. For brain surgeons, it takes about fifty thousand hours of working on our craft to get into this realm.

The facts are known and positive tools for us to use whenever we need them. The truth is known and tremendously positive. We've been here before and we know just what to do. It seems as if we were made to be here at this moment, doing this thing.

This is flow.

You are in the land of *MacGyver*, the television hero who can defuse a bomb with bubblegum and a paperclip. Everything you see is a tool because you are operating in a place of high competence and craft.

So, in these rare moments the trick is to not place your focus on Brain 2.0. Let Brain 1.0 drive the bus. Its fast thinking is accurate and on target. That's because your deliberate slow-thinking Brain 2.0 has so much memory about how to deal with this environment that it does not require "stop-gap self-doubt thoughts" to stand in its way. Former Major League Baseball pitcher David Cone explains it this way during the flow state, "When you think, you stink." What he meant is that a pitcher has to do the work necessary to build his skills to such a high level that he can trust himself when he pitches in a game. Once the pitcher does that work (ten thousand or more hours learning the craft), he must stop thinking about what he has to do and trust that his Brain 1.0 and Brain 2.0 don't need him and his "mind" consciously second-guessing their simultaneous operation. The mind must relax and allow the pitcher to pitch.

The way to do this—and it's far easier said than done—is for the pitcher simply to remind himself he has the craft to succeed. (He wouldn't be pitching in Major League Baseball if he didn't have it.) He should just proceed as planned on his mission. He should just keep moving with confidence because he is operating inside his genius—the place where he is supposed to be. He's survived the minor leagues, strived to get into the majors, and is thriving in the arena. All systems are on go. So let it go.

The flow state is what Joseph Campbell meant by "following your bliss." Once you've done the work (invested intense cognitive energy over thousands of hours of skill building within your particular craft) and thus have built a territory for yourself that is super familiar, you'll find yourself in that space and should follow your "gut." Your "gut" is Brain 1.0 and it's fast-thinking processing.

Here's a passage from Csikszentmihalyi's *Flow*, "There comes a state of being after intense deliberate practice that manifests itself as autotelic, an activity that has a purpose in itself." Csikszentmihalyi goes on to state that when we can achieve the state, "technique is transcended and the art becomes the artless art grown out of the unconscious."

After reading those words years ago, I thought of that day with the lady from Texas and my first Jannetta procedure. At the end of the operation, I walked out of OR 8 and after eight years of hard work had finally attained a place of confidence that I was going to be a competent neurosurgeon.

TWENTY-FIVE
The Calm Before the Storm Quadrant

We all think we'd love to live in the flow quadrant world every waking moment but without obstacles to our goals, drop-in unexpected Phere events that derail us. The experience would prove to be very King Midas-like. If everything we did turned into gold expressions of creation, we'd soon tire of creating. We'd get bored. We'd take our hard-won acquisition of a unique set of skills that level up to an ephemeral expression of transcendence for granted.

Eventually, we'd begin undermining ourselves, destroying our gift with ancillary distractions that satisfy the dark side of previously unexplored desires, short-term dissipation at the expense of long-term creation. Pick up any newspaper and you'll read about men and women who made terrible choices at the height of their powers.

They didn't recognize the Pheres in their lives, the signs, that the time had come to leave their super familiar world and set off into the dark environs of the unknown. The qualities of the Pheres inside the calm before the storm quadrant, the one just below flow, lead us to contemplate the ideals we've set our sights on. Is our macro "being" goal really achievable? Or is it counter to the realities of everyday life? Do we need to refresh the top of our value hierarchy? If we're experiencing the emotions associated with the calm before the storm quadrant, chances are we need to take a good hard look at what we're shooting for.

It was a common expression for my neurosurgery professors to say: "If it was easy, they'd be doing it at Kmart." These words would typically be delivered when consoling a resident who had reached his technical limit in an operation and called for help. All of the residents were high achievers and we wanted to perfect our skills rapidly. When we did not, we, or at least I, would experience a deep feeling of micro failure that would morph into macro impending doom.

Another attending once told me at lunch after I'd struggled with a difficult case of his, "We're kind of teaching you how to ride a new bike. It's a shitload more complicated than the one you rode in first grade, but essentially, it's a bike. You and your fellow residents will all learn to ride it at different rates, but by the end of your residency you'll all be capable of riding that bike. You'll be competent and safe. You'll all know the rules of the road, know the levers and the gears, and be able to travel from Point A to Point B, but you probably will not be slick. It will take you years, many years, to actually become a skilled rider."

That seemed to help.

After completing my residency and fellowship as well as watching and performing myriads of different surgeries in the multiple subspecialties of neurosurgery, I reasoned that I had all the cards and tricks of the trade in my pocket as I entered my first professional practice. There was nothing more I could do to prepare for my job. I had climbed to the top of the mountain and now it was my plan to enjoy the view, do my work, and maintain a calm and logical approach to whatever challenged me in the future. Easy peasy.

So why did I feel so uneasy? There was a nagging uncertainty beneath my facade, an apprehension that something was going to happen to me soon that would derail everything I'd worked so hard to attain.

I had landed a great practice with wonderful partners, exactly the kind of surgeons I had dreamed of working alongside. I believed I had completed my journey from what was to what should be. I truly believed Julie and I would live there happily ever after.

To add on to the positives, my cases were going well. There were no major complications and I fit into the hospital community. People liked me.

And yet, my performance was not living up to my expectations. I almost never felt comfortable in the OR. I was always on high edge. I was constantly churning, thinking and preparing for anything that could go wrong. I wanted to be ready for the unknown.

I just didn't realize that I already was.

When my internal professional satisfaction wasn't happening, I began to feel anxious. I kept telling myself it was a confidence issue. The more experience I had, the more confidence I'd gain. And that was true in part, but not exactly. This disquietude had more to it than that. Something in my future would knock me over… take me down. I sensed it deep in my bones, but I had no idea what it was. I was locked into that notion that Bruce Springsteen so perfectly captured in his song "When You're Alone." "There's things that'll knock you down you don't even see coming." Knowing that truth is not easy to live with, especially when people's lives are in your hands.

In retrospect, I believe it was an assumption I had when I took on the responsibility of opening up a person's skull and fiddling around in there. I could not behave like everyone else. It was an intractable determination that I had to handle any case that came in at the highest level of competence. Not just handle it, but handle it as well as my teachers had. Better even. I had to hone my skills to a point where they were automatic, machine-like and incapable of letting me down. I had to be in flow all of the time and I would grind myself into dust until I was.

I never felt I had enough training for certain cases. Even though I did more of these cases than other residents graduating at the same time, it wasn't good enough for me. This assumption that I wasn't ready, not good enough, nowhere near the quality of my mentors—unexamined—grew into an unhealthy and damaging force I'd need to confront and metabolize before it destroyed me.

That story I told myself didn't sit well with my Brain 1.0 simply because Brain 1.0 refuses to accept Brain 2.0's, for lack of a better expression, narrative bullshit. Brain 1.0 was the place inside of me that kept reminding me of that Springsteen lyric. I would not immediately know what to do about the unknowns in my future. Would they be obstacles? Would they be tools? There was just no way to predict. Life is a combinatorial explosion problem ad infinitum. To believe you can parse out every contingency is madness.

The human mind can't do it. So shooting for that impossible goal is ridiculous—thus the Brain 1.0's jolts of apprehension coming my way.

The calm before the storm quadrant usually arises during the times in our lives when we've attained a high-level goal. We've worked and worked and worked to achieve something we believe will change our lives forever. Once we X, the rest of my life will be smooth sailing... we think. We all come to understand just how wrong this assumption is soon after we've been handed the trophy or awarded the new title and raise. We have a rush of joy when we hit the finish line tape and then soon after, sometimes immediately after, a surge of discontent arises. In real estate it's called buyer's remorse. Or as Peggy Lee once sang so well, we experience the "Is that all there is?" syndrome. Our gold medal just doesn't feel as great as we thought it would.

So let's put on our cognitively dominant glasses and take a look at this quadrant with higher resolution. Here are the four cells within what I call the calm before the storm quadrant.

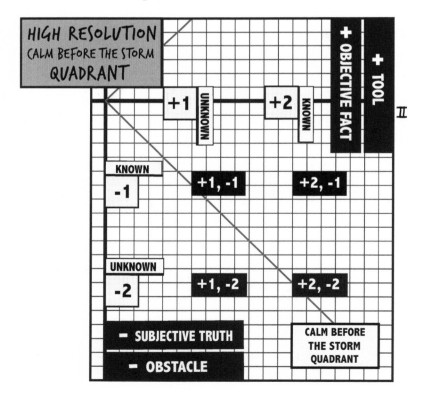

Just listen to any post-big athletic event interview with the winning athlete. They'll be asked how it feels and they'll stumble for words. Usually they'll say, "It's surreal. It hasn't sunk in yet." But the truth is that what they thought would happen—incredible long-lasting bliss—is very evanescent and is soon followed by a *sinking feeling, an emptiness.*

This experience is a palpable collision with the second quadrant of Phere. My belief was that with a high-powered brain surgery residency and fellowship, I would have the tools to be confident. But in fact a part of me constantly compared my performances to the virtuosos above me, which did not help my confidence. Remember that Pheres are simply instances when what we think is going to happen isn't what's happening. Our fantasy is not our experiential reality. I thought I was going to be confident and inoculated from fear. That proved naive.

The bottom right-hand cell of the calm before the storm quadrant (+2, -2) most clearly represents this moment in time. It's a double positive fact—I just won the US Open!—matched with a double negative truth—my navigation system (Brain 2.0 narrative story machine) is lacking a new destination. My story has come to an end. What do I do now?

I call this quadrant the calm before the storm because after the freeze-orienting response to the Pheres within we must retreat and reassess our target goal. We can't proceed as planned if we don't know where we're going. So we must reconsider what we want next. What's the next big goal to direct ourselves?

Sure, we can shoot for winning the next big tournament and adding some more trophies to our trophy case. Or work ourselves up to the highest desk in the corporation, CEO. And for a while those goals are enough to keep us directed and secure on our path. We get better and better and better. We level up our craft to a place where when we're in flow, inside our chosen territory, and no one can touch us.

But what about after you've cashed out all the territory has to offer? What do you do then?

This is the crux of this quadrant. Recognizing that you are inside this calm before the storm quadrant will be immeasurably helpful. The way to recognize it is to map the emotional state that Brain 1.0 is signaling to you. Now let's look at the quadrant with the emotional qualities from our gradient of fear mapped.

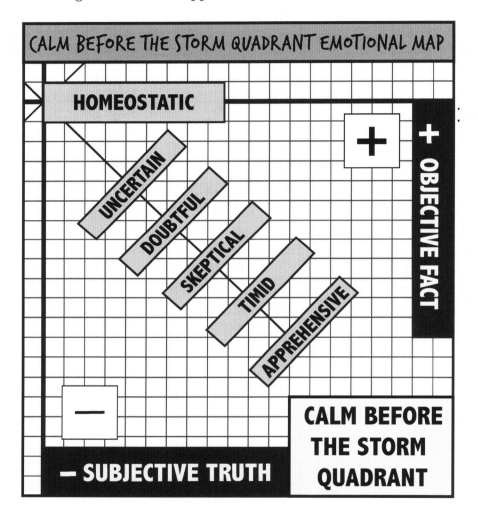

This realm is the familiar-strange environment, characterized by the rise of facts that tell us we've reached a big goal. We've hit the familiar finish line tape. But it's also a strange place in that the subjective component of the Phere is telling us we're facing an obstacle too. The obstacle is that we need a new narrative. That requires us to reference the top of our value hierarchy and come up with a new goal that is consistent with our most firmly held principles of conduct. If we don't do that, we'll feel apprehensive about our place in the world. We'll sense a foreboding storm in the future.

Let's go back to that young woman at Harvard to flesh out this notion. She was the experimenter who took Daniel J Simons and Christopher Chabris' psychology class, the class that explored the experimental methods of psychology by running the invisible gorilla experiment. She was one of the students tasked with finding subjects to run through the protocol.

We can imagine that before she decided to accept Harvard's offer, she was back in her hometown hitting her stride. Her drive to achieve pushed her to excel academically and contribute to her high school and community in such a way that it would grab the attention of the country's most recognized higher education institutions. It took her years of struggle to create a story about herself that would appeal to these institutions in such a way that they'd offer her admission. She valued these institutions as the kind of place that would be good for her to be a part of, so she targeted them to enter.

After the good news arrives in March of her senior year of high school that her hard work has achieved what she set out to achieve (admission into a famous school) she has a rush of elation that her hard work did indeed pay off. But then—perhaps an hour, a few days, or even a few weeks later—she finds herself deeply apprehensive about her future.

She can't sleep very well and she's lost her appetite. She's having serious second thoughts about this whole "superwoman, super achievement person" she concocted in order to be selected as worthy to attend some silly place that seems to alienate friends and family when she lets them know she's going to there in the fall. Everyone treats her differently now in her hometown. They're being more formal, more deferential, more passive aggressive, more negative to her and her big deal ambitions. While she's still in the familiar hometown world, everyone knows she doesn't belong there anymore. Especially her.

She's fallen into the calm before the storm quadrant of Phere, the pit of an objective double positive known tool that carries with it a double subjective unknown negative.

Admission to Harvard is a known objective tool to jump to the head of the line in American life. That's just a fact. Claiming otherwise is silly.

But Harvard is also a double negative subjective obstacle.

How can that be?

Well, the Harvard woman will have to leave her familiar hometown and face a supercharged competitive environment in which no one is deeply emotionally invested in her success. She has to leave all of her attachment figures (family, friends, and the boyfriend she cares deeply about) behind in addition to all of the positive and negative known elements of life in Smalltownsville. All those Harvard positives now look like negatives and the small town negatives now look like positives in the light of this new information.

So, should she retreat and reassess her global goal of "going to Harvard so that she can get recognition as a super smart person capable of great things and all of the advantages that go along with that"? After all, Harvard is also a double negative subjective unknown. What will it actually be like to have to compete at a place like Harvard? The place is teeming with people as ambitious as she is. Competitive people. Maybe she should go somewhere else instead? A place where she will be at the top of the hierarchy the second she steps on campus?

Or should she proceed as planned and just ignore all of that double negative subjective obstacle stuff?

Chances are, she doesn't formally think about any of these facts and truths. Because of the cultural valence attached to Harvard, all of the thousands of hours she put in to get admitted, the superior feeling she gets when the people who used to bully and ridicule her are now the ones being most solicitous to her, she'll be able to shove down that Brain 1.0 subjective negative emotional messaging by distracting herself with other mini-goals. Like "having a relaxing and fun-filled summer."

At least until Labor Day rolls around.

But for the sake of argument, what if she did recognize this unforeseen negative feeling and spent some time unpacking it before she set out to Harvard? Would that do her any good?

Remember, this is a person interested in psychology, so she very well may consider that the negative feeling had more meaning than the proverbial "nerves about leaving home." And perhaps she'd walk it back to her exact moment of personal crisis, the freeze moment of the orienting response when the Phere rises and Brain 1.0 shoots out its negative affect. That is, the moment when the joy of admission dissipated and apprehension rose within her.

The freeze moment (getting the admission letter) comes just before the crisis, and the crisis comes in the form of a question. Should I proceed as planned? Or should I retreat and reassess?

Obviously, the young woman proceeds. She's not going to run away from a factual opportunity of a lifetime that she had to sacrifice a great deal to attain. She's already sent back her acceptance of the offer and she's thinking about what stuff to take to Cambridge.

But she's not an idiot. What about the "as planned" and "reassess" elements? How about thinking more about those?

She thinks about her plan after Harvard. Her plan up to this point was just to get into Harvard. That's done, so now what? She really should reassess her global goal now that her previous global "being" goal (being a Harvard student) has been achieved.

And she does.

She sets a new "being" goal. She wants to explore X at Harvard so that when she's done at Harvard she can move to Y. She sketches out the micro goals that will be necessary to get into that X path, like taking the introductory course offered by Simons and Chabris to learn about how psych experiments are structured and how they work. She'll sign up for that one for sure. She's now reconfigured her target from "getting into Harvard" to "graduating with a degree in psychology."

With this schematic of something to explore that could lead to something else done before she ever arrives for her freshman year, our

Harvard woman arrives refreshed and excited about her the new opportunity-filled environment. So, when she does fall into the deep freshman funk like every freshman, when she discovers she's out of her depth, she's not going to pull out an "A" in every course and she has no idea what to do about it…she'll have something to hold on to. *Oh, right! Psychology, that's the thing that appealed to me before all of this mess fell upon me. Let me keep my focus there and not sweat the "C" in the required literature course.*

The calm before the storm quadrant concerns those moments when it seems like you should be flying high, happy as a clam, and yet something deep down doesn't feel all that great. There's a numbing uncertain apprehension beneath your achievement and you just don't know why. If you understand this is a signal from your incredibly astute Brain 1.0—that what you think will happen isn't what's really happening and that you need to pay attention to the Phere of the experience—you'll be able to metabolize that negative emotional state productively. You'll reassess your global goals, come up with a new story to pursue, and get back on track.

You'll set new, higher goals. You'll put your focus on the micro steps necessary to achieve those new, higher goals. You'll understand that starting a new project that you believe will help you achieve that new higher goal will be as exciting as it is frightening. And you'll be prepared for the inevitable difficulties that arise with that new pursuit because you certainly met the challenges that arose when you successfully set out to achieve previous goals.

Because you know that fear is a signal to pay attention, you'll reconsider the plans (the ends) and reassess the micro actions (the means) you think will get you to a new higher destination than the one you just achieved. But if you do not recognize the Phere valences Brain 1.0 is signaling to you, and you choose to ignore the signals, you'll make no new plans. You'll stagnate. And you might experience fear freak-out.

Without goals, without plans, is not a good place to be. How will you know you're making progress or what micro actions to take to get what you set out to achieve if you don't know where you're going? You'll need to reset your "what is" to "what should be" map using cognitive dominance as your compass.

That's what that bottom right-hand Phere quadrant is about. It's a familiar-strange weigh station that prepares you for the unfamiliar and extraordinary world to come. It's filled with unknowns that can overwhelm you. But by setting a clear new goal, writing a new narrative for yourself during the calm before the storm stage, you'll be ready to confront the darkness ahead.

For me, I lived in the calm before the storm mostly in my first two years of practice in western Massachusetts. It culminated in my experiences with Jesus and Anthony, who I introduced at the start of this book. If only I'd known I was in the calm before the storm quadrant when I operated on both patients, I think I could have avoided a lot of personal sorrow.

TWENTY-SIX
The All Is Lost Quadrant

The unexpected Phere events that pop up in this quadrant are extremely disorienting. They will drop you into a funk that will seem practically impossible to get out of. This is when we need our Brain 2.0 to work overtime because Brain 1.0's fear signaling is constant and intense.

No one likes this place. It's equivalent to living inside an internal hell. The reason is that our worldview, the way we've been able to navigate from our micro negative states to incrementally more positive ones, doesn't seem to give us any satisfaction. Yes, we can make it out of bed, make it to work, complete our tasks, etc. but, we've lost the thread of why we're doing all of these micro actions.

The ordered worldview that our Brain 2.0 had spent years refining gives us no consolation. Our present state is so baffling and chaotic that we can't get a grip on what matters anymore. We've literally fallen into a dark pit of chaos in this quadrant.

We panic here. Our fear freak-out is easily triggered by even the most mundane of Phere events. Being unable to locate our car keys feels as if it's a confirmation of our complete inadequacy in human endeavor. A sink full of dishes symbolizes everything we can find "wrong" about ourselves. These journeys into the pit tempt us to look for easy fixes to buck up our emotional state of mind. We find ourselves drinking too much or returning to old nasty habits. These distractions provide short-term relief—self-medication—but they end up pushing us deeper into the abyss.

Coping with the all is lost quadrant is probably the very reason you decided to give this book a try. Living inside of it is extremely painful and stressful. And if you don't pull yourself out of it (and unfortunately, while there are tools to help you ascend, the only person who can lift you out of the crevasse is you), you can lose the absolute truth about yourself. And that truth is simply that you have an inner gift. You must creatively express that gift throughout your lifetime with all of the vim and vigor you can muster. That is the simple path to generating meaning amidst chaos. Here are the cells of the all is lost quadrant in our Cartesian graph.

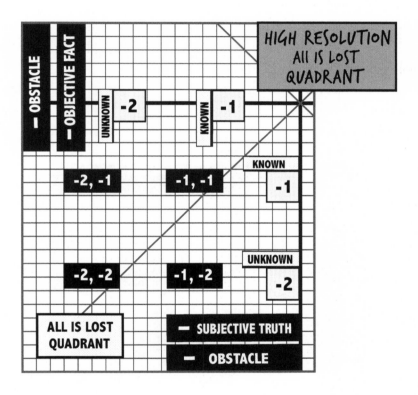

We can't make sense of this foreign land. Objective facts are small (-1) or large (-2) unknown obstacles and our subjective truths are small (-1) or large (-2) unknown obstacles too. We haven't been exposed to any "matter" like it before and we don't know the "meaning of the matter" either. The only information we have comes from our "threat Geiger counter," Brain 1.0, and it's telling us that both components of the unexpected Phere event—the matter and the meaning of the matter—threaten us.

This is because we've never been in this environment before. This environment is equivalent to the realm of the phenomena Nassim Nicholas Taleb wrote about in his book *The Black Swan*: *The Impact of the Highly Improbable*.

This super-unfamiliar territory requires so much exploration and cognitive energy just to function that we can easily lose our bearings. And because we're operating in the dark and can't get a grip on our location, we lose our conception of our global "being" goals rapidly after being dumped into its metaphysical cold black water. We don't know which way is up, which is down, which is left or which is right. Nothing makes sense anymore.

Here is the all is lost quadrant with its corresponding map of fear emotions.

What to do?

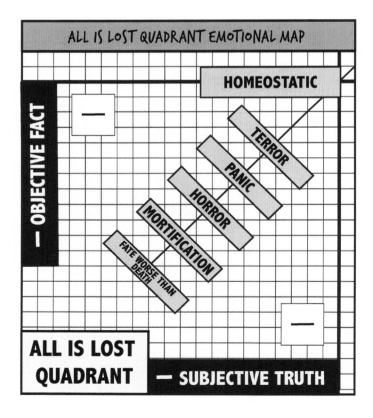

We need to find a place of metaphorical shelter. We must retreat and reassess, giving our Brain 2.0 time to think through the situation. Hold our tongues. Refrain from taking actions. It's difficult to do this because we're feeling like we have to do something. We're drowning and internally thrashing to such a degree that we're compelled to externalize it.

While the following prescription is far easier said than done, I have found this to be my most effective coping mechanism.

1. Think about the highest value you live by. For me, it's a commitment to "creation" versus "destruction." So when I fall into the pit, I tell myself to formulate actions that conform to my notion of what creation means to me.

2. Think about a single micro goal that can conform to the global macro goal of being an agent of creation.

3. Enact the behavior that I will accomplish the micro goal with the highest degree of probability for a positive outcome.

4. Repeat steps one through three.

5. The North Star is my highest value on my private pyramid of value.

We accomplish these micro goals one by one and thus slowly transform the unknown chaotic territory into a more and more familiar one. Our actions bring predicable results.

Let's flesh this out more with an example.

Let's think about our young woman at Harvard again. On the day she arrives, she has no idea where she fits into this community. She has no idea how well she'll match up to her classmates. She doesn't know where to go to sign up for classes. She doesn't know what to do.

The facts are all unknown and the truth is unknown about how she'll be able to cope with the fact because she's never faced these sorts of facts before. She doesn't know what to do. So the anxiety and fear Brain 1.0

pumps into her Brain 2.0 is getting incrementally more pronounced as she approaches campus. There are so many things she doesn't know that she delays checking in to her dorm until the last hour.

Should she proceed as planned for her global goal to study psychology and get a PhD right now?

Obviously, no, not right now.

Right now, she needs to convert a lot of micro unknowns into knowns without getting so obsessed with compiling the answers to the unknowns that she doesn't pay attention to the experience itself. Seems simple enough.

The problem, though, is that Brain 1.0 will experience more unexpected Phere events as she's coping with the earlier ones. The roommate "type" of person she expected to have proves to be untrue. The bed she expected isn't what she'd hoped for. The new building she'll be living in is strange. That bathroom is in a weird configuration. All of the sensory input is unique.

So she should make notes, pay attention to these unexpected Phere events, but not get so obsessive that she can't process them all. She should take them in, give them a moment to lodge in her short-term memory.

She turns her Brain 2.0 to think about fundamentals. Food… where do I go to eat? What's the process? She asks that question of the proctor. She gets an answer and then heads out to accomplish the goal of eating.

You get the idea…small conversions of unknowns into knowns. Drip by drip.

And yet, an all is lost moment for her is inevitable, even if she takes the Brain 2.0 processing to heart.

This is simply because her brain will overload. She'll melt down at some point. Her Brain 1.0 will revolt and tell her it's too much. It can't handle all of this stuff. All is lost. There is no way she'll be able to use the way her Brain 2.0 navigated Smalltownville here. She'll have to change behavior…not just one behavior, but a lot of behavior. The people are just too foreign. They don't react the way she thinks they'll react to her "funny" jokes. They don't like the stuffed animal she brought to put on her bed. She's a stranger in a strange land. And on and on.

Believe it or not, just knowing that the all is lost quadrant will sink her down into a degree of fear freak-out panic will be incredibly helpful for her. My all is lost Pheres commonly involve losing a patient or receiving a malpractice letter. Now when I get them I fall back to my cognitive dominance standard operating procedure of remembering my purpose on Earth, remembering the oath I took, and acknowledging that I am in a very difficult business with huge risks.

The fear freak-out stage isn't just inevitable when we head into the darkness inherent in a brand-new extraordinary world. It is essential for us to recognize just how much courage we are displaying as we willingly face a tremendously powerful fear state. Dark unknown extraordinary worlds are the Goliaths that we Davids must confront.

Our young Harvard woman will come to understand that she's put herself in a place where she has never been before. And she's starting from scratch. She'll come to realize that having to figure out the simplest ways to accomplish the most primal goals (where to go to the bathroom, where to eat, where to sleep, etc.) takes a lot of her Brain 2.0 energy. She didn't have to expend this energy when she was in the super-familiar flow quadrant or in one of the familiar-strange quadrants. She'll understand that this drain of energy increases the effects of Brain 1.0's messaging system, which means she'll get more emotional responses to unexpected Phere events than she normally would. Having that information beforehand allows her to steel herself, like David did, before facing the powerful dark force.

Knowing about the cognitive drain associated with the all is lost quadrant will allow her to recognize that she should really limit her goals. She should focus on the micro while keeping the macro available for reference, but not in a punitive way.

Within a few months, or even weeks, she will recognize that her macro goal before she got to Harvard was her "best guess" taken at a time when she needed to guess a goal for the future. It is not set in stone. She can revise her macro being goal as new information becomes available to her. But it's a good start. So, she should take it seriously, but not so seriously that she'll want to drop out of school because she failed the first quiz she took. She'll keep herself open to other "being" options while doing her best within her "best guess" goal.

Oftentimes we run away from the all is lost quadrant. We quit and run back to the familiar. We regress. We incessantly check in with our posse. We play videogames for hours. We watch TV or endlessly scroll through our social media channels. We abandon something we're actually quite capable of doing.

It's understandable and it's something we all do sometimes. A good idea, though, is to watch yourself and ask yourself why you might be reading pulp fiction into the wee hours of the night when you should be doing your work. Could you be in an all is lost quadrant? When you know why you're doing those things, you're in a better position to recognize that you need to go back and sort out more of that chaotic unknown environment. Then you may take some micro steps to convert little objective unknowns into knowns. Drip by drip you turn the dark water into clear.

And eventually, the clear water begins to overtake the dark.

You've learned how to convert the easy unknowns into knowns and the world is becoming more and more familiar to you every day. This is how you'll pull yourself up out of the darkness…one small micro step at a time. It's easier said than done, of course, but just recognizing behavior as representative of an all is lost experience will help you turn your Brain 2.0 attention to those little tasks at hand. Over time those drips of effort will add up and they'll form a channel out of the darkness.

The all is lost quadrant is not an easy one to pull yourself out of. But when we do—and people do it all of the time—we find ourselves stronger, more malleable, heroic even.

TWENTY-SEVEN
The Birth a New Skill Quadrant

It's 2003. I've left western Massachusetts and returned to New Jersey. I've pruned my practice down so that I am no longer performing pediatric neurosurgery. I still can't shake the experience I had with Anthony, but I'm living with it. As Clint Eastwood as Dirty Harry Callahan once said, "A man's got to know his limitations."

I've realized that to be my best I need to focus on areas of neurosurgery that suit my temperament. Pediatrics doesn't align with it. And after pulling myself out of that all is lost experience, I am much more competent and confident. Today I marvel at the alacrity and aplomb that I approached my focused surgical niches after making that important and appropriate specialty choice. I found my groove and I honed it with rigor.

This night, I am in the middle of a craniotomy for a colloid cyst case. It is a benign viscous proteinaceous tumor about the size of a grape. It is blocking the fluid pathways of this patient's brain and is damaging his memory. If I can remove it completely, the thirty-four-year-old patient will be cured.

I have parted the frontal lobe tissue down to the ventricle, the cavity that houses the cystic fluid-filled tumor. I'm scrubbed without an assistant. Only the anesthesiologist, the scrub nurse and circulator are in the room. My partners are long gone from the bustle of the hospital day.

I open the ventricle and advance the two emery-board-sized malleable metallic spatula blades down to hold the brain tissue away and spread the field open for me. I bring in my microscope.

I have handled many of these cases, but I'm a little rusty as I haven't performed one since the end of my residency three years prior. I've been in this brain area a couple of times since I finished training, but not dealing with this particular lesion. As I ease into my seat and zoom in the microscope, I can't find the tumor. I scan from front to back and central to peripheral. It's just not there.

I pause.

What's going on here?

I begin to ask all of the objective factual questions silently to myself. Is this the right patient? YES. Am I on the correct side of the head? YES. Could something have happened since the scan and today when you did the surgery? Possible, but not likely. Okay, keep that on the list. Could you have punctured the cyst on your way in? Possible but unlikely. Okay, keep that one on the list. Am I looking in the wrong place? Maybe.

I keep my cool in silence. No one knows I am lost but me. I again scan from midline to the side, from the front to the back. The anatomy looks normal. The blood in my ears begins pulsating. Judging by this internal feeling, I know this unexpected Phere event is growing.

I get up from the chair and fold my arms to keep from contaminating my hands. I go back to the MRI scan on the wall. Let's step back and collect some macro objective information. The tumor is there. I see it. The scan was done two days ago. The cyst still has to be there. Think. Could I have punctured it? I would have had to be off by three or four centimeters with my entry point—miles in neurosurgery—but it's still a possibility. But the tumor is thick walled. And I had only my forceps opening the ventricle. That sort of implement would be hard pressed to pop that kind of tumor.

Why can't I find the cyst?

I go back under the microscope. Rescan. Nothing. Normal anatomy. Now I'm nervous. Really nervous.

Steadying my shake on the phone held to my ear, I ask the nurse to call my partner. Back in Massachusetts, my colleagues Kamal or Chris would have dropped everything and come to help. They were blood brothers to me. But they were four hours away and no longer my partners. They couldn't help.

I get on the phone with my new partner. I explain my predicament. Embarrassed, but knowing it's the right thing to do for my patient, I ask him to come in and take a look.

He tells me he's out having a nice dinner with his wife and that he won't come in. His attitude is basically "figure it out yourself." I'm shocked that's his point of view, but what can I say? I know he's out with his wife. That's why I did everything I could think of before I called him. Eventually he tells me to put a tubing in to bypass the fluid, leave the rest alone, and close. It's a solution, but not a great one. Because of the location of the tumor (or invisible tumor from my point of view) I'd have to place two drains, one on each side of his head to keep it from growing. Then he'd be dependent on the tubes for the rest of his life and still have pressure on his memory apparatus. The whole goal of the surgery was to relieve him of that pressure and leave no foreign substances that degrade over time in his body.

I ask the nurse to hang up the phone.

I walk back to the MRI with a new subjective truth about my partner and rethink my role here at this hospital. I haven't operated here all that often and I don't want to become one of "those surgeons" hospital staff have little faith in—the kind no one wants to be in the same OR with.

Back to the objective facts. I scan the film again. I have to keep it together. I have to get myself out of this jam because, at this moment, I realize I am the only one who can figure this out.

I go back to the microscope. I want to be mad at my partner, but I have to swallow it. There is no place for anger in an operating room. I back my retractor blades out. I announce to the room. "I'm a little disoriented here and I'm not seeing what I expected to see. We're going to take this slowly." I go into lecture mode—a neurosurgeon's coping mechanism I later learn I share with Sanjay Gupta, who calls it "narrating the room." As Gupta explained to me, something happens when you give voice to your thought process to others. When you explain your actions and decisions to others who share a common goal, it frees you up from the sense of being alone. Because you aren't alone. Everyone else in the operating room wants the same outcome you do and their concern and energy are on your side, processing the ways in which you are approaching the problem. This transparency almost magically leads to an insight.

No longer do I have a room of people I perceive to be judging me as the "lost" new guy in town. Now I have a bunch of fellow warriors intent on terminating that tumor. I show them each layer as I slowly dive down toward the ventricle. "Coronal suture, middle frontal gyrus here, midline here. Deep white matter here, ependymal of the ventricle here," I say reassuring myself.

I retrace every step aloud. I slide the blades in carefully as if it's the first time. I move the microscope to look south. I see that is not the way to go. I move my view to the north. I identify the thalamostriate vein and the choroid plexus as I did the last time, only this time it's aloud. I announce to the room that this is where the tumor should be.

The foramen looks just like it did the last time.

But at this moment, my gut tells me to head deeper. I listen to it. I move my forceps and spatula into the foramen. On the left side of the foramen is the fornix, a crucial structure in memory. I move my instrument more aggressively, with a little more decisiveness. I see a film, which looks more familiar. I dissect around it. I see the wall of the tumor, deeper than I had expected and smaller, but it's there. The size had thrown me off. This cyst is a third of the size I was accustomed to taking out in Pittsburgh. It was tucked deeper and slightly off the center than I'd seen it in the past.

"I got you, you little fucker." The room broke up and the tension was released.

The case went perfectly from then on. I removed it completely. And despite having that experience of being lost in a very straightforward surgery only two hours earlier, I walked out of the OR knowing that from then on I was the best neurosurgeon in the area. I was the "go-to" person all of my colleagues in the room would want to work with. They knew I wouldn't quit and I wasn't an egomaniac either.

It was a huge breakthrough for me. I learned through the humility of the experience and by being transparent I could think my way through it and figure it out. Not only did I grow, but I earned the staff's respect. I did that by not hiding my anxiety, but admitting to it and then using my Brain 2.0 to get me out of the mess.

This is how we can surface from the cold black water of the all is lost quadrant.

After we've lived inside the extraordinary world for a while with its endless unknowns, it slowly transforms into the world of the strange-familiar. We still don't have our territory figured out, but we have the subjective knowledge that we figured other unknowns in our life out before, so there's a favorable probability that we'll be able to figure out what to do about this difficult obstacle in front of us too.

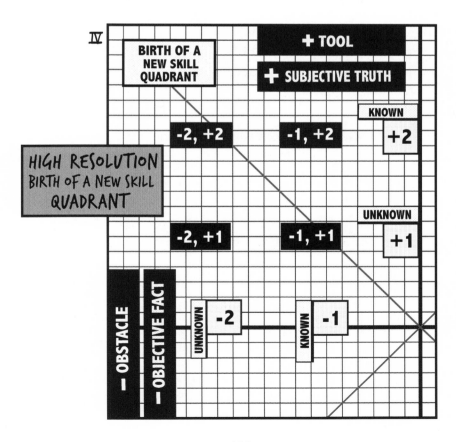

Here are the particular cells in the rise above the x-axis into the birth of a new skill quadrant.

Let's pick up our story about the young Harvard woman enrolled in Simons and Chabris' psychology experiment class. She's been assigned the task of heading into Harvard yard and convincing other students like herself to give up about an hour of their time to submit themselves as guinea pigs for Simons and Chabris' conformational testing of a phenomenon delineated in the 1970s by Ulric Neisser. She'll serve as the experimenter and will walk the subjects through the gorilla suit experiment.

After a passage into the all is lost quadrant upon her first arrival, our young Harvard woman has built up an understanding of the new territory in which she's found herself. She knows where to eat, where to sleep, where to go to class, where to do her laundry, where to find a friendly face, etc. By no means has she mastered the "Harvard game," but she's got enough of it figured out that she can turn her Brain 2.0 to serve more important micro goals than just feeling relatively comfortable. After half of a semester, she now has a bit of surplus cognitive energy.

However, the obstacles set before her—to convince self-absorbed collegians (potential subjects) to drop everything and agree to be used so that she can advance in class—are formidable. These subjects are both known and unknown obstacles. Plus, the environment is still foreign to her and the motivations of the people she's encountering are unknown too. But, in all likelihood, these subjects' goals are in direct opposition to her goals. They're on their way to something important to them and will not be interested in abandoning their goal-directed paths in order to serve hers.

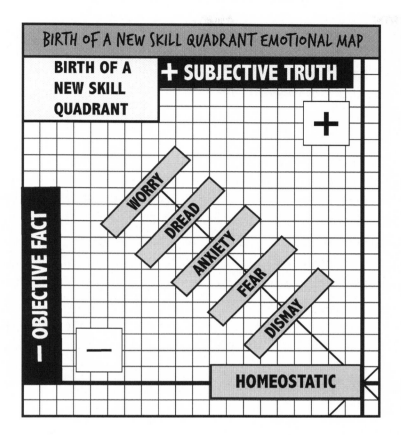

Here is the emotional map of what she's experiencing in this fourth quadrant.

So why doesn't she run back to her dorm room, pull the blankets over her head and hope to God that nobody notices she didn't complete the assignment? Chances are, she probably did that for a day or two after she'd been given her assignment as an experimenter. But now, enough is enough, and she's decided that she's not a wimp and she'll trust that her past experience dealing with these sorts of challenges and getting through them are going to prove useful for this problem.

Her subjective experience solving difficult problems is a known tool. She was so effective solving these kinds of problems before that she was admitted to one of the top colleges in the country. Why not rely upon that truth to get her through this problem?

Our Harvard experimenter reminds herself of her mission—to do well in her class, ideally get an "A." In order to achieve that goal she has to attain a micro goal to do well in this segment of the class. What she expects to happen is that she'll be able to walk into Harvard yard and simply ask a "nice" looking person to help her out. Because everyone at Harvard puts "learning" above everything else, she'll be able to get volunteers without too much trouble. Plus, the professors have told her that they'll give the volunteers large bars of chocolate in return for their time. So the motivational "being" goal of "being one who supports the advancement of science" and the "having" goal of getting a nice big bar of chocolate ought to do the trick. Her job is to just clearly state the request and the inducements on the table to get the subjects to come along.

What she discovers is that her projected fantasy about how easy it will be to get people to drop everything and go with her to another part of campus, spend forty-five minutes with her and her colleagues, just for a large candy bar and the "good feelings about being an asset to science" isn't so easy.

And unexpected Phere events hit her with extraordinary frequency.

Person after person won't even make eye contact when she cordially and then forcefully asks, "Excuse me, sir?" Or, "Excuse me, miss?" These unknown beings objectively all look like fellow students but they're behaving so negatively she can't even be sure of that fact anymore. They just won't give her the time of day. With each blow-off, our Harvard experimenter grows more and more anxious. If she doesn't get volunteers, she won't do well in this part of the course. If she doesn't do well in this part of the course, she'll not do well in the entire course.... And so on.

To pull this scenario back to an abstraction, her mission is to contend with Pheres that are objective obstacles—either (-1) knowns (students she recognizes from her classes and her dorm) or (-2) unknowns (students and/or nonstudents she's never met before). She knows she has subjectively succeeded in solving this category of problem before. Back in high school she was in charge of getting volunteers for the annual blood drive and she'd been able to wrangle friends (+2) and strangers (+1) alike to sit in a chair and have a nurse prick them with a needle to take their blood. So even though her Brain 1.0 fires negative feedback to her every time she doesn't hook one of these unexpected Phere events to comply with her request, she presses onward because she knows the truth about herself. She'll figure out how to convince someone… eventually.

But her failure rate is extraordinary and the anxiety turns to fear of failing this part of the course, failing the course, and failing her ultimate desire to get her PhD. She can't seem to get anyone to listen to her. She freezes. Gets a dry mouth. Should she proceed as planned and just keep doing what she's doing? Or should she retreat and reassess what she's doing?

This scenario is a classic "sales call" panic situation.

And then she spots one of her classmates across the way, pulling in a live one. She watches and sees what her classmate is doing to draw people's attention. Her classmate is pushing the reward… "Get a free sixteen-ounce chocolate bar!" to get people's attention and then springing the hidden cost on the stranger once they perk up and ask about the freebie. She doesn't feel comfortable doing that. So, she asks her Brain 2.0 to think about what she might do that would not make her have to push the chocolate but give her a better chance at scoring a subject.

Her Brain 2.0 goes into overdrive. It comes up with a whole list of micro tasks to perform that could increase the probability of success. She sorts through the list and picks two tasks to employ, with the expectation that they'll be the special sauce to bring her what she wants—someone to watch the Invisible gorilla video and answer some questions.

She decides to only pick out people she thinks look like "nice," reasonable and friendly people who'd be fun to have a cup of coffee with. And then she decides that instead of trying to get them to hear her from the periphery, she'll actually step into their path, sort of block the path but not be so nasty about blocking it that they can't easily sidestep and keep moving.

And then she'll simply ask them a question.

And, what do you know, in the still strange environs of Harvard yard, she's able to approach a friendly looking young man, get his attention, and then ask him a question. She's bootstrapped a new skill, one that will serve her during her quest to ace her psychology course and move her one step closer to a degree in psychology, but also one that will help her get what she wants in a host of other life categories. The nice looking young man agrees to go with her, and after they've finished the protocol he asks her out for coffee. She does so and finds out that they grew up only a few towns away from each other. They agree to meet up later in the library.

Life spent in this strange-familiar quadrant of Phere slowly morphs, through the acquisition of more and more skills, back around into the familiar-familiar. And in that realm our young woman's gifts find their best expression. She shines and gets that feeling there's nothing coming her way that she can't turn into a tool to achieve her PhD in psychology.

Until, of course, she actually receives that PhD. And down into the familiar-strange she goes again.

This Harvard woman's four-quadrant movement from one to two to three to four and around again represents what Carl Jung described and Joseph Campbell delineated into stages as the "hero's journey." Simply stated, the hero is a person called to adventure. That call requires her to leave her ordinary/familiar/known world and step into the extraordinary/ unfamiliar/unknown world. Now through a series of problematic tests, she figures out how to express herself creatively. Her creative actions contribute to her professors' experiment, which shifts the way a large number of people view the world. Once our hero learns that she has a gift for psychological research and figures out how to express that gift, she returns to the familiar world again. Harvard has now transformed from extraordinary to familiar. She shares her gift in that now familiar environment.

But once that gift has been expressed consistently and effectively to such a degree that it becomes second nature to her—i.e., it flows from her with little cognitive energy—our heroic woman must venture into the extraordinary/unfamiliar/unknown world again in order to birth new skills.

Here is that progression again:

Quadrant I: Familiar–Familiar–Flow: Proceed with global, mid-level, and micro goal-directed behavior with minimal retreat/reassessment unless a catastrophic "black swan" Phere arises. (More on this in the chapter about Carla.)

Quadrant II: Familiar–Strange–Calm before the storm: Proceed with Global Goal Resolution and then retreat and reassess new global goal and its underlying mid-level and micro goals. Level up your global goal and prepare for leaving your home territory to pursue it.

Quadrant III: Strange–Strange–All is lost: Proceed with fundamental micro goals to familiarize with new territory. When inevitable failure and foolishness arise, branch into mid-level goal acquisitions. Don't cascade upward or conclude that the new global goal is impossible to achieve. Realize you are in a chaotic environment and you need to preserve cognitive energy in order to think clearly without emotional floods constantly overwhelming you. Here you must identify and extinguish poor coping strategies of avoidance and distraction. When the emotional flood comes anyway, realize you're exactly where you should be. Hang on. This too will pass.

Quadrant IV: Strange–Familiar–Birth a new skill: Proceed with mid-level goals directed toward larger global goals by reassessing Brain 2.0's toolbox. Retreat and reassess when obstacles arise and then proceed trying new tactics until a fresh new tool emerges. Do not run away but press on and know you've been here before and you'll be here again. It's how we learn.

We discussed the hero's journey, which Carl Jung-defined as a lifelong struggle to create a meaningful life. Joseph Campbell later popularized it in his seminal book *The Hero with a Thousand Faces*. The hero sets out on an adventure to accomplish a task and then finds her way back home more experienced and more skilled. This four-quadrant Phere navigation is the process by which you undertake that journey using your cognitive faculties. You simply do that by listening intently to your Brain 1.0's fear signals, which will tell you exactly what kind of Phere you need to contend with. Then you use your Brain 2.0 to break that Phere into two pieces—the objective factual piece and the subjective truthful piece. Those pieces in turn can be categorized as knowns or unknowns and then as tools or obstacles. Knowing the essence of the Phere converts it into something you can think through and manage using the top of your value hierarchy as a guide.

This movement, over time, looks like this:

Let me circle back to the opening of this chapter.

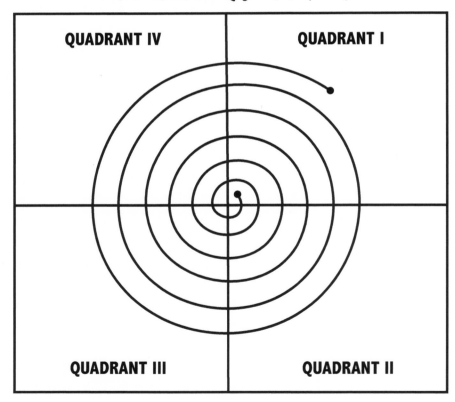

THE HEROIC JOURNEY

QUADRANT IV	**QUADRANT I**
QUADRANT III	**QUADRANT II**

In my colloid cyst operation, I experienced a very troubling unexpected Phere event. I knew where to look in the brain for the tumor, but I couldn't find it. The location and appearance of this particular tumor were different from my previous catalogue of experiences with this sort of pathology. Forced to step a little out of my comfort zone to dig deeper with my Brain 2.0, I used my subjective past procedural memory and narrated the room. That process allowed me to birth a new skill set. I now had another step to follow when I found myself struggling to locate tumors—and a successful story to back it up.

When I had the breakthrough, the experience was a different kind of high than the flow I experienced when I worked on Dr. Jannetta's patient. I did not have the superhero confidence or "can't miss" experience from quadrant one. Instead, at the end of the operation, I felt relief and mental exhaustion. Acting in a way consistent with courage (feeling intense fear and acting anyway) and dampening Brain 1.0's fear signal is liberating and enlightening. But it is also exhausting.

You'll know when you've birthed a new skill because you'll be ready to rest.

PART THREE

Practicing Cognitive Dominance

TWENTY-EIGHT
What We Need

It's 9:38 a.m. on a cold Saturday in January. I'm sitting shotgun in my wife Julie's truck parked outside the front of the school. I'm trying to stay warm while I'm waiting for a Trenton school bus to pick up me and my youth wrestling team.

The dichotomy between the towns of Princeton and Trenton has always fascinated me. Princeton, in my mind, is a twenty-first-century mini Athens with all kinds of intellectual resources at your fingertips. It's a community of people with the necessities under control, striving to stretch themselves. But just twelve miles down the road is Trenton, a prideful blue-collar town with far more fundamental needs at the forefront of that community's mind. Managing the duel challenges of poverty and violence is the standard operating procedure. I was drawn to Trenton to start up a youth wrestling program because I found the structure and discipline inherent in the game a great escape from other external and internal challenges. It was my dream to build a Trenton youth wrestling program just as I had created one in Princeton sixteen years earlier.

Wrestling was my sport as a kid and it helped me in innumerable ways. Among other things, I believe the sport instills a goal-oriented operating system into kids' brains that enables them to pursue excellence throughout their lives. It taught me just how much strength I have inside me (and that all people have that potential strength inside of them too) and how to summon that strength on demand. That's why I'm so committed to coaching the sport. The more kids who get a feel for what power they possess internally, the more of them will summon that power and change the world.

I also reasoned that Trenton parents would jump at the chance to get their kids involved in an activity that could keep them off the streets and away from gangs. A lot of them did, but due to unexpected events I hadn't planned for, many simply couldn't.

But alas, idling in the car with Julie I realized I'd overscheduled the day. Unlike my surgical planning, which I plot out down to the second, when I'm wearing my coach's hat, I'm more of a ready, shoot, aim kind of a planner. I like to pile stuff on. So, in the early morning, I had a radio interview to do about cognitive dominance, and then I would go to Trenton to pick up the team with Julie. Then we'd bring my Trenton kids back to Princeton for the meet. Then after the meet, I would accompany the Trenton team back home. Tight, but doable!

The bus ride was a very important part of the experience. I remembered back in my early wrestling days just how nervous I'd get moving from the territory of my home school onto a bus and then ending up in some alien arena across town. And eventually across the state and country. The bus is the transitional period that can play with a young person's mind. He or she can lose their inner fortitude just on a six-mile trip. They would move from the familiar into the strange-familiar. I began coaching the Trenton kids three years earlier and while they were certainly physically ready for the meet, they needed some reassurance mentally.

In Princeton my vision had come to fruition fairly easily. There was a thriving youth program now in place with a dozen outstanding coaches and engaged volunteer parents. The kids coming out of the program were stellar, not just on the mat but academically and socially too. Many attended great colleges and some of them had even continued the sport at that elite level. I was proud of my involvement in creating something that could stand on its own without me. Now it was time for me to do the same in Trenton.

But I was struggling.

While our fledgling club was making some inroads, I had encountered many more challenges in getting the new program established. Because the schools in Trenton were so spread out, transportation was a major obstacle. We couldn't have practices at night, either, as we did in Princeton. And because of my surgical and office hour schedule, the evening was the only time I could regularly commit to coaching. Add on that the sport is very physically and mentally grueling—there is no way to wrestle at 70 percent effort—we had a lot of attrition as the grind of the season rolled on.

But my biggest challenge was getting the parents to buy in and support the program, something that was easy for me in Princeton. Even when I brought in an Olympic gold medalist to teach a clinic in downtown Trenton, the local turnout was marginal. I had a hard time understanding why.

A few superstar parents in Trenton had embraced the program and were getting involved, but they were few and far between. And we would need a lot more of them to begin hosting meets, manning scoring tables, and organizing logistics if we wanted to stay in the league. The lack of engagement just didn't make any sense to me. Why wouldn't a parent support a program that teaches and reinforces hard work, dedication, and grit?

The bus arrived and I took my spot at the top of the stairs, next to the driver. A twelve-year-old boy climbed the steps of the school bus. I gave him a big smile as I noticed he was the first one onboard two weeks in a row. I met him with a handshake and plopped a banana in his hand.

"Good morning, sir. Remember, what you put in the fuel tank will affect how you perform."

Julie had loaded me up with a care package of bagels and bananas. She'd noticed the Doritos and Skittles the kids were eating after practices and took it upon herself to change up that routine, especially just before a meet.

"Coach? Will you sit with me?"

My heart stirred. "Sure, Ricardo. I'd love to. Let me get everyone checked in and I'll come back. What do you want to talk about?"

"Anything," he replied.

Over my many years of coaching at Princeton and learning from Julie's amazing example, I consciously worked to engage kids in conversation. I'd developed a knack for building a dialogue with them based on mutual respect and they'd responded better than most adults. I sat down next to Ricardo.

"Hey, what are you looking at?"

Ricardo fiddled with his smart phone.

"If you want to have a conversation, you need to put that away. I want eye contact." I smiled. He put the phone in his bag.

I peppered him with my standard series of school and wrestling-related questions: "Do you know who Pythagoras was? What did you learn today? What's going to be your first move off bottom?" The previous bus conversation we'd had was about the difference between a goal and an objective. Ricardo loved to get into it.

We arrived on campus in time for the annual Tiger Classic, a youth meet held in historic Dillon Gym at Princeton University. The match went flawlessly. The kids were getting the wrestling "bug" and they executed the moves they had learned with daring and energy. They were scoring and often winning matches. Best of all, they were smiling. At the close of the match I was flying high after another week of progress on the mats. And I was even more thrilled that an event I had created sixteen years ago was now part of my old and new programs. I knew the more parents who experienced the thrill of seeing their kids work hard and achieve, the more momentum we'd build.

At the end of the wrestling match all the teams celebrated with a pizza party in the back of the gym. Our Trenton kids had a blast but they were getting tired and rambunctious. A little push here and a little shoving there told me it was time to head back to the familiar. They had started their day at 10 a.m. and it was now 4 p.m. They were ready to head home.

The only problem was there was no sign of the bus and I couldn't get the driver on his cell phone. I became anxious.

"Well don't they have an emergency line?" I asked a fellow coach. We were using a Trenton bus company offering a price that was within our tight budget, but we didn't count on the unreliability.

At 4:30 p.m., there was still no sign of the bus and the previously well-behaved kids were running all over the gym. They had nothing to do. A football game broke out. It was a great way to pass the time, but I began to worry about what would happen if somebody fell and fractured a wrist? Or got a concussion? This was not what the kids were there for. I had to bite the bullet and allow the game. It would be torture to make them just sit in a group and await further instructions.

A few Trenton parents had attended the meet and were helping out. Some drove their own cars and had left after the pizza party with their children. A few more had ridden the bus with us and were lingering with the rest of the crowd. But based upon my calculations, we had at least twenty kids who had no parents present, and I was responsible for all of them.

I began calling a list of backup companies, including two limo companies I'd done business with. My contacts had buses but no licensed drivers available. The two other local companies were trying to track down a driver.

By 5 p.m. I was worried. I didn't have a bus, there was no sign of the original bus, and it was getting dark.

I began to ponder how this scenario might play out and began to sweat. We had picked these kids up at three different schools, which were our rendezvous points. Most of them lived a few blocks from their school and had walked to school to catch our bus. Now I started to realize that if I didn't get these kids back to their school soon, it would be dark when we dropped them off. Would it be safe for them to walk back home in the dark?

Thank God Julie was helping out today because we were short on coaches. She and I were figuring out how to solve this problem when a cold, hard rain began to fall.

"Mark, Jamal is a third grader," Julie said. "His eleven-year-old brother is keeping an eye on him but there's no parent here for them. What are you going to do when we get the boys back to school?"

I didn't know. I didn't even have a bus yet. "We may have to carpool them back." Julie pointed out the impracticality of that with twenty kids. But she added, "We better get going if that's what we need to do."

It was a poor option, and it would take a long time. Between Julie, our assistant coach, and me we would have to make at least ten trips. It was a twenty-minute car ride. The math didn't add up. We needed a bus.

Then the assistant coach of the university walked in to begin setting up for the college meet that was to follow ours. He had the number of a bus company in New Brunswick. I called. These guys were the real deal with a fleet of vehicles and an available driver. I hung up the phone. A bus was on its way. Now we had to figure out how to get these kids home.

"We need all hands on deck. Julie and Matt (my assistant coach), I need you to follow me down to Trenton behind the bus. I need your help making sure these kids get delivered to the front doors of their houses. We can't just drop them off at the school. It's too late."

The rain poured. The entire team huddled outside the gym under the portico, waiting. The bus had made it to campus but now the driver was lost. I chastised him for not following directions.

I am an extremely precise person, and I expect excellence from myself and from people around me, even when it's not a life-and-death matter. I can be unforgiving when I see performance less than perfection. It's a major weakness.

Here I was yelling at this bus driver who was bailing me out, demanding that he get to the gym in an unfamiliar area at night in the rain.

The condescending arrogant neurosurgeon tone is inappropriate in nearly every circumstance. But I can't always suppress it, especially after a long Saturday preceded by a tough work week.

And then out of the darkness and mist appeared the luxurious stretch coach bus. It was a sight for sore eyes. But it was never meant to be on the campus's narrow winding roads and it now faced the wrong direction to get us out of here.

First, I apologized to the driver. Then he did an incredible job and turned the large bus around in the tiny space. Now with the bus turned around and on the safe side of the street, we boarded. The kids were accustomed to utilitarian school buses and had never ridden in something like this before. I stood at the front of the bus and saw their eyes light up as they climbed in. They weren't mad or upset. They were excited. A few were carrying soaking wet pizza boxes that contained leftovers from the party.

Ricardo climbed on. He looked tired. Our eyes met. Today had been an adventure and now we were finally heading home. I summoned a grin to let him know we'd made it.

When we arrived at our original pickup point at the school, I told the kids we would walk each of them home. As they walked off the bus Julie directed where they would go. We had contacted some of the parents, who were waiting in their cars. Others had no parents there. Julie, Matt and I divided up the assignments to get the kids delivered home safely.

Ricardo came up to me and tactfully got my attention.

"I can walk home alone," he offered. "I don't need somebody to come with me."

"No way, Ricardo. I made sure I'd be the one to get to walk you home." Is there anything better than a twelve-year-old smile?

We walked nine blocks to Ricardo's house. As we approached, I imagined a scene similar to the one from my own childhood when I'd get home at dusk. Warm yellow lights would be streaming out from the kitchen. The smell of Mom's dinner would waft out when I opened the front door...

Instead, we faced a dark house. Surrounded by frigid black rain puddles, the front door was locked. Ricardo pulled out the phone he'd buried in his bag that morning. He pressed a few buttons. Then a light turned on and Ricardo's sister cracked open the door to let him in.

I thought I would get them safely home and then they'd be warm, dry, fed and safe. I gave Ricardo one last smile before his door clicked shut.

It took one of my former wrestlers who grew up in Trenton, now pursuing his PhD at George Mason University, to explain to me why it was far more difficult to get parental buy-in like I had in Princeton.

"Parents are more focused on keeping the heat on in their house and getting the rent paid. They're not thinking about the camaraderie of a wrestling team. It's not high on their priority list. They're just trying to survive."

Obviously, I coach for selfish reasons too. The ones I teach end up teaching me.

What do we need to make our way in the world? If we had to boil life's mysteries down to fundamental goals to attain, what would they be?

Psychologist and a founding member of the humanistic school of psychology (which focused on exploring fundamental motivations that drive human behavior) Abraham Maslow came up with a theory in 1943 to answer these questions. He called it the Hierarchy of Needs. It's a simple pyramid of five requirements to survive, strive and even thrive in our environment. Maslow theorized that attaining satisfaction of each need would command our primary frame of reference until such time as it was satisfied. Once it was taken care of (the person got what was needed within a specific category), the person would work up to the next level of need and pursue its satisfaction.

There's a lot of debate about the details of Maslow's theories, but as an overall guide to the progression of how Brain 1.0 and Brain 2.0 work to solve the too-much-information problem in order to attain a generally satisfied existence, it's extraordinarily helpful.

It looks like this:

ABRAHAM MASLOW'S HIERARCHY OF NEEDS

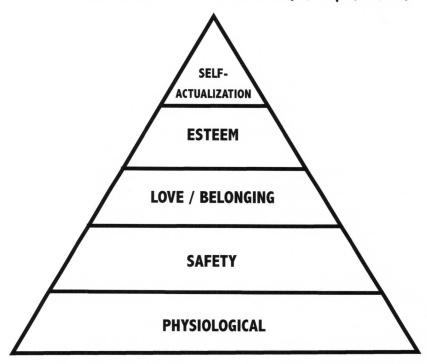

SELF-
ACTUALIZATION

ESTEEM

LOVE / BELONGING

SAFETY

PHYSIOLOGICAL

The floor of the Hierarchy of Needs is physiological. These needs would include our bodies' requirements for air, proper regulation of body temperature, water, sleep, food, and excretion in that order of priority. Just pure external survival needs. Getting these needs met first is Brain 1.0's bottom line. And it motivates Brain 2.0 to put them at the very top of the priority list with heavy doses of emotion. The microsecond these needs come under threat, in some unexpected Phere event or events, Brain 1.0 shoots very large doses of negative affect (fear) to our bodies and Brain 2.0. These necessities will lead to death if left unattained, so all other needs above the physiological ones take a back seat until they are met. These Trenton parents were tightly focused on these needs first…before they could add on anything else for their children.

Brain 1.0 is the sentry between our internal and external environments, zeroing in on every Phere that threatens our survival and places the primal level of need at the top of its priority.

The next floor up is the need for safety, a multifaceted requirement with its own levels and micro levels of satisfaction that extends through time and space.

The need for personal safety is primary. If our own lives are threatened by another being or an impending environmental crisis, Brain 1.0 treats that reality as Code Blue. If a tiger or a serial killer is on the loose in our neighborhood or we're in a cave with a limited reserve of air that is slowly being depleted, our personal safety is threatened in a short window of time. The longer the window of time our safety is threatened (we're all going to die, but that's a larger time frame that we can effectively understand) the less Brain 1.0 fires fear.

After our individual bodies are safe, the need for safety for our most intimate relationships is next. If we're an infant, our mother is primary. Without her, we won't survive so when we don't see her, we worry for her safety. Next would be our father, siblings, relatives, friends and so on. If we're the mother or father, we work to put our children's safety before our own.

The need for our community/group/tribe's safety is next up the pyramid. If we're in the marching band and the school board threatens to cancel the program, all of us in the band see that development as a disaster and thus we all get together to save the program.

Higher and higher levels of identification with larger and larger groups take the safety need to its limits—from town identification to state and ethnicity to country, all the way up to Homo sapiens as a species. Our safety need is met only as far as these units' safety are also being met.

Safety issues extend into the metaphysical too.

If it is unsafe to express one's thoughts, beliefs, and opinions, Brain 1.0 takes notice and pushes Brain 2.0's negative emotion. The social constructs that create a sense of safety, like individual rights and law and order, are crucial to the individual attaining his or her need for safety. If one metaphysical need trumped all others, it would be authenticity, both empirical (objective fact) and metaphysical (subjective truth).

Securing authenticity (a bond between an internal commitment to perpetuating a particular value and externally acting in support of that value) is crucial for our sanity. Authenticity is the realm of the objective and subjective in harmony. We need everyone to express what they hold to be true (their highest value) so all subjective value systems and their individual frames of reference can be thrown into a vast metaphysical ocean of observation and experience. If we all seek authenticity, more unknowns become known. More light shines into the darkness. You can see how important it is then to consciously choose what to hold as the pinnacle of your value hierarchy.

What you'll find is that the higher you move up the pyramid, the more influential the metaphysical (internal mind) needs become. So, the essential state of being at the bottom of the pyramid is reflective of core Brain 1.0 processes, and as we travel further and further up the pyramid, we get more into the Brain 2.0 determinative structures.

The middle of the pyramid, the need for love, is the transitional need that is part physical and part metaphysical. Our love need connotes a combination plate of Brain 1.0 and Brain 2.0 working together in a complex way. The need for sexual expression is biologically driven. It's a primal need embedded in our DNA. If we don't reproduce, we die off as a species. And since primal needs are the realm of Brain 1.0, sexual desire comes with extreme emotional release. But it is not without metaphysical character too, or all of us would couple indiscriminately and monogamy would seem ridiculous. Sex would then simply be a bodily function like breathing or eating.

The metaphysical need to commune sexually requires subjective truth attached to it. Objectively, we all know how important sex is. Without it, the human race would not survive. So, the objective truth is that sex is positive because it is the means by which we reproduce. But subjectively, the sex and love combination is extremely complex. It requires a Brain 2.0 function on top of the Brain 1.0. We all understand the biological need for sex, but what of the need for "love." What's that about?

Perhaps love is about becoming "known," belonging to something larger than oneself. It's a need to find a being that can be relied upon as a consistent truthful force.

Becoming "known" is a process that reveals the myriad parts of oneself to another in such a way that the other person accepts and appreciates both our potential and limitations, with empathy and care. Acceptance and being known requires a shared value system, though. If what I believe to be true and what you believe to be true are not similar, conflict is inevitable. So, knowing our own bottom-line core value system is critical to our ability to manage all of our other higher rung needs. Sex is a "having" goal while love is a "being" goal.

The next level on the pyramid is the need for esteem, a metaphysical quality. We all want other people to have a high opinion of us. When they do, our lives go more smoothly. The path to esteem also relies upon other shared beliefs. It begins with our conception of what we believe in and how well we've held true to that belief in the progression of our lives. If our actions match our beliefs and we have faith that our beliefs are objectively and subjectively "true," we can achieve our need for self-esteem. Self-esteem is a "being" goal.

However, the siren song of third-party esteem (those in our lives tangential to our secondary attachment group, i.e., our family and closest friends) is a very heady melody. We want those not connected to us to admire us. We want their esteem too. Oftentimes the desire to get that third-party validation can blind us to the most important need in this slice of the pyramid, and that is self-esteem, a holistic appreciation of our own being. Without self-esteem we're in trouble metaphysically.

We don't "feel right" about ourselves and so we ask that big Brain 2.0 to use its keen analytical toolbox to determine what is wrong with us. We then spend a lot of time fixing the "what is wrong with us" punch list from our Brain 2.0, always hoping to achieve that elusive combination of self-esteem, family-approval esteem (second party) and what we consider the big win, third-party validation. However, that search for esteem outside of our core system (our self) can derail us time and time again. We lose the "being" forest for the trees of third-party validation.

When we get off course, we sacrifice our focus on our fundamental belief about the world, the thing that makes sense of the entire hierarchy of our values, in order to attain the micro goals necessary to get our lower needs taken care of. We cheat on a test to get into the best college, and then cheat in college to get the best job, and then we cheat in the job to get into the executive suite thinking that once we get there we'll get the third-party validation necessary to complete our pyramid and reach nirvana. However, we soon find that too much is never enough. We don't find our attainments meaningful because they are not serving a higher value or purpose.

Alas, unless our core belief aligns with the notion that the world is a zero-sum game, the goal in life is to be recognized as the best player in the game, and to be the best player means getting the most prizes and the most material goods no matter the cost or method, we find ourselves unsatisfied. Troubled. Often that trouble leads to personal turmoil and ultimately despair.

But if instead our core belief is that the world is an environment made up of extraordinary potential and not a zero-sum game of consumption, we can find meaning. This creative value system puts forth that the best way to navigate the world is to work to move environmental potential into the realm of actuality. If a fundamental truth says human creation is the primary reason for us being here, it's possible to make "something" that remains in the world after we've left. So creating the something that only we can create is the reason we're here.

This approach is the opposite of consuming the greatest share before there's "nothing" left. It replaces *getting my fair share before there is nothing left* as the top-of-the-pyramid operating principle with *working to create something to leave behind for the next generation*. I put forth that there is far more prescriptive meaning to the latter idea than the former. Something is better than nothing.

Whether they consciously know it or not, our two students in Harvard yard who helped Simon and Chabris with their invisible gorilla experiment share the "something" value system. Our experimenter believes the psychology investigation she's participating in will aid in the production of universal knowledge about the human condition. It's a belief the young man shares or he would find the attractive young woman's core "unattractive." If he didn't share the belief in the notion that the purpose of going to Harvard is to increase the probability of creating something that lasts longer than the life of an individual, her silly experiment would be nothing to him. While he may be objectively and physically attracted to her and he'd be willing to go through the motions in order to trick her into spending time with him, the two value systems would inevitably clash. His desire to find true love with her would fail.

This brings me to the next level up on Maslow's hierarchy—the need for self-actualization. Maslow believed that the purpose of life is creation. The meaning we seek is revealed in the active work we do to create things. So, it makes sense that he put self-actualization at the top of his pyramid of needs. It's the ultimate thing he believed we all need. It's finding the thing the individual self is supposed to "do" on Earth... and once the individual discovers that thing, her ability to realize that work (actualize it) is how she satisfies the need at the top of the pyramid.

An actualized person, someone doing the work she was meant to do, would by Maslow's theory find life on Earth more meaningful and have a higher level of Brain 1.0 positive emotion. Put another way, she'd find her experiences more meaningful as they contribute to her eventual discovery of her purpose. Meaning thereby contributes positive emotion. **The paradox is that finding meaning in life requires the courage to tangle with the negative emotions inherent in the hero's journey—especially the all is lost negative state of quadrant three.**

So, we've sort of backed into the highest need necessary for human beings—the big kahuna need that will direct the global value system of the individual. This is a need for meaning, a belief in something as opposed to a belief in nothing.

It is important to accept that it is very reasonable to believe in nothing, especially in the twenty-first century. Some very intelligent people see the world as a random series of events with no baked in "meaning" to it. They are not necessarily malcontents either. They simply see all life on Earth as a grand accident and subscribe to the value system that the role of the individual is to make the best of things here. The less suffering for everyone the better. And the path to less suffering is personally held values and a code of ethics and morality that puts the reduction of suffering as its primary focus. That's actually believing in something, even though these "nonbelievers" would argue otherwise.

Those who truly believe in nothing are the ones your Brain 1.0 must be attuned to. These are the nihilists who find the fact that there is suffering (and plenty of it) on Earth as a sign that not only is there no meaning to be had, but that human life itself is not just meaningless but malevolent. In their eyes, the whole planet would be better off if humanity was tightly controlled or eradicated. The belief in nothing, meaning it would be better if we were nothing rather than something, is a serious problem.

The problem with the belief that humanity is meaningless is that we are biologically programmed to act out our beliefs. We require a consonance between our internal beliefs and external behavior. If we believe the truth of one thing and are forced, coerced or induced to act out its opposite (put into a state called cognitive dissonance), we must somehow reconcile the system.

We have to return to cognitive consonance, a state when our highest belief works in concert with our external actions.

Either we adjust our beliefs to match our actions (this is usually what we do) or we refuse to act as instructed so that we don't betray our beliefs. This latter choice is extraordinarily difficult as it requires Brain 2.0 to suffer Brain 1.0's alarm system firing at its highest level every waking (and probably sleeping) moment. We'll explore the evidence for cognitive dissonance in the next chapter.

Because we face the confounding knowledge that our lives are limited and that they will inevitably cease (the dilemma of death), Maslow put forth that our highest need is to understand the meaning of our life. If not understand it, we must at least have a singular definition that works for our singular purpose. At the minimum, at the most boiled down, we will either believe there is meaning to our life or there isn't meaning to our life.

Either one of those will "work" as a guiding principle. Committing to believing in "creating something" or "the depletion of the world to nothing" guides our actions. We simply need to believe in something, even if that belief is that there is nothing. This belief in something versus nothing or nothing versus something will give your Brain 2.0 and Brain 1.0 a global operating principle to navigate the world. That is, it will give you the mechanism to evaluate the positive or negative nature of things (judge and assign value) and beings that pop up in your life that you didn't see coming (unexpected Phere events).

This is obviously why subscribing to a particular religious doctrine can be such a tremendously helpful choice. When you don't know what to do about something or someone, you can move on up to the top of the pyramid of your needs and the possible choices available to you based upon how they would affect your adherence to a core belief. And as the core beliefs are strictly laid out for you in a religious affiliation, you always have something to refer to. The problem with that, of course, is in the fallibility of "totalitarian and comprehensive" dogma.

For example, if an authority figure (someone higher up on your chosen territorial hierarchy of competence) says you'll get ahead at work and they will guarantee you are never found out if you agree to lie about something, and you're not sure how to handle that situation, you reference the top of your need pyramid, the need to believe in X in order to feel as if you are acting consistently.

If you believe that lying is a negative action because it inhibits the proper way to create a positive world, you just align your action with that belief and pass on the opportunity to rise in company rank at the expense of your belief. You'll positively benefit in gaining a clear indication that this working environment is not the best place for you, but negatively you'll need to get that résumé together and look for another place to work.

Or if you believe the ends justify the means and getting the most out of life for yourself is fundamental, you'll have no problem taking up the offer. Your belief in the limitations of the world's resources allows you to do what's necessary to secure the most for yourself. And your actions do not conflict with that belief by "lying." You'll see the "lie" as a tool, not an obstacle.

While self-actualization was something Maslow defined in terms of his belief in the potential of the world and our mission to create as a means to free that positive potential, the "something" value system still works as a concept for those who believe in the opposite. For those who believe the world is in the process of degenerating, meaning there are limited resources on Earth and because their consumption is inevitable, the best strategy is to position oneself at the top of the consumption chain in order to secure the richest life possible, that process—rising to the top of the material world—is what self-actualization means for those who believe in the "nothing" value system.

Our biology (the way our brains function) is such that we envision goals according to our frame of reference. Our frames of reference are determined by our value system. If we were to categorize value systems all the way up the chain of belief, we would arrive at a fundamental bedrock choice that boils down to a binary question.

Do you believe life means something? Or do you believe there is no meaning to life, and the random nature of existence reduces it to meaninglessness and nothingness in its finality—death?

Something or nothing. That's your fundamental choice.

It's important to make a choice between those two core beliefs. Because if you do not choose one, you will be rudderless when it comes to generating goals and evaluating how close you are to attaining them. You will live in chaos. Not to mention the fact that Brain 1.0's messages to Brain 2.0 will be muddled and far more difficult to categorize and comprehend without a core value system. The longer Brain 2.0 takes to engage with the unexpected Phere events that Brain 1.0 brings to its attention…you guessed it, the more fear bears down on our bodies and minds. When fear is allowed to circle back and forth in ever-increasing levels of negative feedback, it is more difficult not to succumb to fear freak-out and retreat into numbing familiarity.

When we panic, we retreat into what we know, the familiar…anything to escape chaos. We're unwilling to step into the dark of the unknown because the guidewire (our value system) that we could use to pull us back into order has been severed.

When we flee from fear, our world contracts. We stay inside our neighborhood. When difficult unexpected Phere events pop up in our neighborhood, we stay inside our house. And when difficult unexpected Phere events pop up in our house, we retreat to our bedroom. And eventually we find it difficult just to get out of bed.

TWENTY-NINE
Proximal Control Leads to Micro Flow

To Carla's college roommate, her mid-morning on-the-couch stupor seemed like symptoms of a hangover after a late night of partying. As she lay there, though, it became alarmingly evident that her breathing was way out of whack—giant suck-ins of air followed by little movement and then more violent suck-ins.

She shook her friend to wake her up.

"Carla! Carla!" No response. It was as if Carla was in the middle of the ocean diving into deep water, only to reluctantly return to the surface every now and then to get a gulp or two more of air, and then back down she would go. There was no waking her up from her dream diving.

After the 911 call, it took the paramedics just fifteen minutes to get Carla into the emergency room where I'd been called in from the road for a consult.

After a quick examination and review of preliminary studies, the diagnosis was clear to me. A blood vessel in Carla's brain had burst and the leaking blood was pooling inside her brain, putting pressure on every system inside, critically the brainstem's regulation of her automatic breathing and circulation.

I pressed my thumb hard just above Carla's right eyebrow, a maneuver that evokes intense pain, transmitting powerful direct stimulation to the consciousness center deep inside the brain. Supraorbital pressure, the technical name for it, is like a triple shot of espresso injected into the brainstem to try and awaken a patient to gauge the level of arousal or consciousness. She winced, weakly gave a guttural groan, and blindly swiped her arm out to stop me.

There was still hope, but not more than thirty minutes of it.

I grabbed the emergency physician by the arm.

"Dave, intubate her NOW! She's not protecting her airway. She needs to go to the OR ASAP."

As the rapidly mounting pressure in Carla's brain was impairing her ability to swallow and breathe regularly, Dave inserted a tube into Carla's windpipe to assist her breathing and then inflated the circular balloon it contained in its wall to fasten it and to prevent saliva from clogging up her lungs. The procedure was completed in four minutes.

The next order of business was to get more precise information about the location of the bleeding inside Carla's head. She had to be whisked back to the radiological suite for a specialized CT scan. Surgeons postulate and then eliminate as many possible unexpected Phere events from popping up and getting in their way when they're inside the body before they actually operate. *You don't want to be doing a lot of thinking in the operating room.* We want what we think will happen to happen with minimal surprises so we can enter a flow state. And for a brain surgeon, the CT scan helps us plot out a plan to make the most straightforward surgical procedure possible. Without it, you're courting chaos.

The scan would be my macro guide to relieve the pressure building inside Carla's brain in the fastest possible time. These more detailed images with contrast dye were critical because it can be disastrous if you land on an aneurysm and are not prepared. If there was an aneurysm, I would need to get proximal control of the feeding vessel. *Always get proximal control...* another heuristic drilled into my head, which means the only way to fix a gushing pipe is to turn it off at its source first and then repair it. I wanted her in the OR fast, but going in blindly was way too risky and increased the probability of a bad outcome.

I waved off a well-meaning student who was delaying Carla's transport to the radiology suite.

"Don't worry about taking her temperature right now, Kelly. That's not important anymore. We need her back to scan PRONTO!"

"But I need to get a temperature for the transfer sheet." Each stage of the patient's movement from one department to the next tracks her vitals so changes to the vitals from one stage to another can be quickly identified. We'll know something happened between X and Y, which will give us clues about exactly what happened, why it happened, and how we can ameliorate it.

Fighting the urge to raise my arrogant neurosurgeon voice, I gently implored the novice, "Kelly, if we don't get her to scan, she's going to be room temperature. Skip it. Help me to get her on the stretcher. Please, she needs your help."

From the emergency room, I called the hospital operator, whom I knew well:

"I need your help fast. Get me the most senior person on the IV team to the CT scanner. STAT."

"You got it."

I knew I could count on him. We had no time for botched IVs and he'd make sure we'd have the best vein sticker on site.

Our medical technologist, Denise, knew the urgency as well as I did (her nickname was the vampire because she was reputed to be able to draw blood from a stone) and had already placed a larger bore catheter into Carla's arm so we could inject the contrast medium with pressure. That one step would ensure the best possible pictures from the CT scan. And because I knew Denise well, it was one less thing I had to ask for. She would simply do it automatically.

The next challenge arose as we arrived unannounced in radiology and encountered an annoyed CT technician. He'd been prematurely pulled from his break and he was not in the mood, nor is anyone ever really, to be talked down to by an arrogant surgeon. Following "standard radiology protocol," he began to scrutinize Carla's incomplete paperwork.

"This scan isn't in the queue. Where are the orders? There's no info here. What's her allergy history?"

My eyes darted down to his name badge. I didn't know this guy, but we needed him on our side right now.

"Jim, I'm not here to be difficult or weird, but if you could look at me for a second I'll explain."

He did. I slowed my pace for emphasis.

"This woman is circling the drain. We're going to get the demographics on the back end, after the scan. I'll write the order. I have no idea what allergies she has. Please skip the consent, draw up the contrast, and get her in the gantry so I can see what bled. I need your help here."

It took me a while to figure it out, like ten years, but that's usually all it takes to get someone on your side—the truth delivered person to person with honesty and a plea for help without posturing. You simply need to acknowledge to critical players in your goal-directed journey how powerful and effective they are in the service of someone else and 99 percent of the time, they'll rise to the challenge.

I quickly reexamined Carla while Jim and I lifted her onto the CT table. Her response to my supraorbital pressure was nowhere near what it was just minutes before. The right side of her face was now droopy, an ominous sign of the clot enlarging.

Jim saw my expression and took control of his territory. He was all in.

"Crap! Let's go! Come on! Let's go!" he shouted to his team.

His perfectly positioned computer-enhanced images revealed that the clot was in her cerebellum, the coordination center of her brain deep in the back of her head. I couldn't see an aneurysm—a weakened blister that could have caused the bleed—but it could still be lurking inside the clot. This clot location made it even more critical to relieve the pressure on the respiratory and consciousness centers in the brainstem. If they were irrevocably damaged, all would be for naught.

While Jim flashed the images on the screen, I called the OR. We were in luck. They were wheeling a hip surgery patient into a fresh Operating Room and the OR team was primed and ready to go. All we had to do was swap out the patients and switch out the sterile equipment.

"Don't let that patient go into the room! I need it."

"But it's a chief case. I can't do that," the OR nurse replied.

I was starting to lose it. The cognitive energy necessary to use just the right tone and the right approach to convince hard-working and dedicated people to do something they weren't comfortable doing… even for very good reasons…was reaching its end. Brain 1.0's emotional responses were starting to bear down on me to do something about these roadblocks. *Scream! Demand! Pull rank!*

I took a breath and just said what needed to be said with as little negative tone as I could.

"Ursula, that's exactly what you have to do. Right now. I have no time. Please stop the train up there. I'm coming up with her now. I'll call Rick."

I called the chief of orthopedics. "Listen, Rick, we need to go to the OR now. I need to bump your case. Now."

"Mark, it's just a hip dislocation. Any chance I could sneak this one in before you go? It'll take me just thirty minutes, and mine is kind of an emergency too."

I lost some control with Rick.

"Rick, this woman's Naomi's age." Naomi is his daughter. "She's got a nasty posterior fossa hemorrhage. I have no time to spare. She has no time to spare. Please, have them call in another team for your case. BUT RIGHT NOW, I'm coming to the OR. Can you *please* help get your equipment out of that room? I need your room, I need your help, and I need it *now*. We're out of time. This is a Hail Mary. Have them open the craniotomy trays and tell them I'm on my way. Thanks!"

Rick knew I wasn't BSing and that I would never use his daughter's name selfishly. So, he became my OR quarterback and rapidly relinquished his room, even helping assemble the instruments with the nursing team for our operation.

There were two more hurdles before I could get into my arena—anesthesia and Carla's family.

I met the anesthesia team in the OR staging area.

"Where's the ER chart? The paperwork? All I see here is a history and physical. The labs aren't complete. There's no consent."

Always helpful, but risk averse, anesthesia demands a complete picture before administering medications to put someone to sleep. Unlike surgeons who frequently have to make decisions with limited information, they do not like taking a patient into the OR without getting a full story, a past medical history, medications, prior anesthesia and family history. But we had no time for that here.

"Here's the story: nineteen-year old previously healthy, now dying. Needs posterior fossa decompression and clot evacuation ten minutes ago. Don't know anything else. Let's roll!"

I looked at Carla's heart monitor. Her blood pressure was rising and her heart rate was dropping. In neurosurgery, this is a classically described phenomenon known as the Cushing Response, named after the man who described it. Harvey Cushing was the iconic father of modern neurosurgery. These conditions are seen when the pressure inside the head rises to deadly levels. This Cushing Response often shortly precedes death.

"We've got a Cushing situation!"

She could hear it in my voice and Carla's monitor wasn't lying. Carla was about to die. Gripping the severity of the situation, anesthesia granted us an immediate pass to the operating theatre. Once I knew Kendra was wheeling Carla back to the OR, I quickly ducked into the family waiting room to get consent for the surgery.

Fortunately, her parents didn't hear my staging area presentation; I needed to frame it a little bit more gently. I entered a nearby "green room" and they lurched up from the couch. Their faces telegraphed dread, a parent's worst nightmare. They knew something was gravely wrong with the girl they had just delivered to college in September.

Aware they would hang on my every word, I rapidly delivered the news. In these types of cases, particularly when patients are as critically ill as Carla was, it's important to leave the family with hope, but not optimism. Carla's odds of surviving were shrinking by the minute; even if we did save her, it was unlikely she would ever be the same. Her father signed the consent as the two of them held hands.

Walking down the hallway to the OR, I glanced at my watch. It had been twenty-eight minutes since I met Carla. I had bought a half-hour of precious time that Carla desperately needed.

Everyone in that operating suite was triple timing it to get her surgery started. There is often a special camaraderie among the OR team, but something was magical about this particular case. It flowed. What were obstacles had quickly transformed into tools. We had given Carla a decent chance at survival. All she needed now was for me to do my part. Everyone else had done theirs.

Now I needed my surgical game to turn ON.

The sink water was numbingly cold as I prepped. Meanwhile, Kendra the anesthesiologist induced general anesthesia and placed important portals to administer medications directly into the blood stream and monitor blood pressure. But her blood pressure remained high and her heart rate low, still indicative of a deadly buildup of pressure inside her head.

Kendra gave high doses of Mannitol, a dense sugar solution that dehydrates the brain and temporarily decreases the pressure. The first surgical step was to drill a hole in the top of Carla's head in order to relieve the pressure by placing a catheter that drained the cerebrospinal fluid.

Similar to Anthony's surgery, this catheter wouldn't remove the clot, but it would make the procedure safer by preventing the fluid buildup and allowing a pressure pop-off valve.

As I dried my hands with a sterile towel and the team gowned me, I slipped into a shortcut to my zone. Over the years I have developed a routine, my formula to get myself together before doing a neurosurgical procedure, to hit my 5 Ps: Pause, Patient, Plan, Positive Thought, Prayer. Because of the severity of Carla's condition, the stakes were high. I really needed some good mojo. Right now.

Pause: "Mark, close your eyes, go to a quiet place in your mind for one moment, and shut out everything around you."

Patient: "This young woman needs you to do your best right now. And her parents need you too."

Plan: "Slam a drain in first thing. That will buy you some time. Then get her positioned prone fast, and get down to the bone like a bad ass."

Positive Thought: "You can do this, Mark. This is a moment in your life to make a difference…a big difference."

Prayer: "Dear God, please help me be my best for Carla. Please help my eyes and my hands to do what is needed to save her. Thank you for this gift you have given me."

To get the team paddling in the same direction, you need to get others into their zone. The only way you can do this is to truly care about everyone, whether you like them personally or not. Caring means helping them to do their best work. To coach and mentor them in their performance is more important than you being perfect. In surgery, even if you perform perfectly, when the team doesn't do the same, there are casualties.

"Denise," I held my scrub nurse's hand as she put my gloves on and I caught the eyes of everyone in that room as quickly as I could.

"This girl needs our best. Let's save her together."

The drain went in perfectly. A spurt of cerebrospinal fluid shot across the room, indicating her intracranial pressure was critical. I sewed the drain in and immediately flipped Carla's body, positioning her head for the craniotomy.

Incision, craniotomy, clot evacuation, everything went perfectly.

Denise was right there for every handoff. I found and cauterized a few small blood vessels at the bottom of the hemorrhage that looked suspiciously like the cause of the bleeding. Some of Carla's cerebellum was bruised from the blood clot, but overall her brain tissue looked relatively healthy and was pulsating with her heartbeat—the first good sign I saw. With half optimism, half anxiety, I closed the wound.

Carla's postoperative scan looked good. It showed the blood clot evacuated, the pressure was diminished and the catheter was in perfect position. As she awakened over the ensuing days and her breathing tube was removed, her speech was thick and labored. A month later I saw her in the office. She arrived on a stretcher from her rehabilitation center for a postoperative check. Her voice was improved but still tongue-tied, a common finding considering the area of the brain that had been injured.

She smiled. I noticed the symmetry of her cheeks. A very good sign.

.... 🧠 ....

Carla's case contains multiple examples of the first quadrant of Phere, flow.

When I got the call to go to the ER, five or so minutes before the ambulance pulled in, I had hundreds of previous experiences just like this one behind me. I was anxious, though, because at this stage I didn't know if I'd need to birth some new skill on the fly. Hope for the best, but prepare for the worst.

I also knew this territory backward and forward. It was an objective known to me. I'd worked in this hospital for years and was familiar with just about everyone who also worked here. More known tools. And I knew my skills had proven their mettle many times before. So this story was subjectively known to me too.

It's a good idea to remind yourself when you're anxious that 1) you're inside a territory that's familiar, 2) that you've been in this situation before and 3) that Brain 1.0 is simply reminding you to pay attention and use your Brain 2.0 to think through the choices you make. What that means practically is to use the methods and systems you've used in the past that achieved similar goals. I call that getting proximal control, another neurosurgery heuristic that in a larger sense means centered and coherent micro goals will add up to your macro goal.

My first micro goal was to quickly diagnose what ailed this woman.

So that's all I focused on in the seconds the paramedics pushed her gurney through the ER doors. She's unresponsive. Check just how unresponsive. Supraorbital pressure reveals a deeper problem than I anticipated.

A Phere. What kind of Phere?

This Phere is an objective positive tool in that it gives me a definitive diagnosis and a definitive time frame, intracranial bleeding that's squeezing her Central Nervous System's most critical structure—the brainstem. This means that by the looks of her reaction, I've got about a half-hour to release the pressure and save her. And this Phere is a subjective positive tool too because I know what to do about that condition. Cut a hole in her head, drain the fluid buildup, and navigate to the clot. Seal it. Clean up and close. Next micro goal step is to ask Dave to intubate Carla to help her breathe because the system in her brain that usually does that for her is getting squeezed.

Next problem to solve is finding the popped blood vessel in Carla's head. I'll need the best CT scans to find it, which will allow me to bootstrap a surgical strategy—a micro tactic by micro tactic plan to get in, fix the problem, and get out with minimal damage.

Another Phere pops up in the form of Kelly the student nurse and her passion to "get the vitals." After I explain the seriousness of the situation, Kelly becomes a positive objective tool and positive subjective tool too. She helps me put Carla on a stretcher to get her to radiology as I call the hospital operator. Because the operator is a known being to me, I'm able to bypass the usual niceties and simply ask for what I need. Knowing he'll get it done, I move on to the next micro goal.

Next up is the Phere of the annoyed CT tech, Jim. I don't know him, so he's an objective and subjective unknown. I'll need to pay attention to him keenly and turn my initial intuition that he'll be an obstacle into him serving the mission as a tool. The trick to getting him on the side of doing everything possible to save Carla's life is literally paying attention to him with seriousness and respect. **Seeing him through that lens allows him to release the best part of himself, which he does very quickly after I've explained the situation.**

You'll notice that my focus is directed to the micro tasks at hand. I'm giving full attention to every Phere that rises, and I have little time to obsess about any Brain 1.0 fear coming my way. It's certainly still there as a background hum for me, but it's not inhibiting my ability to make decisions and act on those decisions. Because the arena and situation are so familiar to me, I'm experiencing the early signs of "flow."

Where the rubber meets the road, however, is in the OR.

Everything up until that point does not compare to the fear jolts my Brain 1.0 shoots my way just before I operate. What I'm doing abstractly when I operate is chasing the penultimate place at the top of Maslow's pyramid, the need to self-actualize. Remarkably, when the rest of the team in the room is fully flowing in their own private self-actualizing processes too, together we get the opportunity to transcend ourselves. And that is the very top of the pyramid...when our actions not only transcend beyond our physical bodies, but actually transcend time too.

To go even higher than the top of the pyramid means to move beyond yourself, to create something that changes the course of world history. I'm sure you've heard of the butterfly effect, in which a small change in a complex system leads to great effect in that same system. Everyone in that OR, through their creative actions, transcends themselves by doing their part to save the life of a young woman who will change the world. Whether we wish to acknowledge the truth or not, the fact is that every single person changes the world.

Together, when we're all doing what we should be doing with intent and skill, the sum is far greater than our individual parts. We move beyond ourselves and transcend into a creative realm.

This is why I came up with my Brain 2.0's Five-P preoperative grounding system, to put myself in the best position I can to transcend myself.

The first P stands for **pause**. It's a way to clear the past and settle the present so I can put all of my effort toward securing the future.

Then I have to focus on the most valuable player in this game, the **patient**.

Next is a super boiled down micro step by micro step **plan**.

Then I remind myself of the truth that what I'm doing is **positive**, meaningful and makes a difference.

And lastly, I say a **prayer** to God.

Because when I get to work inside the flow quadrant, I'm in heaven.

THIRTY
The PGC Rule

"Vhaaat is this?"

"Vhaaaat?" he said it louder.

"*VHAAAAAAAT IS THIS?*" now bordering on a yell.

Dr. Enrique Gerszten theatrically asked the question in his booming signature accent, one-part Sigmund Freud and one-part Mel Brooks.

Strutting around in a white coat and gloves, he proudly displayed the oddity to us as if he were a waiter offering a gourmet dessert at a fine Manhattan restaurant. He offered each medical student a peek at the metallic cookie sheet in his hands.

Only the platter didn't hold anything sweet. On it lay a brownish tan, leathery meat-like specimen the shape of a desiccated wineskin.

"Vhaaat is this? *Vaaaaat is ze diagnosis?*" he repeated.

With the first year of normal human studies completed, it was now traditionally time to pivot toward studying the abnormal. We would spend the hot Virginia summer and much of the next year in and out of this cold smelly lab, slogging through tissue and diseases illustrating everything that has ever gone wrong with the human body.

Dr. Gerszten employed the Socratic method to stump the class regularly. In an intellectually intimidating manner, you never were quite sure if he was as irascible as he presented himself or just playing a part. He would regularly present us with a rare pathologic specimen that demonstrated the hallmark features of a disease process.

Pathologists hold a unique position in medicine. Rather than care for patients, they examine the anomalous pieces and parts that have been excised from them. Sometimes they work under a microscope and sometimes by "gross" examination or with the bare eye. They don't fear the Phere. It's why they got into the profession in the first place.

But I had no interest in lab work. My grandfather made sure of that.

Like professor Gerszten, Grandpa Pizzi was right out of central casting, an old-school surgeon and raconteur. I began my Pizzi-apprenticeship when I was in kindergarten, tagging along with him when he made house calls throughout our New Jersey neighborhood. Some days, he'd even let me carry his black bag, but those were the rounds portion of my early education. Mostly I just hung out with him in his living room snacking on medical stories and being quizzed on scientific minutiae while everyone else was outside playing ball.

"Mark, in your practice of medicine you will make two types of mistakes: errors of commission and errors of omission…" he'd begin in the comfort of his living room La-Z-Boy chair as he held a lit match to the tip of his fresh cigar and puffed up a perfect ring of fire. "OMISSION… those are the ones that haunt you…"

The smoke encircled me inside his perfect precision of oratory pause. And then he'd begin…

"It was a routine appendectomy. For an apprentice to an exquisite Italian tailor named Thomas Iannucci…"

Back in the old days before CT scanners and MRIs, when patients got appendicitis they usually presented with classic achy and diffuse abdominal pain, beginning around the umbilicus (the belly button), and then progressed over the course of hours to localize as severe stabbing pain in the right lower quadrant of the belly. The presentation is no different than it was one hundred or one thousand years ago.

The difference though is that if you got appendicitis one thousand years ago, you would crawl off to some edge of your village and die. But some ninety years ago, back when Gramps was practicing, if you came down with appendicitis and could get to a surgeon, you had a fighting chance.

Thomas Iannucci did just that. Then twenty-one years old, he gingerly managed to get to the emergency room at St. Mary Hospital in Orange, New

Jersey, late Thanksgiving evening in 1931. His complaint: severe abdominal pain and fever.

Holding very still on the stretcher, guarding his gut with crossed arms, he was exhibiting all the signs of an acute abdomen. Then and now this behavior presents a surgical emergency. Grandpa, a young on-call general surgeon two years into his practice, knew exactly what to do.

"I made a midline incision because his symptoms were diffuse. I needed the room to look around. First, I went to the appendix and sure enough it was the culprit—red and enlarged. Fortunately, he had not perforated his bowel, which would have been a much worse problem. I removed the inflamed appendix."

A few puffs of the cigar and another pregnant pause. Just when I was about to beg for more...

"Then I began to do a once-over on the belly."

This was his story's turning point.

"Wait a minute, I thought you said you *missed* the opportunity... It sounds like you *saved* him," I interrupted.

Grandpa held up a hand and continued, "I palpated each organ in the belly. First the liver and gall bladder. No gall stones, liver good, spleen good, no masses in the pancreas. Then I ran the bowel."

"Running the bowel" is a systematic palpation and inspection of the length of the intestines from one end of the alimentary canal to the other. The surgeon manually slides their fingers beginning from the bottom of the sigmoid colon, gently making their way back through the small intestine back to the stomach. They use their fingers as mini "scanners" to palpate any polyps or growths from the outside of the organ.

Although somewhat crude and not as accurate as scans or scopes, it's a practice still in use today. But back then, there were few diagnostic or imaging tests that could be done on patients. So, if you had someone under general anesthesia and you had their belly open, you had a golden opportunity to take a good look-see "under the hood." It was a way of screening for any yet undiagnosed diseases that could be lurking in other areas of the abdomen.

"The entire bowel looked and felt good," Grandpa said. "No masses, no inflammation anywhere else. But the stomach felt a little tight, like it was spasmed. It wasn't a major abnormality, but I just remember it didn't feel like others I had felt when I ran the bowel in my training and early practice. I felt it a second time. It just didn't feel right. I paused and thought, what do I do?"

Grampa then reasoned his way out of the crisis.

"Then I thought, look, this kid didn't come in with a stomach problem. He had acute appendicitis. You fixed his problem. The firm stomach is probably nothing. It's late. Christ, it's Thanksgiving. You're beat, and you fixed the problem."

He gave me a good hard look in the eyes, another puff and then...

"I closed and went home."

The difference between surgeons like my grandfather and pathologists like the brilliant Dr. Gerszten is that the surgeon's decisions are in medias res while the pathologist's decisions are after the fact.

Don't get me wrong. Pathologists are indispensable and their intellectual rigor and exploratory nature bring forth innovations in medical technology like few other medical concentrations. These doctors are a different breed. In my experience, they (at least the generation cut from Dr. G's mold) generally have more detachment, are somewhat blunter communicators and can be authoritarian in their proclamations.

Does the witch choose the wand or does the wand choose the witch?

The personality and detachment of pathologists surely comes in part from their environment. The pathology lab in med school is a macabre "show and tell" kind of a place. Along the shelves lay formalin jars containing evidence of human diseases that destroyed people, stole loved ones, inflicted excruciating pain, and frequently devastated the human condition. Each specimen has a story to tell and serves as a lesson for the medical student.

Pathologists tend to be superlative lateral thinkers too. As opposed to surgeons who think more linearly. Lateral thinking is a thought process first described in 1967 by Edward de Bono, an expert in critical thinking. It's used by organizations and individuals to enhance problem-solving and decision-making. Lateral thinking is a more creative, right hemispheric, and indirect approach rather than one relying strictly on logic and pattern recognition.

Hugh Laurie in his role of Dr. House in the TV series demonstrates the value of lateral thinking. If we can dislocate the pattern ingrained in our mind such that new and novel solutions can be generated, we can perhaps arrive at better solutions than previously possible.

The human body, and the world for that matter, is so incredibly complex and interconnected that our tendency to think and behave in linear ways needs to be augmented by other ways of thinking.

If this, that: *if that, this* must be broadened to *This could mean that or that or that.*

The Biblical story of King Solomon and the two women both claiming to be the mother of a baby can be considered an example of lateral thinking. It was the king's job to determine who would take the child home. He ordered that the child be cut in half, knowing that the real mother would give up the child rather than have it killed. A manufacturing example also illustrates the style of thinking. When the really strong adhesive invented at 3M turns out to be a dud, in fact a very weak adhesive, what do you do? You find a use for the weak stuff—and Post-it Notes are born.

In my neurosurgery practice, Grampa Pizzi and Dr. Gerszten inspired the PGC Rule, which is, "Name at least three other diseases than the one you are absolutely sure is causing this patient's problem." PGC is an example of the lateral thinking process in medicine. By exploring multiple levels of possibility, we can find novel discoveries and avoid the constraints of rigid single cause, or single effect thinking.

In my grandfather's medical era, practically all of the patients coming to his office with tumors would have surgery to remove the entire abnormality if possible. The excised specimen would then be sent to the pathologist. In those days the pathologist would have a large piece of tissue to work on.

Nowadays with sophisticated imaging and more effective chemotherapy and radiation, many tumors do not need to be resected, or removed. With a simple same-day needle biopsy, a diagnosis can be posited and a nonsurgical or minimally invasive treatment regimen can be established.

When a biopsy occurs, either in the operating room or more often now in the radiology suite, the specimen is sent in a medical-grade Ziploc baggie down to the pathology department. The pathologist opens the bag, takes the specimen and traps the tissue in a liquid that turns to gel once frozen. Then the tiny chunk of tissue is placed on a cryostat, a highly sophisticated lab equivalent of a delicatessen meat slicer.

The thin layer of stained tissue is then placed on a slide and dipped into various dyes. Then it's put under the microscope for analysis. A pathologist will scan the microscopic field looking for telltale signs of disease. Are there waves of tiny blue cells suggesting a tumor called lymphoma? Or are there light purple cells with multi-shaped centers that suggest infection? These subtle distinctions can literally mean the difference between a month of antibiotics for a patient or six months of chemotherapy and radiation. Tens of thousands of shapes and colors have been drilled into the mind of a seasoned pathologist.

In Grandpa's day, as today, the pathologist trumps all other diagnosticians.

"The diagnosis is [Insert disease here]," they often say with complete certainty. It's understandable. The buck stops at the pathologist. When their diagnosis is made, it overrides all other clinicians' decisions or hypotheses.

The GI doctor may think his patient has Crohn's disease, but when the pathologist looks at the biopsied tissue under the microscope, her call is the final call. If she says it is cancer, it's cancer. If she says it's not, it's not, unless there is a sampling error when the biopsy is performed.

A sampling error occurs because characteristics of the entire lesion are estimated from the small needle aspiration or a tiny piece of tissue from the lesion in question. If the biopsy needle doesn't enter all the way into the tumor, it can skive off and catch the edge. Or if it hits the center of the target but the center is already decomposed and doesn't yield any definitive clues, there can be diagnostic inaccuracies.

Sometimes it is possible that the sampled tissue is not a representative example of all the cells in the total mass. Sometimes a tumor can have heterogeneity where parts of it look more benign and other parts look more malignant. Whenever this occurs the default is to the more malignant diagnosis.

Therefore, needle biopsies can sometimes be a bit of a wild card. So oftentimes we repeat and compare data to get the most probable diagnosis.

"Vhaaat is this? *Vhaaaaat is ze diagnosis?*"

Dr. Gerszten jammed the slab of meat on his cookie sheet just beneath my chin to give me the most intimate vantage point.

He stepped back as I nervously put some gloves on and picked up the oily specimen. It looked and felt like a deflated football left out in the rain. The formalin preservative marinade burned the back of my throat.

"Vhaaaat is the diagnosis!" towering over me, Dr. G. screamed.

I blurted, "It's a classic case of diffuse infiltrating adenocarcinoma linitus plastica type."

The words came effortlessly the moment I recognized the shape and felt the rubbery nature of the meaty tissue, as if I'd just gone back in time to the lazy afternoon with Grampa Pizzi and returned with his gift.

"The next day, the kid looked great and a few days later I discharged him home, happy as a clam. I went back to work and forgot him…until he came back two years later with advanced stomach cancer. It was a kind of cancer that grows and infiltrates the muscle walls of the stomach. It made the stomach wall seem like a leathery wine pouch. I must have been feeling the early stages when I opened his belly two years before. The pathologist told me after the fact that it was diffuse infiltrating adenocarcinoma linitus plastica type. And If I had recognized the mass and removed it when he presented to me with appendicitis two years earlier, I might have saved him. But, of course, I did not. The twenty-three-year-old young man died a few months later from widely disseminated cancer."

"Acts of omission, Mark. They will haunt you," said Grampa.

Twenty years later…

"Cooooorrrrrrect," Dr. G. said, haltingly.

THIRTY-ONE
The "C" in the PGC Rule

A groggy, preoperative Rob Conenello looked up from his OR stretcher and saw me hovering above him. He reached out his hand to grab my own before I began my work.

"Doc...I've always told my kids, even since they were little: 'Do great things'... Now it's your turn."

I'd met Rob at my office on a spring morning in 2012. He was about my age, a graying and magnetic podiatrist. He'd brought with him a diagnosis of glossopharyngeal neuralgia, a rare disease of the ninth cranial nerve that is characterized by irregular and sudden electric shock-like lightning bolts of pain in the tongue and deep throat. Often triggered by swallowing (try to stop swallowing for a while and see how fun that is), when the jolts come and how often they come is impossible to predict.

Amazingly, Rob experienced the symptoms for almost a full year before he came to see me. At first, he suffered in silence. "It's as if you stuck your tongue in an electrical socket," he quipped. "It's invading my life and my work. I have to duck into my side office between patients just to get psyched up to put a smile on for them when I enter their room. I can't do it much longer."

In his supporting medical history paperwork, I reviewed other physicians' evaluations and the biopsy and work-up of that area of his mouth. When I asked him about it, he said the biopsy reported benign inflammation, hence his grin and bear it strategy. He'd had two other consultations before coming to me, with a neurologist and an ear nose and throat physician in New York City. They'd both concluded that he was one of the unlucky victims of glossopharyngeal neuralgia.

He had all the classic symptoms. Intermittent quiescent, or dormant, periods of no pain. The traditional triggers that set off the electric shocks. Response to suppression of the pain with Tegretol, the mainstay drug that classically halts lancinating nerve pain in its tracks.

Rob also brought a high-resolution brain scan. I stared carefully at the pictures of his brainstem where the origin of the glossopharyngeal nerve lay. The images showed a small blood vessel digging into the axilla or underside of the nerve as it headed straight toward the painful side of his mouth.

My evaluation, along with the other two consulting evaluations, confirmed that it was obvious he was suffering from glossopharyngeal neuralgia due to the blood vessel irritation. Three subjective points of view all coming to the same conclusion—the unexpected Phere event Rob suffered from was a known subjective obstacle (-1) derived from a known objective fact (the phenomenon called glossopharyngeal neuralgia). And the solution to that problem was the objective known tool (+2) that I could provide, the fact that I knew how to perform the surgery that takes care of the glossopharyngeal neuralgia problem.

He wanted the surgery to fix it.

He was a busy doc running his own business and needed to be on his game. He was tough and he said he could take the pain most days, but he couldn't tolerate the sedating effects of the medications on the days he couldn't. He had to be present and in full control of himself with his patients. That's the commitment he'd made to them when they trusted him with their bodies, and there was no way he'd not live up to that code.

He wanted a definitive solution. He wanted the blood vessel moved so he wouldn't be distracted any longer.

I obliged.

Soon after I released his hand that morning in the OR, I drilled a fifty cent piece-sized window of bone just behind his left ear. Under the microscope, I deftly found the offending blood vessel, dissected it, and moved it away from the underside of the nerve. Then I placed a fluffy felt pad the size of the head of a Q-tip between the vessel and the nerve to permanently displace it in a slightly different direction. The surgery went exactly as planned.

He woke up in recovery pain-free and all smiles. I discharged him home two days later and he did wonderfully in rehab. We weaned him off all medications, and three months later he sent me a family picture at Disney World.

The caption read, "Thanks for making this day possible. AND keep doing great things!"

Rob was back to his old self and we'd occasionally text back and forth sharing war stories about challenging cases. He'd become a colleague and a friend. One of his sons was a wrestler and with two of my sons wrestling in college, our connection tightened. The doctor/patient divide was over and a friend/friend relationship had replaced it.

And then, about a year into our new friendship, I got a text from him: "Hey, is this supposed to come back?"

"Unlikely," I confidently replied. "I saw a good artery compressing the nerve. I moved it away permanently. There's no way that could have shifted."

He came in for a check. His pain was returning. We started back on medications.

I held his hand, reassured him. It'll blow over. Keep an eye on it, keep the meds on for now. My confidence was infectious and he left in good spirits, ready to tackle the world again.

Six months went by.

He came back. More pain. Now the meds weren't working. I ordered a repeat brain scan. It looked clear. Phew, I breathed a sigh of relief. Nothing I did wrong, I selfishly thought. Everything is in its place where it should be.

Over the next six months Rob persisted to pester me with his recurrent pain complaints. And I listened, reassured and comforted, and kept telling him it would go away. The nerve was healing. The nerve would recover and this was just a minor setback.

But Rob was not getting better. He was getting worse.

I began to wonder if Rob was crazy.

Some facial or throat pain patients who come for an evaluation can have an element of psychiatric disease. I've never been sure what comes first: the excruciating pain that can potentially make anyone crazy or the mental illness that can sometimes manifest itself as a facial pain syndrome?

Ultimately, over the phone I suggested maybe he consider biofeedback or possibly even a re-exploration of the area....

He returned to my office with an idea. How about a Gamma Knife procedure? It was a possible option. The Gamma Knife is a radiation device that utilizes focused radiation to block pain impulses that run through nerves. It's delivered by attaching the patient's head to a guidance frame that looks like an upside-down crown. Once the frame is attached, the patient's head is essentially stuffed into a radiation unit and the beams are focused on the tiny region of the nerve right where the pain originates. By delivering radiation to this spot the size of a pencil eraser, it somehow suppresses the firing of the nerve.

Since this procedure aimed at the glossopharyngeal nerve was somewhat experimental and not a procedure I performed, I sent him to a former professor of mine who specialized in this type of treatment.

During Rob's work-up they noticed that his tongue was deviated and atrophied in the left side, a new finding I had missed when he was at the last office visit. They got a new brain scan. On their scan, at the very bottom slice of the picture, they found a shadow deep in the back of his throat under the tongue. This discovery prompted a neck MRI scan to get a better look.

I still remember the first image Rob texted me with what they found.

I felt a deep chill down my spine and broke into a cold sweat as I scrolled through the images he texted me.

Now I could see the problem, the truth and proof that Rob was not crazy.

Now I wondered if I was crazy.

It was now so obvious. There was a large mass in the back of Rob's mouth under the base of his tongue. Previous brain scans did not show this because the lesion was just below the field of view of the scanner, deep within his throat.

There was a cancer in Rob's throat, and I had missed it. Not only had I missed it, I prolonged his suffering and delayed his diagnosis and potential therapeutic window for at least a year. And I had probably performed an unnecessary craniotomy on him too, a procedure geared toward a totally different diagnosis.

Oh my God. Oh my God... I thought. *I missed a throat cancer. I just sentenced this man to death. Oh my God. His life...his wife...his children...*

My inner critic flooded my head. *How could you miss this, Mark? How could you? You have signed his death certificate. Everything you trained to be...everything you believed you were has spiraled right down the drain.*

Critical self-narration, an indispensable part of our conscious thinking procedure, can easily spiral out of control when anomalous information like a tumor arises in challenging times.

"You're a bad doctor," kept breaking through all my other thoughts.

I tried to defend myself against the internal assault. The first stage was to blame the victim. *He told you at your first office visit that he had a lesion there and it was biopsied and proven negative. He told you that. Remember? He said it was nothing. It's his fault.*

But these hollow words couldn't suppress my damnation. I knew they were lies.

The inner voice was incessant in the car on the way to work: *I should have revisited the "inflammation" possibility problem.*

At wrestling practice with my students: *I should have considered a sampling error when it was biopsied early on.*

In the operating room between procedures: *I should have gotten a neck MRI scan long ago.*

At the dinner table with the people who cared about me most: *I should have assumed the worst.*

Nassim Nicholas Taleb in his book *The Black Swan* states, "Memory is a self-serving revision machine." And blaming the victim is just one of its revisionary tactics. Over the course of two weeks I went through the full Kübler-Ross Model of grief: Denial, anger, bargaining, depression, and at long last acceptance.

Denial: Was my memory playing tricks on me? Did he say biopsy or did he just say it was inflammation? The diagnosis was benign so it's not my fault I didn't double check it.

Anger: How could anyone blame me for something I wasn't responsible for?

Bargaining: If I were to consider that perhaps I could have done more for Rob and let him know about my sincere regret that I didn't double check that inflammation or order a larger field of vision scan, maybe he would forgive me and maybe he'd even survive my error.

Depression: That's all well and good, but the fact is that I am not a good doctor after all of these years I lied to myself about being one.

Acceptance: I made a mistake. I didn't think about Rob's condition in the way I've told myself to think about diagnoses...laterally. I should have been thinking laterally... what three other things could have caused or contributed to Rob's pain that I didn't think about? As a consequence of my human error, Rob needed help dealing with the actual problem, not his feelings about the problem or mine, but the problem. I needed to put my ego aside and use my skills now to help him with the problem he was facing now...not the ones he'd faced in the past.

My worry and fear about my status and my opinion of myself was the signal to me that I needed to place my attention on, you guessed it, the problem, the present Phere—his newly diagnosed illness.

Sure enough, Rob did indeed have throat cancer with metastasis to his lymph nodes. As Rob explored his options for treatment, we kept up a text and phone dialogue where I did my best to laterally help. It was shocking to me that Rob was still willing to keep talking to me. I thought for sure he would have pushed me off. Or his family would have told me to go away. I was sure they thought I had done enough damage. But like Rob, his family was dealing with the problem, and I could help with it. So if I was someone they could use to solve it—a tool— they'd use it. Simple, but extraordinary.

The macro plan that came to the fore was to perform an en bloc resection, that is, to cut the entire tumor mass out, as was done in Grandpa Pizzi's days. The operation would permanently disfigure Rob and this kind of surgery opens up the possibility of a number of complications.

Rob wisely decided to keep that option on hold a bit longer and press on exploring more about the actual problem—the cancer cells themselves.

Thankfully, after a few additional biopsies to really unpack the nature of the thing, it turned out to be a tumor that his oncologists thought would be sensitive to simultaneous radiation and chemotherapy. Great! That was the good news.

Rob proceeded with those treatments without surgery. But those treatments, while his best chance, are nevertheless taxing physically and mentally. A prolonged period of excruciating pain no less. But Rob underwent that soul-pounding gauntlet of fifty rounds of radiation plus chemotherapy with a forbearance that left me in awe. The treatments waged an Armageddon on the deep-seated tumor and also on his previously athletic build. Because of the needed aggressive treatments, he suffered the extreme side effects of his therapy. This included more pain in the throat than he'd ever felt before. He described it as if he were swallowing shards of glass with every swallow combined with constant nausea and unremitting bouts of vomiting.

During these awful days, Rob described himself as a professional vomiter.

After a fifty-five-pound weight loss, he turned a corner. Determined to return to his practice, he pulled on an ill-fitting white coat five months after this odyssey and dragged himself to the office to see patients. And somehow, just six months after beginning the therapy, Rob finished a Memorial Day 5K race wearing a T-shirt that read, "Do Great Things."

To this day, my misdiagnosis and the delay I caused not confronting the unwanted truth that Rob kept informing me about haunts me. I had done exactly what my grandfather warned me about way back when I was his five-year-old sidekick. I had committed an act of omission. I failed to order a test that would have picked up Rob's cancer earlier. In retrospect, it seems so simple, so blatantly obvious. I was an idiot, and Rob and his family had to pay for my ignoring a fundamental law of medicine two brilliant men, my grandfather and Dr. Enrique Gerszten, went to great trouble to teach me.

In retrospect my hubris blinded me to abandon the lateral thinking rule my grandfather told me when I was five years old and my medical school professor reinforced when I was twenty-five years old. If not for the heroic behavior of Rob Conenello and his genius to think through the information presented to him and find the best possible solution to it, and somehow doing that without blaming others for being flawed human beings, my mistake could have cost someone's life.

Rob never expressed anger toward me. He just went with the experience. He thought it through and acted cognitively dominant. He focused on doing great things. I did my best to stick with him and follow his lead. Every few weeks, I would send him a positive thought. He would give me an update. We stayed in touch.

And he just kept going. Remarkably, he responded beautifully to the torment from the treatments. The tumor shrank and after four months of misery, he began to eat again without the horrific pain. Rob remains in remission two years since his last radiation treatment. We sat down to dinner in his hometown last winter. In an awkward and uncomfortable beginning to an evening that I had initiated, he led with the $64,000-dollar question.

"Mark, do you think I ever had glossopharyngeal neuralgia?"

My entire career, I had been told by lawyers and insurance consultants to avoid this kind of conversation. And if pressed, just to never admit to personal error. But I had to. I couldn't live with myself any other way.

"No, I don't think so."

Rob broke down. "It's all coming back to me tonight. I'm so sorry to be so emotional. The pain was so bad. It was awful. I thought about ending it all. There were times before the tumor diagnosis that I just didn't think I could go on. And it was like nobody was believing me. Not even you."

I sat silently. Sometimes there are no words to soften truth.

After a while I said, "I'm sorry I wasn't a better doctor for you."

Let's look at Rob's story in terms of Phere.

Objectively, he bravely presented the facts of his symptoms over and over again to me. And as it first presented, scans and other opinions confirmed that what ailed him was an objective known obstacle (-1), a diagnosis of glossopharyngeal neuralgia. And subjectively, it was a known obstacle (-1). I had plenty of experience with the diagnosis. The (-1, -1) Phere character placed Rob in the all is lost quadrant and he wisely chose to do whatever he could to rise above it.

And after the surgery, he and I both believed we'd accomplished that task.

Soon after, however, Rob's symptoms reemerged. A Phere that we both believed had been identified and metabolized had come back to torment him. This is where our subjective experiences diverged.

I convinced myself that the truth of Rob's pain had to be false. He had to be crazy. There was no way he could be experiencing pain because I did everything "right."

I did not move up my own hierarchy of values and abide the single value I hold dearest—creation over destruction. Instead, I held firm to my "esteem" need. I told myself the story that I was the expert here and I had the proof of my expertise on all three levels of the esteem need (first, second and third-party validation, especially third party). These "I know better" accomplishments were the only proof necessary. One of us, Rob or I, had to be mistaken about the success of my operation. And since I was the one with all of the fancy medical degrees, I had to be the one in the right.

Rob was clearly stating that he was in horrific physical pain and had fallen even further down the all is lost quadrant. He was now experiencing an objective unknown obstacle (-2) and a subjective unknown obstacle (-2). We had no new diagnosis and no one believed he was actually experiencing the pain he was reporting.

Let's go back to the nature of the Phere again and how it transformed.

Originally, it was an objective known obstacle (-1) and a subjective known obstacle (-1) and from our four-quadrant graph we can see it's in the all is lost quadrant, the place where we need the most help getting out of that black arena. The trick to contending with these sorts of unexpected Phere events is to look at them from different perspectives. But if one perspective rises above all others it must be the search for deep veracity (fact and truth together). I failed to place that value above my commitment to maintain my self-esteem and it could have cost another person his life.

A very useful tactic when you find yourself in this horrific quadrant is to do what Rob did. He used lateral thinking to unpack the possibilities inherent in his symptoms piece by piece. Because I feared a blow to my reputation as a surgeon, I steadfastly refused to think about Rob's symptoms other than as reflective of my diagnosis and intervention. I made an error of omission, just like my Grandfather Pizzi warned me about when I was a boy. Instead I should have looked at the Phere as the opportunity to unearth truth and put my energies toward creating more life for Rob.

But luckily for me, the man I let down refused to quit. I turned into his Phere (I was behaving unexpectedly when he told me about his symptoms) and he brilliantly chose to seek multiple other opinions to figure out just what his pain meant. My locked-in belief that since there was no reason I could detect that he should continue to be suffering, his suffering wasn't occurring posed a vexing obstacle to Rob. If his own doctor told him it made no sense that he was in pain, his pain was "invalid."

Rob nudging me eventually transformed me into a source of aid to him. To appease Rob, I thought, I offered a referral and recommendation to one of my mentors, who proved to be the deciding factor in catching Rob's cancer before it was too late.

With my experience with Rob, I came up with a rule I use whenever I find myself not listening to the objective facts of a case in favor of relying upon my experience. I call it **The PGC Rule**, which is dedicated to my grandfather Doc Pizzi, my pathology professor Dr. Enrique Gerszten and to the heroic Rob Conenello. The PGC Rule simply states... when you find yourself feeling all is lost, come up with multiple levels of looking at the Phere event that precipitated the feeling. Dissect each and every possibility with Mr. Spock-like precision as if someone's life depends upon it. Because it probably does.

THIRTY-TWO
Cognitive Consonance

On the first cool evening of September 1944, five years after the Soviet Socialist Republic seized the river town of Stryi in southeastern Ukraine as part of the German USSR invasion of Poland, the father of a nine-year-old boy thumped his fist on the front door of a modest home inside the town's fourteenth-century-era perimeter.

The thirty-two-year-old matriarch inside knew what she was about to hear before she'd even touched the latch. The threat of punishment, knowing it would come but not exactly when, had become an ever-present reality for her.

The man whispered into the widening seam of the opening door that guarded the space between the town's public space and the owner's entryway.

"Get out...run...NOW! They are coming for you."

The woman's five-year-old daughter clung to the back of her mother's skirt, shielding herself from the man and his news. While she did not completely understand his message, his urgent hush told the little girl everything she needed to know. People whispered just before the soldiers came.

Only hours before all had proceeded as prescribed by the authorities.

The performance space at the town's gymnasium filled to capacity with parents and grandparents, uncles and aunts, and the special honorable guest in attendance. A representative from the Soviet Republic had come to evaluate the elementary indoctrination of the town's youth into the global Soviet system.

Thankfully, the schoolteacher's direction of the student assembly executed flawlessly. The songs expertly curated, the play energetically delivered and exactly as ordered, and the pinnacle of the performance—a beautiful ode to Father Stalin—hit just the right note with a remarkably memorized recitation by a boy with a pitch perfect sense of drama.

You could feel the pressure in the room release with the completion of his last poetic syllable. They'd passed the test.

But in the microsecond between the end of the performance and the final round of applause. . .just as the monitor was about to signal his approval with his departure. . . the boy went off script.

"I just recited you a poem that I was ordered to read," he announced. "Now I will sing you a song that *I* want to sing." The faces in the crowd flushed.

When the boy finished singing *Shche ne vmerla Ukrayina* (*Ukraine has not yet perished*), he looked directly at his father to gauge his approval. Upon seeing his stunned and ghostly expression, he turned and looked directly at his teacher for her validation.

The boy's desire to be acknowledged gave her resistance to the occupation away.

But for the one hundred and twenty odd seconds it took the boy to sing their song, her underground rebellion remained undetected. The monitor had failed to look on the back of the school room's brand new "official" map and find the teacher's secret curriculum. And he had missed the Ukrainian national flag that she'd neatly stashed in the bottom of her shoe bin. All such contraband would now be discovered as he ransacked her classroom with a fresh eye.

The teacher glanced at the frowning Soviet official. She winced a nervous, apologetic *kids these days?* kind of smile. But she knew by his expression that all was certainly lost. He wasn't buying it.

She understood that in the end she'd be held responsible for the boy's brazen performance and now everyone in the school and in the community would pay for it dearly. She was proud of her young pupil and yet devastated that his naïve courage would result in the destruction of her and his home.

She told this to the whispering father now at her door.

The trembling man put his hands on her shoulders to deliver the inevitable.

"We are sorry. But the monitor beat him and insisted on finding out what you were teaching. He told him everything, the map, the flag, everything," he turned to leave, muttering over his shoulder desperate pleas. "You must leave. They are coming for you. Quickly RUN! Get out!"

The schoolteacher's clinging daughter understood the words "get out." But the six-year-old did not understand their impact or magnitude.

A verdict of dissident activity was a certain ticket to the Norilsk "reeducation" camp…if you were pitied enough not to be shot. More and more of Stryi's townspeople disappeared as the days fell under occupation one after the other.

The schoolteacher took a moment. Then she put her mind to how best protect her family and her daughter.

"Sit…over there at the kitchen table." She shepherded the girl away from the front door to her favorite chair.

She needed to gather their indispensable things and leave in the remaining minutes before the authorities arrived.

Her husband was still at work at the warehouse, which was just at the end of their cobblestone road. He'd be home soon. She retreated to the bedroom and pulled the family trunk out from under the bed. She loaded in photo albums, embroidery, clothing, her jewelry box and important documents. She grabbed her daughter's clothing and all the dry food in the house.

Then she pulled the kilim from the hearth in the living room. Her mother had woven the rug by hand.

In her last act before leaving her birthplace forever, she pulled a chair up to the front door and stepped up to gently lift a wooden crucifix off the nail above the transom. The growl of her husband's truck rumbled to the front door.

She did not take the time to wipe the tears streaming from her eyes as she hurriedly told him the story. He embraced her and together they worked a quickly charted plan. While she draped the red and black kilim into the bed of the truck, he grabbed the handles of the overstuffed trunk and heaved the heavy box on top. They stuffed the passenger side of the cab with potatoes and bags of wheat and flour. In twenty odd minutes, they'd gathered and packed the essentials.

The truck sputtered and spat, struggling with the extra weight as it grinded up the first hill heading west. With no room in the cab, mother and daughter lay in the bed of the truck. The space was enough for the little girl, but the mother's knees ached, her legs propped on canisters of gasoline. The cool fall air began to penetrate through their coats, so mother and daughter rolled the edge of the rug over their bodies to shield them from the draft as the truck heaved forward.

They traded their truck and remaining gasoline for a wagon and two oxen on their second day on the run.

The days grew shorter. Fall turned to winter.

Her mother's kilim kept them warm in the woods. They'd moved into the mountains to escape detection. Now there was no more food for the oxen. So they traded the oxen to a mountain man for a two-wheeled handcart to carry their dwindling family heirlooms. Then they traded the heirlooms for meat, bread and a dry night's sleep. All the while they evaded the Nazis moving into the territory from the west and the Russians squeezing in from the east.

It was deep winter now.

The food was all gone as were most of their possessions. The kilim was now draped over the cart, straddling both sidewalls, and the daughter lay nestled between a layer of the wool inside the cart with the rug on top as her father pulled it along. The only benefit of the cold was that the frozen ground made for easier pulling. Until the snow came...

One night, as dusk approached, they had managed to stay hidden in the woods while a passing German troop formation marched by. The temperature dropped as they made their way into the abandoned Nazi encampment. They would scrounge for food scraps as another miserable night lay ahead. The father set the cart down, quietly conferred with his wife and crept away to survey the abandoned area. He came back without food but he had found a warmer place to sleep.

They walked over to the area that had freshly dug dirt and logs. Water vapor came from a small hole in the soil. The ground was warm and soft. Then a cold breeze turned the vapor toward them.

The father continued his work.

He began by laying some small logs over the fetid hole and then some pine boughs for cushion. His wife and daughter gagged as they sat nearby, but the covered over latrine hole would serve as a warm heating duct that would vent into their bedding. Just as the father finished setting the pine boughs and prepared the area for them to sleep, another family of three came through the trees.

The father raised a hatchet above his head as a show of force, as these were desperate times, but the situation diffused when the male stranger spoke in Ukrainian.

"We mean no harm. It's Christmas Eve. God Bless You. Can you spare us some food?"

They had no food, but father, mother and daughter offered them a place next to them in their encampment. They knew six bodies would be warmer than three. But the stranger's wife couldn't stand the smell and the guests retreated.

The father, mother and daughter covered their noses with dirty shirts from their bags to mask the smell and settled in, bundling up with their worn rug. The father joked to the mother that the rug smelled worse than the piss and shit as he and his wife engulfed their daughter.

They awoke the next day with a thick blanket of snow covering them. Father quickly stood and shook off the kilim. His stiff leg cracked from the bitter cold, but after a few stomps the blood flowed again and he recovered.

He then roused his family. He knew they had to keep moving in this cold just to stay alive.

As they walked out of the camp and deeper into the unknown, they spotted the family that had visited the night before leaning up against a large tree trunk. They were still. The daughter noticed there was no vapor coming from their mouths. Three inches of snow sat upon their bodies.

The mother checked the inner breast pocket of her coat and then approached the frozen family.

Afterward, the family pressed onward.

That night, their luck ran out.

A Russian sentry ordered them out of their makeshift shelter at gunpoint. He stared briefly at the three, assessing the threat. He was used to finding these sorts of ragged leftovers from the bitter fighting. People had scattered everywhere. Their homes had been entered, commandeered for Russian or Nazi officers, their food stolen, their loved ones shot or raped. Those who escaped headed for the hills. People like this were everywhere in the woods.

He separated them from their cart that held their meager belongings and marched them toward his encampment.

The mother looked at the father as she kept her hand on her little girl's head. They knew their time was short. She was thankful that a Russian had found them and not a Nazi. They would already be dead if the Nazis had found them.

During the interrogation, they were asked to produce their citizenship papers, which they'd been forced to leave back at their cart. They were not allowed to retrieve them.

In a matter of minutes they were declared enemies of the Russian state and condemned to death. The officer ordered the young sentry soldier who'd found them to take them to the usual place and carry out the sentencing.

Now as they walked to their deaths, the mother sank her right hand inside her coat pocket.

The clearing was about three hundred yards away.

She tried to speak to the guard.

"Silence. Now!" He jammed the barrel of his gun into her back.

As they approached the site another terrible stench preceded their arrival. It was worse than the teeming life smell of days ago above the latrine.

As they reached the heaped-up dirt she peered over the edge and saw a jigsaw jumble of decaying bodies—a grotesque collage of corpses with arms and legs and necks and backs contorted and intertwined. They'd all been sprinkled with white powder.

She wouldn't beg.

She heard the sounds of the sentry lifting his rifle.

The mother spun around to face him.

"Wait, wait, wait, please. Can I say a prayer? Please have mercy and let me say a prayer." Then she recognized the sentry's young eyes. He was a teenager, barely strong enough to lift his weapon.

"Nyet."

"Please, please. For my child, please."

She pulled the crucifix out of her coat with her right hand. She held it over her husband's head. *In the name of the Father and the Son and the Holy Spirit.* She held it over her daughter's head. *In the name of the Father and the Son and the Holy Spirit."*

Then she held it toward the boy holding the gun.

"In the name of the Father, the Son and the Holy Spirit."

He lifted his gun and pulled the trigger.

He pushed the father into the pit.

The soldier raised his rifle again. Fired a second round.

He pushed the mother into the pit.

Then he fired a last shot into the air and pushed his gun around to his back to free his arms.

The little girl didn't understand.

The soldier picked her up and then handed her down into her mother and father's waiting arms. And then he was gone.

When my wife Julie told me that story about her grandmother and grandfather, Iwanna and Volodymyr Medwid, and the little girl sandwiched in the cart like a burrito who became Julie's mother, I knew this was a family I needed to be a part of.

To have the presence of mind to make the decisions that saved her family's life, Julie's grandmother was just the kind of thinker I longed to be.

How did she do it?

How did she out-think the fear throughout those horrifying all is lost experiences?

As a thirty-two-year-old married young woman with a six-year-old child (Julie's mother was born a year before the German and Soviet invasion of Poland) and an incredibly stressful job as a schoolteacher facing the wrath of the German and Soviet war machine in 1944, it is nothing short of miraculous that Iwanna Medwid did not succumb to the horrific fate of tens of millions of lives obliterated by those two evil empires. Add the fact that she never surrendered her foundational trust in her belief in an ideal is even more astounding.

How did she manage to triumph under such terrifying circumstances? How did she avoid fear freak-out?

This is the core question we set out to explore, finding the best possible way to metabolize the most primal emotion of human experience—fear.

So, let's examine the story using the cognitive dominance methodology.

The knock on the door from the boy student's father was an objective known obstacle (-1) and a subjective known obstacle (-1). This situation pushed Iwanna right into the icy waters of the all is lost quadrant.

She knew that her teaching the Ukrainian national song to the town's youth as a tool of resistance to Soviet occupation radically increased the probability of her being discovered by the Soviet Authorities. It was a fact that the people who resisted were arrested and sent away to labor camps, if not executed right then and there. And she knew that her religious devotion also put her at risk with the Soviet authorities. Those are objective facts and subjective truths.

So even before the father of her student knocked on her door, Iwanna was operating in a chaotic environment, the fourth quadrant of Phere. When thinking itself is controlled by a capricious external power, you're living inside of a chaotic world. What's more, she was required to live in a state of cognitive dissonance too, when her hierarchical values and her actions were at odds. What she believed in (her country's right to exist and in a higher moral authority) could only be acted out in secret. She no doubt suspected that the time would come when she and her family would need to leave, but until that time she decided to work toward resisting the occupation.

Living in that constant state of the threat of being found out is exhausting, but when the time came to leave, she was prepared. She simply focused on the micro tasks and goals to survive. The anxiety and fear could now be directly confronted because her beliefs and her actions were now cognitively consonant. She had a global goal—escape for her and her family to a place that valued what she valued—and the micro goals to reach that goal took on a laser focus for her.

Her fundamental belief in a higher power, her worldview, then allowed her a comprehensive reference point to contend with the progressive complications of her family's escape. When the end was virtually certain, she didn't succumb to fear freak-out. Instead she relied on the top of her hierarchy of values—her faith in her God and in abiding her God's teachings.

And that faith allowed her not to behave in the way that would make her and her family's deaths certain. If she had panicked and begged for mercy from a soldier just wishing to do his duty and get it over with, the soldier would not have had to confront the cognitive dissonance he was experiencing. Because he was focused on a lower level of need (belonging to the Soviet system to survive) he did not (and could not if he were to remain sane) recognize that his behavior did not match his fundamental belief.

Let's look at the final moments from the point of view of the Soviet soldier. What he expected to happen was this family to plead for their lives, to hysterically break down as he led them to the pit filled with executed refugees. But then the unexpected happened instead. The matriarch blessed him, pulled out a symbol from his past that he still felt an attachment to, just as he was preparing to shoot her.

This Phere represented a factual objective known obstacle to his goal to be a good soldier and do as he was told in order to survive and perhaps later on thrive in the Soviet system. And it also represented a subjective known obstacle. He was raised with faith and being reminded of the abandonment of those ideals was an obstacle to him doing his duty. Iwanna's behavior forced him to fall into the all is lost quadrant too, to tumble into the world that made no sense.

His choice to abide by his higher value hierarchy and not kill them, like Iwanna's to continue to teach the Ukraine song and to attempt to escape, was consistent with the human need to live in cognitive consonance, a match of belief and action. It's heroic action in the moment.

Also fascinating is that the shared experience of both Iwana and the soldier navigating a chaotic environment in the all is lost quadrant with the same fundamental value system proved to be a salvation for both. I'd argue that Iwanna saved the soldier as much as the soldier saved her and her family. At least in that moment, he felt a rush of positive emotion as his Brain 1.0 registered the cognitive alignment of his beliefs and actions. He chose creation instead of destruction and acted out that choice.

So the takeaway is that when you fall into the all is lost quadrant, focus your Brain 2.0 energies at the top of your value system. If you fail to connect with your core value system, you will find yourself at the mercy of a desperate Brain 1.0, which will continue to jolt you with fear until you find yourself spiraling downward into panic. Brain 1.0 needs your beliefs to align with your actions or it will force you to believe lies are truth.

The way out of the spiral is to grab ahold of one thing you firmly believe to be your most prized value and use your Brain 2.0 to drive actions to match your beliefs. When that happens, you'll still feel the fear, but the cognitive consonance will fill you with meaning. For that soldier in that moment, his fundamental belief in the sanctity of life was an act of creation in a world falling apart. Saving the lives of the refugees gave him a rush of positive emotion, equal in measure to the gift he gave Iwanna and her family.

That soldier changed my life. Without Julie's gifts in the world, I would be nowhere near the person I am today.

When your very survival is at stake, use your fundamental belief in something as your north star. Just as Rob Conenello's belief in "doing great things" guided him through a gauntlet of horrific pain, so did Iwanna's commitment to her faith allow her to operate under extraordinary fear.

THIRTY-THREE
IRISE

66 "Jumping to conclusions is risky when the situation is unfamiliar, the stakes are high, and there is no time to collect more information. These are the circumstances in which intuitive errors are probable, which may be prevented by a deliberate intervention of System 2."

– Daniel Kahneman, *Thinking, Fast and Slow*

Daniel Kahneman and Amos Tversky won the Nobel Prize in economics in 2002 for their work they did unraveling the centuries-old rational behavior paradigm of economic models. Creating a number of fascinating experiments akin to the invisible gorilla experiment, Kahneman and Tversky hypothesized to explain how and why people behave irrationally in two ways of thinking.

The first way they described as the "gut instinct" fast-thinking approach, relying upon instinct and jumping to quick conclusions. They called this System 1.

The other way they described is slow, deep, analytical, reasoned, problem-solving thinking. They called this System 2.

For our cognitive dominance framework what we've been calling Brain 1.0 is what drives System 1 thinking. When we're feeling a "gut instinct" to take one action or another, it is based upon the emotional influences of Brain 1.0. We "feel" it as opposed to deeper thinking it through. We have a hunch.

Similarly, Brain 2.0 drives System 2 thinking. This is the grunt work of going back and forth between Brain 2.0's right and left hemispheres, thinking up stories and then analyzing them to figure out the probabilities of our expected story happening in light of our past experience.

Obviously, it takes far more energy to use Brain 2.0 than to let Brain 1.0 run the operation. And as we're built evolutionarily to conserve energy (why waste energy on thinking when we already "know" what to do?) we rely upon Brain 1.0 to run us through our everyday habits. We don't have to use Brain 2.0 when we're driving to the supermarket or when we're mopping the floor. We've done those things so many times before that we're on automatic pilot. Brain 1.0 is in charge.

A good rule of thumb is to rely on Brain 1.0 when you're operating inside of quadrant one, the flow quadrant. Remember that everything in quadrant one is familiar. The obstacles and tools that arise you've seen before. They are not unique black swans. They're things we've faced before. For me, getting a family's consent to operate is an obstacle, but it's not a difficult one to figure out how to negotiate. I've done it so many times before that my Brain 1.0 can dive into easily accessible memory, and based upon the "feel" of the people I'm speaking with, it can direct me with the right set of words and actions to get the consent.

When we move down to quadrant two, the calm before the storm, our Brain 1.0 is sending a signal that it anticipates being outside of its element. Something weird is going on that it doesn't understand. It sends a jolt of fear to our Brain 2.0 to tell it to figure out what's going on. Something unexpected has happened or is happening (a Phere) and it's not quite sure what it is.

If Brain 2.0 refuses to do any work after the first jolt for help, Brain 1.0 will keep nudging and nudging until it does, or until the Phere snowballs into such a monster that it overwhelms us and we freak out. That monster can become so frightening that it'll shoot us into the all is lost quadrant.

And in the chaotic all is lost environment, we really need to unleash the power of our Brain 2.0. Brain 1.0 simply has no idea of what to do, hence the constant firing of negative fear emotion, so it's up to Brain 2.0 to figure it out. Brain 2.0 has to heroically take up the challenge.

Brain 2.0 has to "slow-think," meaning use all of its resources and energies to go back and forth between its right and left hemispheres until it can settle on the "best possible choice." Julie's grandmother Iwanna from the Ukraine used her Brain 2.0 to figure out what her "best possible choice" was during the very real crisis of being held at gunpoint and what she felt was the inevitable climax of her death.

She put her Brain 2.0 to work and decided it would be best to leave the world consciously, if not willingly. She'd reassert the top of her hierarchy values, her faith, and voice that commitment just before her death. That way, her actions and her beliefs would be in sync until the very last moment of consciousness. Being cognitively consonant allowed her to quell the fear. So, **while she had zero control over when she was going to die, she did have control over how she would die.** That's a Brain 2.0 function using Kahneman and Tversky's System 2 thinking model.

But what about black swans? Unknown unknowns.

What about when things you've never seen before happen very quickly? There is no progression from flow to calm before the storm. Things move from "flow" to "all is lost" in a heartbeat.

Bluntly, sometimes shit happens that we've just never seen before, when we least expect it. In terms of our quadrant system, we move from one to three in a flash. And no matter our fifty thousand hours of experience in our particular profession, we don't know what the hell is going on...all of the sudden.

We just cannot predict personal black swans like the one I faced with Oksanna back when I was doing my residency—the wisp of red in a fluid that I'd always experienced as clear, colorless transparency caught me completely off guard. Thankfully, my mentor in the room (Dr. Albright) had seen that phenomenon before and stopped me before I allowed my intuitive Brain 1.0/System 1 fast-thinking response (pull out the endoscope!) to rule the moment.

Dr. Albright saved Oksanna's life because he'd seen this rare phenomenon before. He used his Brain 2.0/System 2 and introduced a subjective known tool (+) into a situation where the unknown reigned.

But what do we do if there is no mentor in the room when we experience a black swan and there's very little time to choose a course of action?

This is the question I've strived to solve since that shocking experience with Oksanna and in the other deeply troubling cases since. In the intervening decades, I set out to figure out a way first to clearly recognize black swans, which evolved into my gradient of fear concept that mapped onto my four quadrants of Phere graph inspired by Walt Langheinrich. And then I put my mind to figuring out how to remain cognitively consonant as I strained to metabolize Pheres internally using Brain 2.0's System 2.

Because you don't have a lot of time to contemplate the universe in an operating room, I boiled down cognitive dominance into five simple active steps for those moments you simply don't have the time to dilly dally.

I call it the IRISE protocol.

1. **Identify**: Have I seen this before? Is this a black swan? What kind of Phere is it—objective unknown obstacle (-2) or subjective unknown obstacle (-2). These will plunge you right into the dark waters of All is Lost.

2. **Reject**: What's your Brain 1.0 saying? When it's a black swan (a code blue unknown unknown Phere) it will be a rush of terror/panic/fear and tell you to do something immediately. Don't trust it. You have to use Brain 2.0 to reject the System 1 response.

   Your Brain 1.0 is trying to protect you. It's answering the challenge of the moment with an answer to a much easier question from the past. What will happen in the future if you listen to Brain 1.0 in this moment is potentially irreversible, i.e., death. You've got to be Arthur Fonzarelli in this moment. Stay cool.

3. **Inventory**: What's the state of the tools available to combat uncertainty? Move from micro personal vision to macro group vision and back again. Check with anyone and everyone else experiencing the same thing. Look into each person's eyes. Have you seen this before? If the answer is no, move back to micro. You're in charge. You're the one responsible for figuring out what to do or not do! So, move on.

4. **Stabilize:** This is the *First Do No Harm* (Hippocrates 101) step. Act or don't act at the lowest possible cost to buy you the greatest amount of time to think through the problem some more. The problem in brain surgery is that sometimes when you don't act, YOU DO HARM. Make sure the vitals are taken care of first...buy time. It's precious and you need it for your Brain 2.0 to go into overdrive.

5. **Evaluate**: What's the problem? How can I solve this problem? Walk through it from the micro fundamentals forward. Just keep picking it apart. Laser focus on the problem, not the way you feel dealing with the problem. Remember the PGC rule and think laterally. What could it possibly be through multiple lenses?

Let's pretend that I had no mentor in the OR that day with Oksanna. Here's how the protocol would have worked.

1. **Identify:** Have I ever seen a red wisp of fluid in cerebrospinal fluid followed by screen darkness on the television monitor before?

No.

2. **Reject:** What's my gut saying? It's telling me to pull out the endoscope so I can see the ventricle better. Don't do that!

3. **Inventory:** Has anyone in the OR seen this before?

Hold steady and ask the room. Narrate the room, as Sanjay Gupta would say, and then ask if anyone else around has experience with the thing you're confronting. Asking the room not only confirms that I'm dealing with a black swan but that everyone else is too (at least for everyone in the room who hasn't seen this phenomenon before). It also reveals that the patient's blood is spurting onto the floor. Remember I was so deeply focused on the micro that I didn't even know that blood was exiting the wound. This move to the macro point of view gives me more information to help me in the next step. Micro to macro will give you more information, guaranteed.

4. **Stabilize:** I have the insight based on the outflow of blood that we need more blood for transfusion. I ask someone in the room to get it. And then we transfuse, transfuse, and transfuse. Holding steady, I've bought more time to think some more. Holding her steady also gives the patient's brain and body time to solve the problem too. Two brains safely dealing with the problem are better than one.

5. **Evaluate:** Shift to analytical mode and think about the black swan. The red wisp must be blood. It's flooding the ventricle and shooting out the endoscope hole. It is flowing so briskly that the blood is absorbing all of the light from my endoscope, thus blacking out my screen. If I pull out the endoscope, the blood will have nowhere to go and it will burst through the ventricle and then crush the brain and kill the patient.

This process would have served me well. And it has served me innumerable times since I put it together. IRISE has become for me a primary mental tool that works with medical black swans and all variety of Pheres in general too—family Pheres, coaching Pheres, and all other ones too.

The trick to cognitive dominance and the emergency protocol IRISE is to remember just how powerful a force you are. You've been in bad spots before and you made it through. Use that Brain 2.0/System 2 thinking and ***don't react to Brain 1.0's fear firings, offering System 1 solutions to complex problems.*** Stabilize the situation (meaning take care of the low levels of Maslow's hierarchy first), which will buy you time to think through the Phere until you metabolize it in the best way possible. That is acting heroically while staying true to the top of your hierarchy of values.

THIRTY-FOUR

The Fifth Quadrant—
The Unknown Known

It's a January Friday in New Jersey.

If I don't call my father's doctor back now, he may not return my call until Monday morning. Then I'll have to wait all weekend to hear Dad's diagnosis.

I call him.

Dad's pathology report is in. He has Acute Myelogenous Leukemia (AML), a blood disorder that starts in the bone marrow. For an eighty-eight-year-old guy, it's a death sentence. He's got maybe six months left. And it isn't likely to be a soft landing either. It's going to be a grinder through chemotherapy just to get that extra time.

The worst news possible.

It's 1:15 p.m., an hour and fifteen minutes before I have to open up someone's skull.

Dr. Parziale, Dad's primary physician, signs off of the call telling me that he's already told Dad his AML death sentence diagnosis.

I'm nauseated when I hit the end call button. A flurry of thoughts assaults me. *What have you just done? You're about to operate and you've just taken yourself out of the right mindset... You idiot! You need to drive up to Short Hills and see Dad. NOW! NO! You have a case to do. You can't do it. You need to see Dad. Can you really give this guy your best? Can you get the job done? Maybe you should cancel the operation. Postpone until tomorrow? Fresh start... get some space from this?*

I willfully shut down the internal chatter and start to think.

Ironically, one of the side effects of AML is the susceptibility to bleeding, exactly the kind of bleeding that I'm trying to prevent with the scheduled craniotomy. How would I feel if Dad's doctor bailed out of a critical operation?

But postponing the operation is a reasonable option. One of my mentors, Greg Thompson, passed along one of his father's adages that seared into my brain the first time I heard it. *It's never too late to do the right thing.*

I think it through.

1. Tomorrow is Saturday and the operating room is typically less staffed on the weekends.

2. I will be on call tomorrow for other emergencies, which could preclude a straightforward beginning, middle and end to the procedure. So tomorrow has challenges.

3. The patient could get into trouble tonight. Trouble is a neurosurgeon's code word for "rapidly deteriorate into a life-or-death situation" but really it means the patient could die.

4. The patient already had a lot of brain swelling due to the angry tumor and I had already waited one night to get him transferred and fully prepped for surgery. He's ready now.

Okay, what else?

The patient's family is waiting for me. At the very least, I need to check in as soon as possible. So, I'll go up there, see him and his family, and explain the situation. I'll see how I feel in that room. How stable is he? How stable am I? If it still doesn't feel right, I'll cancel it right then and there. Call it in the room, not in this car.

I've got my marching orders.

Moving through the hospital calms me. It's my domain. I know where the best coffee maker is, the high-test Keurig in the surgeon's lounge. I make myself a cup. I put on my gear in the locker room. I can feel a sense of purpose and calm come over me from the thousands of times I've done this before. It's comforting. I'm like a hamster on his exercise wheel—moving and not thinking too much. *You don't want to be doing a lot of thinking in the OR.*

By the time I arrive at the patient's bedside, my energy is up and my nausea has passed.

He's got his three kids hanging on to his left arm and his wife is hand in hand on his right. I can't help but smile.

"You ready?" I ask.

"Yup!"

"Let's get going."

I'm in my scrubs now, peeling the stick drape and positioning it over the patient's head. As I'm stapling it to his scalp, my inner panic comes back. *You're tired and stressed out... How are you going to do this? You may feel okay now, but what about in three hours when the real pressure bears down?*

I'm used to this, but it never gets easier to combat.

What I have now that I didn't have when I was younger are some tools to silence this inner underminer. I step back from the sterile field and talk to myself like my dad used to talk to me when I got hyper before a wrestling match. Talk yourself through the best mindset and center yourself on that. Reorder reality to suit your goals if necessary. That's how your brain works, so use it to your advantage.

It's 7:30 a.m. You've had a great night's sleep and you've had your perfect fill of coffee. You'll be done by 2:00 p.m. and you'll reward yourself with a great meal.

Do I fall for this "as if" hook, line and sinker? No. But it gets my mind out of negative land very quickly. It helps me center on the target... focus.

I follow up with the right music. I cue up John Hiatt's "Through Your Hands" and play it out of the OR speakers at a volume just below the anesthesiologist's threshold of annoyance. And just before I step back into the sterile field to begin work, I recite a stanza from another poem my dad sent me years ago... *If–* by Rudyard Kipling.

If you can force your heart and nerve and sinew
To serve your turn long after they are gone,
And so hold on when there is nothing in you
Except the Will which says to them: "Hold on!"

Five hours and fifty-two minutes later, I slouch in the circulating nurse's chair by the computer in the corner of the recovery room. I take a deep breath and rise. The patient's anesthesia is wearing off and there's one more thing I need to do.

"Mr. Holder!" I shout the patient's name to break his fog. "Wiggle your toes!"

There's equal movement in both legs.

"Now...squeeze my hand!"

He does.

It's now a week after Mr. Holder's case. I drive Dad home from the "rehabilitation" hospital. He's physically depleted and too weak to ride in the front seat. His skin is sallow and his eyelids heavy.

Just four weeks before this ride, he'd sent me a comprehensive analysis of a lecture I gave that had been posted on YouTube. The time stamp on his email was 5:10 a.m. That brightly burning passion was still inside his body. I knew it. I just needed to help him get out again.

When I got Dad home, my brother John had already transformed the bedroom into a makeshift hospice. I lifted him out of the wheelchair and laid him on Mom's side of the bed. If anything could get Dad to rally, it would be Mom's psychic energy. But I wasn't prepared for how Dad's muscular body had mutated into a frail sack of jelly and bones.

I assessed his general condition. His breathing was labored. His speech was soft and shallow. I propped a pillow under his head and he wretched a deep rumbling cough...what doctors recognize as "the old man's friend."

Before there were antibiotics or pharmacological goodies like morphine or Ativan, death exacted an excruciatingly painful price on the just barely living. So when a sick old man developed pneumonia, doctors left it untreated. The disease would run its course with the patient slowly lapsing into delirium and gently passing away from overwhelming infection, which was far more merciful than painful organ failure.

Often on rounds in medical school, when confronted with an older person with pneumonia, my Internal Medicine attending Dr. Tickoff would sigh and remind us… "It's not a bad way to go." Hearing Dad's cough brought those words back and steeled my nerve.

I settled Dad in bed and stepped out of the bedroom.

Why had he gotten "the dwindles" so quickly? A month ago he was the healthiest eighty-eight-year-old I'd ever seen. His cell counts weren't that bad, which meant that his undiagnosed AML hadn't wreaked havoc yet. His hemoglobin was normal and his oxygenation was good.

So why was he going down the drain?

Obviously, either at the hospital or at the rehab he caught some bug that his body would have beaten off easily before the AML came. It lodged itself into his vulnerable lungs and rapidly reproduced.

I resolved that once he got his feet under him, I'd get him back to the hospital and tank him up with IV fluids and antibiotics. He'll be back to his old self in no time and I could reassess from there. I mean this guy lived by Dylan Thomas's beseeching to "*Rage, rage against the dying of the light*." I wasn't going to let him down.

I continued to think it through as I made my way to the pharmacy. He needed diapers, cloth wipes, towels, a memory foam mattress pad to prevent pressure ulcers, and a bunch of other palliatives.

I'd explain it all to him when he woke up. This spiral doesn't make sense. It's too fast. Why no fever? Just a deep cough? Why no abnormal chest X-ray?

Before I burdened him with my doctor talk, though, I called his primary doctor again, Mike Parziale. I explained my thinking to him in my usual machine gun way.

"Mike, you know how strong he is. Hell, he was walking two miles a day a month ago. His labs are good. Normal hemoglobin. You should feel his radial pulse. It's as strong and regular as a metronome. The two times he's been back to the hospital we've pumped him full of fluids and he's rallied…"

"Mark," he kindly cut me off, "I've been following all of this. And I think you're right. Your dad probably has the early stages of pneumonia, which is accelerating his decline. I have one question for you to consider, though." He waited a moment to make sure I was listening.

"Yeah…what?"

"How many times do you want your dad to die?"

The hospice comfort kit arrived the next morning via UPS. Atropine to treat wet respirations. Haldol for agitation and restlessness. Compazine for nausea. Tylenol suppository for fevers. Ativan to ease anxiety. Morphine for pain.

I knew Dad was still all there that night because at one point the cat, Sara, a being he long ago banished from his presence for her habitual indiscretions on mom's favorite rug, jumped onto his bed. She came to pay her respects.

"Hey, Dad…Sara is here to see you," I told him.

He motioned with his hand and patted the bed by his right hip. She curled up next to him and gave him a good full body rub.

The next morning, the extended family arrived. Dad didn't have the energy to talk about much. He told us where his self-authored obituary was. He told us where the tax returns and bills were and where he wanted his funeral mass. He reminded me about Ulysses.

"Yes, Dad. I know. I won't forget."

Dad had given me the poem six months before. We were in his study when he handed me a set of seven green, coffee-stained three-by-five index cards. The edges were worn and frayed, but the words were written clearly and crisply. "*Read this at my funeral*," he told me and then just as abruptly he changed the subject and went on about a biography of Churchill he'd just finished reading.

I now sat in a chair at his bedside and Mom lay beside him. She told the story of the night they met and of how he fell in love with the girl in the blue dress. Dad smiled. No more history lectures, no more big ideas seized him. His energy was dissipated and he wanted to remember the most important moments in his life. Mom knew that instinctively.

The pneumonia had him. It was like watching a drowning man pulling himself up for air, but after Dad broke the surface and got a breath, he'd expend it by saying, "I love you," to whoever was in the room.

In the hall, I trembled in front of my wife Julie and son Trevor.

"I don't want to give it to him. I can't give it to him. I just can't."

"It's okay, Mark. It's your time to be the son, not the doctor. Let the nurse do it. Be the son." Julie, like always, was there with the perfect words of advice.

But the hospice nurse wasn't there every moment. And I knew she needed to walk the fine line between making a dying patient comfortable and accelerating death to shorten suffering. Hospice nurses have to err on the conservative side.

Because of loved ones just like me, who have great difficulty letting go.

I sat back down next to him.

"Dad, I have the morphine. Do you want it?"

Head nod yes.

"If I give this to you, you're not going to wake up. You're not going to think clearly anymore. Your mind is going to go."

Please say no. Not yet. Please say no. Give me another moment of unclouded consciousness.

"Yes…Mark, I want the morphine."

"Okay, I'm with you. Dad, you'll always be with me. I love you. I love you so much."

I held the small syringe and fitted its tip tightly into the vial and pulled back. And then I pinched his chapped lower lip and pushed down on his jaw. I parked the tip of the syringe gently under his tongue. I pushed the plunger down.

I grasped his soft clammy hand.
My grip was firm and calloused.
Squeeze...
Squeeze.

. . . .

The fifth quadrant of Pheres aren't really unexpected. They're unknown knowns. We know they're coming, but we don't know when. We can successfully put off these inevitables for long stretches of time without immediate negative consequences.

We don't worry about our grades even though we know that if we don't have good ones, our choices will be severely limited when we get older. We don't set up a retirement fund because we're only twenty-five years old. We don't think that extra beer every night is going to hurt us. We don't think about what our family will do if we get hit by a bus.

There's a reason we don't deal with these unknown knowns. It's because we can't think of any positive emotional release by doing so. We only see the negative experience thinking about them and as such load these unknown knowns with more anxiety and fear with each passing day. Kahneman and Tversky detailed this proclivity in their 1979 paper "Prospect theory: An analysis of decision under risk."[7] Unknown knowns revolve around big existential problems—death primarily. And all of its varieties. The death of childhood, the death of singledom or independence, the death of a marriage, the death of a job, career, or lifestyle, and ultimately the death of a loved one and eventually our own death.

Knowing that death and destruction is inevitable is extremely disturbing. It's not something we want to dwell on in the present, as we put our energies toward creation, but we really should.

So how do we?

The answer is found by the habits we build dealing with the other

---

7 *Econometrica*, 47, 263-291.

micro unexpected Phere events of life. If we refuse to acknowledge and then confront and finally metabolize unexpected Phere events that Brain 1.0 tells us are real and need to be looked at, then what happens when the big unexpected Phere events come in the form of death or destruction or change? We'll run from them too.

And when we avoid unpacking discomforting unexpected events, our world gets smaller and smaller and smaller until we come to believe in our own particular "terrible knowledge." And slowly but surely we begin to doubt all of the things that used to mean something to us. We start to believe in "nothing."

We begin to believe that destruction is the most powerful force on Earth and that all the platitudes about creative forces and positive goods being born into the world for the betterment of a higher plain of existence are nonsense. The only thing we can absolutely be sure of is death and destruction.

The problem with coming to that conclusion is that it increases suffering and misery, not just for yourself, but for everyone around you. From the personal to the family to the community, the belief in "nothing" just makes the "meaningless" days we spend here of even greater torment. This is the very dark side of refusing to contend with the things that give rise to fear.

So, why not… for the sake of argument… simply choose to make life less tortuous and meaningless by taking the heroic creative approach? It's a lot harder to act out than the destructive and nihilistic approach, but it will certainly make your days here a bit more bearable. That just seems like a reasonable and "thinking person's" conclusion to the paradox of existence. Life is hard enough. Why not work to bring a little more light and creative energy into it before you leave?

That's what my father taught me as the key to getting a grip on this world. And it's what I'm hoping to pass on to my own children. Not with words, but with actions. Just like my father did for me.

So, the creative heroic course of action I'm recommending throughout this book is a way to make that constant life companion "fear" representative of what it really is. It's simply a signal from your inner warrior (my inner Jack Nicholson-Jessup) standing on the wall between your fantasies and reality. And the signal he's sending you is simply to pay attention to something that just happened that you didn't expect. Unpack that thing, dissect it, figure out what it means. And do some deep thinking about how it relates to what *you* want out of life, what *you* need out of life, what *you* firmly believe in and what *you* value.

I hope my take on cognitive dominance derived from the last twenty-eight years of my life dealing with high stress, high anxiety, high fear situations in brain and spine surgery helps you frame and metabolize those things that trigger your fears.

EPILOGUE
After Anthony

Which brings me back to Anthony.

While working on this book, I decided that I needed to explore what happened to him. When he left my care, I did my best to put him out of my mind (even though I'd given his photo a prominent place in my office). I convinced myself that he probably passed away. With little hope for a positive objective fact to have come out of my operation, it took a lot of inner fortitude to summon the courage even to just search for the family restaurant on Facebook.

But lo and behold, I found the page and scrolled around. Among the photos was a twenty-four-year-old man sitting in a wheelchair with his family at Rockefeller Center.

I called Mr. Liquori, Anthony's father and asked him if I could come visit. He graciously agreed. The next Sunday I went to their pitch perfect pizza parlor and sat down with Mr. and Mrs. Liquori and Anthony. He's cognitively compromised, most likely related to the postoperative radiation and chemotherapy. But it was obvious from the second I walked in that he was still the number one helper and a formidable source of love and pride to his whole family.

When I left to go home, Mr. Liquori showered me with gifts—takeout pizza, fresh bread, a beautiful purse from Italy for Julie, a plant split from the mother plant in his restaurant window from thirty-three years before... Lastly, Mrs. Liquori came out with a copy of a photo I never knew existed. In fact, in my deep all is lost depression—the experience that had me swear off pediatric neurosurgery entirely—I'd completely failed to store the memory of the memorialized event.

It's a photo of a younger me holding Anthony after he'd returned home from my surgery. I'm sitting with my own young family in a booth at the Liquori restaurant finishing a meal.

What I realize now is that what I thought was a quadrant three experience—a fall into chaos and the contemplation of the dark truth of the random nature of life and my failure as a surgeon—was actually a quadrant four, the birthing of a new skill.

What I didn't do then was to unpack the nature of the unexpected Phere event that befell the Liquori family.

The objective known fact about Anthony when I met him was that he had a very serious tumor that would in all likelihood take his life. And the subjective truth was not that I didn't have the skills to save him, but that, thanks to Dr. Albright and a slew of other mentors, I had the experience and the work ethic to do everything in my power to try. I meticulously proceeded to plan the operation. I got my good friend and wonderful surgeon Kamal to spell me when I knew I would get tired. And in the end, I scraped off every last molecule of that terminal tumor. Anthony survived.

It is no doubt that Anthony profoundly affected me in ways that I still haven't been able to come to grips with. I used to look at Anthony's plaque in my office and get sad. Now I look at the new photo, the one Mrs. Liquori was so kind to give me, with pride. The young surgeon in that picture gave it everything he had. And even when he failed to live up to his own expectations, he released his gift to the best of his ability. I'm now proud to have been that guy, instead of ashamed.

That's what the pursuit of cognitive dominance taught me. And I know it will do the same for you.

ACKNOWLEDGMENTS

This book is the culmination of fifty-four years of life, over half spent learning and practicing the art of neurosurgery. I have been privileged to know and to have learned from hundreds of intelligent, inspiring people who have given me their time and knowledge, shaping me into who I am today and nurturing the person I can still become.

First, there are no words that can encompass the depth of the love and gratitude I feel for the people who inspire me, daily, to be the best husband and father I can be. My amazing wife Julie and our talented, loving children, Kaleigh and her husband AJ, Alex, Patrick, and Trevor are the light of my life. They have endured many iterations of these stories and I appreciate their thoughtful input, love, and support.

Special recognition goes to my mother and father, Mary Jean and the late John J. McLaughlin, for the strong foundation they gave me and their indomitable drive and loving support. My uncles Walter and Francis Pizzi, Jr., and my late grandfather Francis Pizzi, Sr., all physicians, influenced my career choice and life. In particular, Grandpa Pizzi showed me what a doctor looks like in thought and action and he is always with me. I also gratefully acknowledge my mother-in-law Orysha Stefaniw for her love and for sharing the story about Ivanna Medwid, her remarkable mother.

My colleagues and partners Dr. Seth Joseffer, Dr. Nirav Shah, and Dr. Matt Tormenti at Princeton Brain and Spine have always been supportive while I was working on this book. They are truly my loyal and caring comrades and I thank them for their support.

I have been fortunate to have mentors and colleagues who have made me a better physician and person. They include Dr. Leland Albright, Dr. Regis Haid, Dr. Peter Jannetta, Dr. Hae Dong Jho, Dr. Dade Lunsford, Dr. John Moossy, Dr. John Povlishock, Dr. Gail Rosseau, Dr. Peter Sheptak, Dr. William Welch, and Dr. Harold Young. I also thank my chief resident and long-time friend Dr. Walt Langheinrich and all the nurses, practitioners, and physician assistants who have taught and helped me along the way, and in many instances played a role in my stories.

I am grateful to all my teachers who have had a formative influence on my life, especially one of the founding fathers of sports psychology, Dr. Nate Zinsser at the United States Military Academy's Center for Enhanced Performance. Dr. Zinsser, who leads one of the country's most prominent sports psychology programs, has been my advisor, mentor and friend for almost four decades. He introduced me to the concept of cognitive dominance, which became the core of the book. Robert C. Brenner, Jr., my first advisor at The Pingry School, introduced me to a way of life I have strived to attain ever since: scholar athlete. I also thank Dean Sluyter, my high school freshman English teacher, who first taught me how to write coherently and who remains a trusted advisor.

I owe a special debt of gratitude to all my coaches, especially to my first wrestling coach John Serruto who forever altered the trajectory of my life by teaching me early on that Determination (with a capital D) trumps everything. I also thank my college coach William Hoffman Pincus who remains an intellectual inspiration in my life and who provided valuable input on an early draft. Wrestling, a passion I've had since childhood, has enabled me to remain in the presence of great coaches and parents at the Princeton Wrestling Club and Trenton Youth Wrestling.

There are many people along the way who helped me function successfully as a doctor, author and coach. I recognize and thank my personal and professional assistants Gil Derry, Kathryn Finney and Terrilyn Nilson for their dedication, advice, and tireless work ethic.

This work would never have come to fruition without the seasoned hand of my co-writer, agent, and editor Shawn Coyne. Shawn served as advisor, teacher, and therapist for me as we stitched these stories into a cohesive theory/antidote on how to metabolize fear in a healthy way.

The stories that make up the book exist because of my patients, specifically Dr. Robert Conenello and the entire Liquori family. They are true professionals, friends, and beautiful people who not only entrusted me with their lives, but also kindly allowed me to include them in this book.

I would like to thank my first readers including Chris Aragona, Chris and Lori Ayres, Tripp Davis, Brian Dwight, Katrina Firlik, Jeff Harrison, Mike Horowitz, Kamal Kalia, Moss Kearney, Karla Schacher, Rob Schmidt, Carol and Bob Smilari, John Tumillo, and John Tydings. Also thanks to Dr. Sanjay Gupta for generously devoting interview time and for inspiring the "Gradient of Fear" chapter with his provocative quote: "I take the word fear very seriously."

Lori Ayres also played an instrumental role in the book development process, creating amazing artwork that made often complex concepts far more accessible. I thank Daniel Somma, one of my clinical assistants, who helped me with research. Authors who inspired many of the concepts in Cognitive Dominance including Jordan Peterson, Steven Pressfield, Carl Jung, Jeffrey Jay, Erich Fromm, David Hume, Iain McGilchrist, Nassim Nicholas Taleb, Abraham Maslow, Joseph Campbell, Daniel Kahneman, John Vervaeke and Simon Sinek. All have had a profound effect on this manuscript. Some of the illustrations in my book were inspired by Jordan Peterson's masterpiece *Maps of Meaning*.

I would also like to thank people interviewed for the book but whose stories did not make it into print. Please know that your contributions informed the content and I am grateful for the time you gave me. Many thanks to Alex Bethea, Marsha Brown, Ed Hochuli, Chris Kuenne, Chief Master Sgt. William Calvin Markham, Ed Meyercord,

Sally Roberts, and Jen Schumacher. Your courageous stories will be included in other Cognitive Dominance publications.

I also express my appreciation to the many professionals who have guided my thinking over the years and provided expertise in my areas of weakness. Ken Davidson, at the consulting company Workability, has helped me grow emotionally and intellectually. Brian Greer, founder of Goimage Media, has been a friend, advisor and colleague. Jim Harshaw Jr. helps me prioritize and execute my goals. Karen Horton has provided editorial support for this book and many other writing projects. John McDaniel, founder of Peak Performance Physicians, helped me launch my company, Princeton Brain and Spine, many years ago and worked with me to shape many of my business practices and principles. Nancy Webster, a longtime friend and communications expert, has advised me since I began presenting medical stories to the public. Sasha Zebryk of SashaSpeaks has been my first and lifelong speech coach. Thanks, too, to my public relations team at Zilker Media for advice and guidance during the launch of this project.

To all of you, I am grateful that you are a part of my life. Indeed, without you, this book would not exist.

Finally, thanks to all who buy and read this book. You are helping Trenton Youth Wrestling, a non-profit organization dedicated to providing inner city boys and girls with opportunities through the sport of wrestling, augmented by mentorships. A portion of the book's proceeds will help fund this important project.

Mark McLaughlin (www.markmclaughlinmd.com) is the founder of Princeton Brain and Spine Care specializing in trigeminal neuralgia and cervical spine surgery. He studied under Peter Jannetta, considered the father of modern neurosurgery.

A former NCAA Division I wrestler, McLaughlin was inducted into the National Wrestling Hall of Fame in 2016. He is in his eighteenth-year coaching the Princeton Wrestling Club and created the non-profit Trenton Youth Wrestling organization dedicated to inner city girls and boys. His commentary regularly appears in Business Insider and other national media outlets.

Made in the USA
Middletown, DE
05 February 2020

84204488R00210